A Buddhist Crossroads

In the late nineteenth and early twentieth centuries, Buddhism in Asia was transformed by the impact of colonial modernity and new technologies and began to spread in earnest to the West. Transnational networking among Asian Buddhists and early western converts engendered pioneering attempts to develop new kinds of Buddhism for a globalized world, in ways not controlled by any single sect or region. Drawing on new research by scholars worldwide, this book brings together some of the most extraordinary episodes and personalities of a period of almost a century from 1860-1960. Examples include Indian intellectuals who saw Buddhism as a homegrown path for a modern post-colonial future, poor whites 'going native' as Asian monks, a Brooklyn-born monk who sought to convert Mussolini, and the failed 1950s attempt to train British monks to establish a Thai sangha in Britain. Some of these stories represent creative failures, paths not taken, which may show us alternative possibilities for a more diverse Buddhism in a world dominated by religious nationalisms. Other pioneers paved the way for the mainstreaming of new forms of Buddhism in later decades, in time for the post-1960s takeoff of 'global Buddhism'.

This book was originally published as a special issue of *Contemporary Buddhism*.

Brian Bocking is Professor of the Study of Religions at University College Cork, Ireland, and formerly Chair of the Study of Religions Department at SOAS, University of London, UK. He has published mainly in the field of Japanese religions and is currently researching early Irish Buddhists.

Phibul Choompolpaisal is Research Associate in Thai Meditation Texts at King's College London, UK. He is author of several articles on Thai Buddhism in the early modern period.

Laurence Cox is Lecturer in Sociology at the National University of Ireland, Maynooth, Ireland. He is author of *Buddhism and Ireland* (2013) and has published widely on social movements. He is currently working with Brian Bocking and Alicia Turner on the strange lives of U Dhammaloka and Capt. Charles Pfoundes.

Alicia Turner is an Assistant Professor of Religious Studies in the Humanities department of York University in Toronto, Canada. She is the author of *Saving Buddhism: The Impermanence of Religion in Colonial Burma* (2014) and editor of *The Journal of Burma Studies*.

A Buddhist Crossroads
Pioneer Western Buddhists and Asian Networks 1860-1960

Edited by
Brian Bocking,
Phibul Choompolpaisal,
Laurence Cox and Alicia Turner

Routledge
Taylor & Francis Group
LONDON AND NEW YORK

First published 2015
by Routledge
2 Park Square, Milton Park, Abingdon, Oxon, OX14 4RN, UK

and by Routledge
711 Third Avenue, New York, NY 10017, USA

Routledge is an imprint of the Taylor & Francis Group, an informa business

British Library Cataloguing in Publication Data
A catalogue record for this book is available from the British Library

ISBN13: 978-1-138-78958-6

Typeset in Helvetica
by Taylor & Francis Books

Publisher's Note
The publisher accepts responsibility for any inconsistencies that may have arisen during the conversion of this book from journal articles to book chapters, namely the possible inclusion of journal terminology.

Disclaimer
Every effort has been made to contact copyright holders for their permission to reprint material in this book. The publishers would be grateful to hear from any copyright holder who is not here acknowledged and will undertake to rectify any errors or omissions in future editions of this book.

Contents

Citation Information vii
Notes on Contributors xi

1. Introduction: A Buddhist crossroads: pioneer European Buddhists and globalizing Asian networks 1860–1960
Alicia Turner, Laurence Cox and Brian Bocking 1

2. Flagging up Buddhism: Charles Pfoundes (*Omoie Tetzunostzuke*) among the international congresses and expositions, 1893–1905
Brian Bocking 16

3. Buddhist councils in a time of transition: globalism, modernity and the preservation of textual traditions
Tilman Frasch 37

4. Three boys on a great vehicle: 'Mahayana Buddhism' and a trans-national network
Shin'ichi Yoshinaga 51

5. The Bible, the bottle and the knife: religion as a mode of resisting colonialism for U Dhammaloka
Alicia Turner 65

6. Ananda Metteyya: controversial networker, passionate critic
Elizabeth J. Harris 77

7. Tai-Burmese-Lao Buddhisms in the 'modernizing' of Ban Thawai (Bangkok): the dynamic interaction between ethnic minority religion and British–Siamese centralization in the late nineteenth/early twentieth centuries
Phibul Choompolpaisal 93

8. Rethinking early western Buddhists: beachcombers, 'going native' and dissident Orientalism
Laurence Cox 115

9. 'Like embers hidden in ashes, or jewels encrusted in stone': Rāhul Sāṅkṛtyāyan, Dharmānand Kosambī and Buddhist activity in colonial India
Douglas Ober 133

10. Elective affinities: the reconstruction of a forgotten episode in the shared history of Thai and British Buddhism – Kapilavaḍḍho and Wat Paknam
Andrew Skilton 148

11. Brooklyn Bhikkhu: how Salvatore Cioffi became the Venerable Lokanatha
Philip Deslippe 168

Index 186

Citation Information

The chapters in this book were originally published in *Contemporary Buddhism: An Interdisciplinary Journal*, volume 14, issue 1 (May 2013). When citing this material, please use the original page numbering for each article, as follows:

Chapter 1

Introduction: A Buddhist crossroads: pioneer European Buddhists and globalizing Asian networks 1860–1960
Alicia Turner, Laurence Cox and Brian Bocking
Contemporary Buddhism: An Interdisciplinary Journal, volume 14, issue 1 (May 2013) pp. 1-16

Chapter 2

Flagging up Buddhism: Charles Pfoundes (Omoie Tetzunostzuke) *among the international congresses and expositions, 1893–1905*
Brian Bocking
Contemporary Buddhism: An Interdisciplinary Journal, volume 14, issue 1 (May 2013) pp. 17-37

Chapter 3

Buddhist councils in a time of transition: globalism, modernity and the preservation of textual traditions
Tilman Frasch
Contemporary Buddhism: An Interdisciplinary Journal, volume 14, issue 1 (May 2013) pp. 38-51

Chapter 4

Three boys on a great vehicle: 'Mahayana Buddhism' and a trans-national network
Shin'ichi Yoshinaga
Contemporary Buddhism: An Interdisciplinary Journal, volume 14, issue 1 (May 2013) pp. 52-65

Chapter 5

The Bible, the bottle and the knife: religion as a mode of resisting colonialism for U Dhammaloka

Alicia Turner

Contemporary Buddhism: An Interdisciplinary Journal, volume 14, issue 1 (May 2013) pp. 66-77

Chapter 6

Ananda Metteyya: controversial networker, passionate critic

Elizabeth J. Harris

Contemporary Buddhism: An Interdisciplinary Journal, volume 14, issue 1 (May 2013) pp. 78-93

Chapter 7

Tai-Burmese-Lao Buddhisms in the 'modernizing' of Ban Thawai (Bangkok): the dynamic interaction between ethnic minority religion and British–Siamese centralization in the late nineteenth/early twentieth centuries

Phibul Choompolpaisal

Contemporary Buddhism: An Interdisciplinary Journal, volume 14, issue 1 (May 2013) pp. 94-115

Chapter 8

Rethinking early western Buddhists: beachcombers, 'going native' and dissident Orientalism

Laurence Cox

Contemporary Buddhism: An Interdisciplinary Journal, volume 14, issue 1 (May 2013) pp. 116-133

Chapter 9

'Like embers hidden in ashes, or jewels encrusted in stone': Rāhul Sāṅkṛtyāyan, Dharmānand Kosambī and Buddhist activity in colonial India

Douglas Ober

Contemporary Buddhism: An Interdisciplinary Journal, volume 14, issue 1 (May 2013) pp. 134-148

Chapter 10

Elective affinities: the reconstruction of a forgotten episode in the shared history of Thai and British Buddhism – Kapilavaḍḍho and Wat Paknam

Andrew Skilton

Contemporary Buddhism: An Interdisciplinary Journal, volume 14, issue 1 (May 2013) pp. 149-168

CITATION INFORMATION

Chapter 11

Brooklyn Bhikkhu: how Salvatore Cioffi became the Venerable Lokanatha
Philip Deslippe
Contemporary Buddhism: An Interdisciplinary Journal, volume 14, issue 1 (May 2013) pp. 169-186

Please direct any queries you may have about the citations to clsuk.permissions@cengage.com

Notes on Contributors

Brian Bocking is Professor in the Study of Religions Department at University College Cork (UCC), Ireland, the first department of its kind in the Republic. Until December 2007 he held the Chair in the study of Religions at the School of Oriental and African Studies (SOAS), London. He is currently researching with Alicia Turner (Toronto) and Laurence Cox (Maynooth) the life of 'the Irish Buddhist' U Dhammaloka; and with Laurence Cox and Yoshinaga Shin'ichi (Kyoto), the career of another forgotten Irish Buddhist: 'Captain' Charles Pfoundes (1840–1907).

Phibul Choompolpaisal is Post-doctoral Research Fellow at University College Cork. He completed his PhD on early modern Thai Buddhism at the School of Oriental and African Studies (SOAS), University of London, UK. His publications include an analysis of Weber's influence on Theravāda Buddhism studies (2008), the significance of the sixteenth-century Sukhothai inscription for Theravada Buddhism (co-authored with Kate Crosby and Andrew Skilton, forthcoming) and a history of monastic education in Thailand (forthcoming). He is also reviews editor of the journal *Contemporary Buddhism*.

Laurence Cox co-directs the MA in Community Education, Equality and Social Activism at the National University of Ireland Maynooth, Ireland. He is co-editor of the social movement studies journal Interface and has written widely on social movements, working-class activism, counter cultures and western Buddhism, including the forthcoming *Buddhism and Ireland* (Equinox) and co-editor of *Ireland's New Religious Movements* (Cambridge Scholars). He is working with Brian Bocking and Alicia Turner on U Dhammaloka and early western Buddhists in Asia.

Philip Deslippe is a doctoral student in the Department of Religious Studies at the University of California, Santa Barbara, USA. In 2011 he edited and introduced the definitive edition of *The Kybalion* for Tarcher/Penguin. He is currently working on several projects about the history of early American yoga, as well as the flagship biography of William Walker Atkinson.

Tilman Frasch is Senior Lecturer in Asian History at Manchester Metropolitan University, UK. He studied South Asian History, European History and Indian Languages at Heidelberg University, Germany, from which he received a doctorate with a thesis on the city and state of Pagan in 1995. His research areas include pre-modern South and Southeast Asian history, Buddhist studies, urban history and history of technology. Among his recent publications are: 'Buddha's Tooth Relic', in Axel Michaels, *Ritual Dynamics and the Science of the Ritual* (2010); '1456: The Making of a Buddhist Ecumene in the Bay of Bengal', in Rila Mukherjee, *Pelagic Passageways* (2011); and several contributions to an eight volume *Globalgeschichte* 1000–2000 AD (2008–2011).

Elizabeth J Harris is an Associate Professor in the Department of Theology, Philosophy and Religious Studies at Liverpool Hope University, UK, specializing in Buddhist Studies. She is currently President of the European Network of Buddhist – Christian Studies. Her publications include: *What Buddhists Believe* (1998), *Ananda Metteyya: The First British Emissary of Buddhism* (1998) and *Theravāda Buddhism and the British Encounter: Religious, Missionary and Colonial Experience in Nineteenth Century Sri Lanka* (2006).

Douglas Ober is a PhD student in the Department of Asian Studies, University of British Columbia, Vancouver, Canada. His research examines transnational Buddhist movements in India, the Himalayas and Tibet, and religious change in South Asia more widely.

Andrew Skilton is Senior Research Fellow in Buddhist Studies in the Theology and Religious Studies Department at King's College London, UK. He also manages the Revealing Hidden Collections Project at the Bodleian Library Oxford.

Alicia Turner is an Assistant Professor of Religious Studies in the Humanities department of York University in Toronto, Canada. She specializes in the study of Buddhism in Southeast Asia with an emphasis on the period of British colonialism in Burma/Myanmar. Her research focuses on the intersections of religion, colonialism and nationalism. Seeking to understand the cultural aspects of British colonialism and how it transformed local ideas and categories, she investigates the key role religion played in the colonial encounter, both as an ordering category for colonial rule and as a mode of response.

Shin'ichi Yoshinaga is Associate Professor of Maizuru National College of Technology, Japan. He specializes in the history of spiritual and esoteric thought in Japan, as well as modern Buddhism. He has been doing research on reijutsu, healing practices of a spiritual kind, which corresponded to metaphysical religions in America.

INTRODUCTION

A BUDDHIST CROSSROADS: PIONEER EUROPEAN BUDDHISTS AND GLOBALIZING ASIAN NETWORKS 1860–1960

Alicia Turner, Laurence Cox and **Brian Bocking**

Single-country approaches to the study of Buddhism miss the crucial significance of international networks in the making of modern Buddhism, in a period when the material basis for such networks had been transformed. Southeast Asia in particular acted as a dynamic crossroads in this period enabling the emergence of a 'global Buddhism' not controlled by any single sect, while India and Japan both played unexpectedly significant roles in this crossroads. A key element of this process was the encounter between Asian Buddhist networks and western would-be Buddhists. Those involved, however, were often marginal - 'creative failures' in many cases - whose stories enable us to think this history in a more diverse way than is often done. In other cases as isolated figures they could pave the way for the 'mainstreaming' of new forms of Buddhism by established actors in later decades. This article introduces the special issue of Contemporary Buddhism *entitled 'A Buddhist crossroads: pioneer European Buddhists and globalizing Asian networks 1860–1960'. The research described in this issue often raises other methodological questions of representativity and significance, while posing important challenges around collaborative research and the use of new technologies.*

A cacophony of voices in the making of modern Buddhism

The period from the later nineteenth to the first half of the twentieth centuries—roughly between the Indian Revolt of 1857 and the withdrawal of most European powers from direct rule in Asia—was one of immense change across Southeast Asia and the Buddhist world. This century saw the emergence of the elements that we now take to constitute modern Buddhism, or the multiple modern Buddhisms: the rise of the laity as practitioners and organizers (including meditation movements), new roles for women, for scholars and indeed for monks, the development of national sanghas and ethno-nationalist Buddhist discourses, and the association of Buddhism with a de-mythologized rationalist and scientific discourse. Moreover, the period saw the creation of new Buddhist institutional structures across Southeast Asia and Sri Lanka and multiple 'Buddhist Revivals' (late nineteenth century, turn of the twentieth century and, finally again, around 1956 with the Buddha Jayanti). It also saw the culmination of colonial empires (British, French, Japanese) and nationalism, decolonization and the creation of multiple Buddhist nation-states. It was the formative century for Buddhism, Asian modernity and their various hybrids.

The histories of modern Buddhism have, with some recent exceptions (Blackburn 2012; Jaffe 2004, 2006; Kirichenko 2012; Tweed 2011) tended to be insular—focused on the unfolding of Buddhism and modernity in a single country, perhaps unconsciously moulded by the ideas of Buddhism as a national entity that came to dominate the twentieth century. Yet, as we showed in an earlier special issue of *Contemporary Buddhism*, this is to write history backwards, taking the institutions and approaches which eventually became dominant, refining their own origin myths and drawing on their texts and archives. These histories are too often written *about* the winners, even if not always from supportive standpoints, despite the possibility of returning to contemporary sources and showing a very different picture. What global Buddhism had become by 1960, on the eve of its mass export to the West, was not at all that which was dominant in 1860. Buddhist modernism had to be *made*; the process whereby it became largely accepted by most of the surviving groups, as at least normative and an adequate self-representation to the outside world, was a long and winding road and the institutions and ideas characteristic of this final phase of establishment were not necessarily either those which started the process or those which appeared most significant at the time.

The more closely one investigates the changes enacted, the more it becomes clear that the creation of modern Buddhisms was not set mainly on a national stage, nor was it the product of local conversations alone. Instead, it was the fruit of extensive interactions and interconnections across a wide variety of national, ethnic, cultural and colonial boundaries (Bocking 2010, Turner 2010). As Richard Jaffe has encouraged us to understand, modern Buddhism was made and remade through a dizzying array of interactions and connections across Asia. The diverse modern constructions of Buddhism:

> involved a wide variety of Indians, Thais, Sri Lankans, Japanese, Koreans, Tibetans, and Chinese who listened and responded not only to what Europeans and Americans said about Buddhism, but who also talked among themselves.... Consideration of these exchanges in Asia reveals the emergence of a tightly linked global Buddhist culture in the late nineteenth century and illuminates the diverse 'complex global loops' through which ideas were transmitted. (Jaffe 2004, 67)

The more we come to understand the significance of these conversations and interconnections, the more the stories of those who crossed boundaries becomes important.

The articles gathered in this issue of *Contemporary Buddhism* shed light on such global loops. They are stories of unusual Buddhist figures who operated across boundaries to create their own hybrid interpretations of modern Buddhism. These stories complicate the picture of Buddhism in its modern modes by asking us to consider voices and conversations outside of the standard histories. They embody stories of Buddhism from the margins, but more than this, they represent the invention and imagination of modern Buddhism as a highly mobile, global, interactive and interpretative process.

Starting from the margins?

The papers collected here offer an alternative way to explore the making of modern Buddhisms. This alternative approach by no means provides a total picture (nor would it help to substitute one over-canonical account with another), but rather highlights a series of dimensions of 'Buddhist Revival', variously construed, wherein a new exploration of sources can offer a different and perhaps more adequate perspective.

Firstly, the authors in this issue approach Southeast Asia (and by extension South and East Asia) in this period as a dynamic 'Buddhist crossroads'. Frequently seen by westerners and by some Asian reformers as the locus of the 'original' teachings, lacking the academic and industrialized resources of the emerging Japanese empire and fragmented between British, French and independent states, Southeast Asia was a particular if diverse centre for *interactions* between different interpretations, organizations, individuals and agendas, interactions which proved fertile in the development of a 'global Buddhism' not controlled by any particular sect.

Secondly, in a period marked in turn by conquest, direct colonial rule, anti-colonial struggle and decolonization, *encounters* between European would-be Buddhists and Asian Buddhist networks (including financial sponsors, lay Buddhist organizations, monastic institutions, teachers and popular audiences) were—as several articles in this issue demonstrate for the first time—key elements in the formation of this new Buddhism.

Thirdly, however, with the emphasis on *pioneer*, those Buddhists—Asian, as well as European—who explored new possibilities were often correspondingly lacking in institutional resources (and hence reliant on such networks in their search for a base). Often they struggled for legitimacy and recognition from both Asian and western audiences, were at times isolated or seen as eccentric and often did not personally reap the benefits that those familiar with the later institutionalization and 'mainstreaming' of the new forms of Buddhism might expect.

The stories told here are less teleological and less rounded than is usual, in that many of the individuals involved were lost to history and the organizations (if any) they founded did not survive. Here, asking the question *why* they were forgotten can tell us much about those forms of contemporary 'global Buddhism' which have persisted. The story is also far more diverse and complex than when written 'backwards' from today's Buddhist high ground. Rather than project the winners of the present back into the past, the articles in this issue highlight the opening of moments of possibility, particularly in the period *before* the new Buddhism became established in lay and monastic contexts, showing the contested nature of the outcome to be something far more than a predestined conflict between 'tradition' and 'modernity'.

Failures and possibilities

On one level, the stories gathered here are studies in Buddhist failures. Most of the 'pioneer' figures and their stories documented here, in many cases for the first time, did not achieve success in conventional terms; at the simplest level, they have not been remembered. Any lineages they founded quickly died out. Their organizations became defunct. Most of their often ambitious projects appear in neither international nor local histories. And yet, their lives and their campaigns are significant for understanding Buddhism as it developed over this period of a century.

The Buddhist figures gathered here offer not simply examples of paths not taken, prospects rejected or options that dwindled away in the history of global and networked Buddhism. Instead, they stand as exemplars of what it was possible to imagine and attempt at different points in Buddhist colonial and transnational history. They represent avenues that have since been closed and abandoned in the Buddhist *imaginaire*, and they tell us something important about the potential that Buddhism was thought to have for cross-cultural understanding and, at times, world historical change. For Dhammaloka, Buddhism was imagined to have the potential to overcome colonialism; for Lokanatha, it had the potential to bring world peace; for Pfoundes it could temper the arrogance of the West. For some of the myriad subaltern whites in South and Southeast Asia, Buddhism offered an alternative culture and belonging. For McGovern, Utsuki and Kirby it offered a new identity. The hybrids of interpretation that these pioneers and border-crossers produced offer a glimpse of the wide potential that Buddhism represented over this century.

In the conclusion to his recent book, *The Lovelorn Ghost and the Magical Monk*, Justin McDaniel begins to reflect on failures as a theoretical lens for Buddhist studies. Referencing the metaphor of a museum that collected hoaxes and failed projects, he reflects on the possibilities entailed in refusing to create 'an ideal or comprehensive gallery of features.' The downside to this effort is that his examples, like the stories assembled here, refuse easy and systematic theorization. He writes, 'There are too many exceptions, idiosyncrasies, too many monasteries, too many agents, too many points to sight. I never have enough tools of analysis in my bag' (McDaniel 2011, 223). What McDaniel produces instead is an insightful picture of the diversity, embraced contradictions and idiosyncrasies of contemporary Buddhism in Thailand.

The stories collected in this issue of Euro–American–Asian and cross-Asian Buddhist encounters and their 'failures' constitute a body of work that can start to produce an equally complex representation of global Buddhism as a persistently shifting, interactive, irreducibly complex concatenation of creative *failures*. The stories of these 'pioneer' figures and their remarkable methods of crossing boundaries do not in themselves rewrite the history of Buddhist modernity. The figures involved are remarkable, for the most part, precisely because they are *not* representative of mainstream narratives, particularly of the sectarian and nationalistic kind; instead they formed their own 'crossroads'. They highlight unusual and otherwise forgotten perspectives and experiences in the cacophony of voices that made up 'Buddhism' between 1860–1960. In foregrounding the unusual, the marginal, we might even pose the question of whether these remarkable figures were only consigned to the past because in some ways they were ahead of their time. Can the sometimes extraordinary, yet forgotten, Buddhist lives discussed in this issue help us not only to rethink the global Buddhist past but also point us towards the unenvisaged and unrepresented voices present in the diversity of contemporary Buddhism?

This raises a general problem around mainstreaming and retrospective legitimacy. The figures discussed here were often able to be 'ahead of their time' *because* they were unusual, marginal, caught between worlds and so freer not only to see possibilities which were being opened up by the forces of social change but also to act on them. Yet, as we know, it took only a few decades for some of the approaches developed by such characters to become thoroughly 'mainstreamed'. Buddhist revival, and indeed anti-colonial nationalism, are in part at least a history of how what were once the strange ideas of marginal or outside eccentrics became the 'common sense' (Gramsci 1971) of whole populations and were adopted by traditional sangha hierarchies and the urban middle class. As such positions became 'respectable', of course, those who had first experimented with them often became something of an embarrassment (particularly if they did not fit into newly-dominant ethno-nationalist narratives), or simply became forgotten as the institutional memories of established Buddhist traditions or the new mass lay movements acquired the power to privilege their own origin stories (Turner, Cox and Bocking 2010). We might almost say that some of these figures were disposable and deniable: if their experiments proved effective, the ideas could be taken up but their originators discarded. If an experiment failed and could be forgotten, established organizations therefore lost nothing in legitimacy.

The methodological issues around such figures go beyond the politics of memory, however. They also raise the question of representativity. The figures discussed here often existed on the margins of what is now visible: unusual in their own time and not central to the 'means of intellectual production', albeit with some notable exceptions (Ober 2013). We regard them as of interest *both* because they are unusual and contradict received accounts *and* because they are sufficiently visible (because of their extraordinary efforts) that we can say something about them. U Dhammaloka, the unwitting progenitor of this particular research agenda (Turner, Cox and Bocking 2010), is exemplary in this respect.

Hence, in most cases, we are not talking about figures who were sufficiently embedded within the mainstream Buddhist organizations of their day for their perspectives to be amplified then or now as authoritative pronouncements; 'representative' in a political sense. Nor are we addressing the larger numbers of those whose involvement made the 'Buddhist crossroads' possible, as sponsors, organizational members, disciples, audiences, organizers and the like (Turner 2011, Cox 2010)—who could be considered 'representative' in the social sense. Rather, we feel, we present figures who offer us a window into worlds that would otherwise remain hidden; worlds whose existence we can demonstrate (Cox 2013) but where it is only the figures who stand in the margins between those worlds and the worlds of power and legitimacy who can readily be grasped. It is perhaps in this light that they are best understood and the specifics of these stories best read; they tell us something about sets of *relationships*; about social groups attempting to become subjects in the public world; about visions of Buddhism attempting to become normative among the wider population and about organizational structures attempting to find a purchase in reality.

A Buddhist crossroads

The articles collected in this issue cover a wide range of topics, all bearing in one way or another on the issues discussed above.

Brian Bocking's article (2013) draws on previously unseen archival sources to offer first a biography of the early and unjustly neglected interpreter of Japanese Buddhism, the Irishman Charles Pfoundes/'Omoie Tetzunostzuke' (Ireland–Australia–Siam–Japan–UK, 1840–1907) and then focuses on the final period of Pfoundes' life, in Japan, showing how his attempts to establish himself as both an academic and religious authority engaged him in the new world of giant exhibitions, congresses and conferences which, from the mid-nineteenth century onwards, formed an increasingly important material structure underpinning religious and scholarly (including Buddhist) networking. The best-known example was the 1893 World's Parliament of Religions, for which Pfoundes reportedly served as an advisor. Pfoundes' scholarly and personal engagement with Buddhism anticipates contemporary participant-observer approaches.

Tilman Frasch's article (2013) asks how new the Buddhist internationalism of the nineteenth to twentieth centuries really was, in the longer historical perspective. Examining more than two millennia of Buddhist travel in the wider Southeast Asian region, he focuses in particular on the councils and synods, noting their historical importance and yet variable standing within particular Buddhist histories and their relatively fixed dual function of standardizing the canon and purifying the sangha. Frasch shows how the 'modern' synods of the period covered in this special issue in Burma and Thailand were indeed innovative, for example in their methods of fixing the text of the Pali canon and in their reaching beyond Theravada.

Yoshinaga Shin'ichi (2013) begins from a recently-discovered cache of temple documents from the early twentieth century which he and his colleagues saved just in time from destruction, to explore a hitherto unknown but significant episode in Japanese Buddhism, the early twentieth century 'Mahayana Association' in Kyoto which brought together William McGovern (US–Philippines–Japan–Taiwan etc., 1897–1964), Utsuki Nishu (Japan–USA–UK–Japan, 1893–1951) and Mortimer T. Kirby (UK–Canada–Japan–Ceylon, 1877–?). Yoshinaga explores the Association's publications, ideas and extensive network of high-level scholarly contacts, its role in disseminating the ideas of D. T. Suzuki and its links to the later Kyoto Theosophical lodge and subsequent Japanese–Western Buddhist networks, offering fresh insights into the modern history of global Japanese Buddhism.

Alicia Turner's article (2013) discusses the 'politics of friendship' within which European–Asian Buddhist connections resisted colonial power, in relation to U Dhammaloka (Ireland–US–Burma etc., ?1856–?1913). Exploring Dhammaloka's analysis of colonialism as 'the Bible, the bottle and the knife', Turner shows how this familiar trope was deployed by Dhammaloka in a different context and how it informed both Dhammaloka's career and his activist programme. Turner asks why religion–in the form of resistance to missionaries and the defence of a 'lived' form of Buddhism–played such a central role, arguing that it enabled Dhammaloka to make authentic connections across the colonial divide. This marks Dhammaloka out from the majority of European and Asian anti-colonialists whose efforts to emancipate the oppressed all too often unwittingly reinforced the dividing categories of colonizer-colonized.

Elizabeth Harris (2013) re-examines, in light of recent discoveries of a number of plebeian early Western Buddhist monastics, the complex figure of Allan Bennett/Ananda Metteyya (UK–Ceylon–Burma–UK, 1872–1923), the Englishman who for almost a century has been represented as the 'first' Western Buddhist monk. Harris argues that far from being a 'gentleman scholar', Bennett's life exemplified a series of real tensions around respectability and the role of esotericism which were central to the western reception of Buddhism in the early 1900s. Bennett's activities included not only Buddhist missionary activism but also opposition to Christian missionaries and an anti-imperialist politics which position him as an early 'engaged Buddhist'.

Phibul Choompolpaisal's article (2013) focuses on the Yannawa (formerly Ban Thawai) area of Bangkok. Nowadays the central banking and business district in the sprawling city but in the 1900s home to a distinctively multi-ethnic and multireligious population ruled under Siamese–British–French treaty jurisdiction which guaranteed religious freedom. The area was packed with Western churches, clubs and consulates (precursors of the major embassies located there today), as well as Buddhist temples serving different ethnic groups. It was here in 1903 that the 'Irish Buddhist' U Dhammaloka opened the first Buddhist bilingual (English–Thai) school in Siam. Remarkably, that bilingual school still exists, though Dhammaloka appears nowhere in modern Thai accounts. Choompolpaisal analyses the complex and wide-ranging colonial configurations that made Wat Ban Thawai, rather than any other monastery, the obvious strategic base for an activist European monk from the Tavoy monastery in Rangoon.

Laurence Cox's article (2013) on 'other Buddhists' in colonial Asia situates lesser-known European monks such as U Dhammaloka in a world of 'poor whites' needed and discarded by Empire. By 'going native' across race boundaries in a period of increasing closure and by developing 'dissident Orientalisms' intended as critiques of imperial capitalism, these individuals formed fragile alliances with Asian networks. Cox suggests that we can see the history of early European conversions to Buddhism as a creative subaltern response to empire; a secondary but by no means irrelevant part of the process of anti-colonial Buddhist revival.

Douglas Ober (2013) explores the transnational activity of colonial-period Indian Buddhist pioneers, in particular Rāhul Sāṅkṛtyāyan (India–Ceylon–Burma–US, 1893–1963) and Dharmānand Kosambī (India–Ceylon–Tibet–Europe, 1876–1947). Both wrote in the vernacular to highlight the rational and progressive or socialist potential of Buddhism, while being themselves connected to a global Buddhist sphere as well as to Indian elites. Their dual outlook generated creative tensions and led to an extensive literary output, as well as presenting a culturally appealing version of Buddhism.

Andrew Skilton (2013) discusses the early British (and first Black British) bhikkhu George Blake/Vijjavaddho (Jamaica–Britain–Thailand–Canada, 1926–) in relation to the failure of the late 1950s attempt to form an independent sangha in England. The cross-cultural encounter of British bhikkhus with Thai monastics in Thailand highlights the tensions and complexities of Buddhism's journey to the west. The previously untold events in which the youthful George Blake/Vijjavaddho was embroiled were to have a significant impact on the development both of meditation techniques and of Theravada monasticism in the west.

Philip Deslippe (2013), finally, offers a biography of the extraordinary Italian-American Buddhist monk Salvatore Cioffi/Ven. Lokanatha (US–Italy–Burma–India etc., 1897–1966) and his dramatic missionary activities in pursuit of Buddhist conversions, love, peace and vegetarianism in India, Italy and the United States, including his involvement with Dr B. S. Ambedkar. Deslippe's paper highlights Lokanatha's changing roles in different periods, cultures and contexts, notably the racialized and sensationalist nature of his media reception in the US, and examines why a figure as committed, devout, energetic and well-publicized (in his time) as Lokanatha was excluded from the conventional canon of western Buddhist history.

Empirical findings

From these papers we can derive a number of empirical findings about the 'Buddhist crossroads' of Southeast Asia and indeed more widely in the period 1860–1960, when 'modern Buddhism' was being shaped.

Firstly, and perhaps least surprisingly, the interactions and interconnections between Asian and western Buddhist modernists—and connections between Asian

Buddhists from different countries and cultures—stand out as central, though as Frasch's article makes clear, Buddhist interactions of different kinds long predated the nineteenth century. As Anne Blackburn (2010) and others have highlighted, international and intercultural connections between Buddhist polities were important for the construction of local authority and Buddhist modernities. Yet more and more we are coming to see that far broader and more diverse sets of interactions played a key role in this period.[1] As the figures and their itineraries mentioned above indicate, many of the people engaged in the construction of modern Buddhism were inveterate travellers, moving not only between East and West but within both, and it is of course precisely this process which made it possible to 'disembed' Buddhism from (some of) its traditional, 'taken-for-granted' features—social context, life course, cultural meaning, ritual, practices, texts—and to construct forms of Buddhism which (to a greater or lesser extent) 'worked' in this wider context.

Secondly, India and Japan appear centrally for very different reasons. Japan from the mid-nineteenth century became a rapidly-modernizing independent Asian imperial power, its egregious success in comparison with other Asian regions symbolized above all by its victories in the 1894–1895 Sino-Japanese conflict and 1904–1905 Russo-Japanese war. Japanese Buddhists, struggling to stay abreast of galloping modernity in Japan, sought to reform Buddhism within while simultaneously launching a 'Buddhist mission' to the West (Bocking 2013; Yoshinaga 2013), while their secular rulers saw Buddhism largely as a means of positioning Japan as the natural leader of its Asian neighbours. India, for its part, was the fulcrum of British imperial power in Asia and marked by the development of new social classes who looked to Buddhism (and to socialism) as viable alternatives to both Christianity and capitalism (Cox 2013; Ober 2013). Moreover, by the end of the nineteenth century, India was being re-discovered and re-imagined as the birthplace of Buddhism and a necessary nexus for international Buddhist connections (Frasch 2013; Jaffe 2004). This is not to say that other countries were absent—*vide* the role of independent Thailand (Choompolpaisal 2013; Skilton 2013) or that of newly-conquered Burma, resistant to its absorption within imperial India (Turner 2013; Harris 2013; Deslippe 2013). Rather, we expected that in studying the Buddhist crossroads of Southeast Asia the imperial powers, particularly Britain, would bulk large. We did not expect that in these articles India and Japan would appear so active as they do.

Thirdly, as the papers by Bocking (2013), Frasch (2013) and Yoshinaga (2013) in particular make clear, we need to identify and take full account of the fast-changing *material* basis for international Buddhist networking and innovation. In this period, new modes of travel were becoming widely available—indeed a map of the places and journeys mentioned in this volume would be largely a map of steamship and railway lines—and such things were becoming accessible enough that, for example, the ordinary traveller's journey from the Shan state to Bangkok had by the early 1900s been reduced from three months to one day—with no identity checks for monks (Choompolpaisal 2013). A friendly railway guard could slip U Dhammaloka's casual acquaintances onto a train in 1905 and Dhammaloka himself could be offered a steamship ticket from Burma to Ceylon in 1909 by the Maha Bodhi Society and even tour Australia alone in 1912. Travel, above all, became more *routine*, something around which it was possible to build viable organizations and networks.

We see too the widespread development of printing presses. Dhammaloka could churn out 'hundreds of thousands' of his pamphlets in Asia as across the world. This spawned a whole ecology of colonial newspapers, missionary and other periodicals, as well as, increasingly, Asian-language papers. All of these could reflect and amplify the activities of such figures, be it by reprinting their own publicity pieces or criticizing their behaviour. It is this same amplification through print media that has made it possible now for us to recover histories which would previously have been lost, as Deslippe (2013) discusses. Along with mass publication went the widespread adoption of new *lingua francas*—most notably English and French—and the development of South and Southeast Asian vernaculars as Buddhist languages in their own right (Frasch 2013; Ober 2013), all of which made a new kind of Buddhist revival possible, scattering copies of the same books and periodicals across the continent(s). This inevitably took scriptural and other knowledge out of the exclusive possession of monks and made it more widely available to the educated laity, whose organizations would become increasingly central to modern Buddhist networking.

Not all of the above are new observations, but the articles gathered here serve as a useful counterpoint to histories of Buddhist modernity that emphasize texts and ideas, by demonstrating that the kinds of debates which could be pursued were shaped and indeed made possible by the practical ability of multiple participants to have access to texts, printed cheaply in a language they understood, and widely distributed. Furthermore, without the ability to travel, recruitment to organizations, meet one's peers at congresses, exhibitions and similar 'nodal' locations and thus encounter, at first hand, other Buddhisms and other Buddhist responses to colonialism, such debates could hardly have got off the ground.

New research technologies and collaboration

In a previous special issue of *Contemporary Buddhism* in November 2010 which launched the forgotten figure of U Dhammaloka, we discussed briefly the new twenty first century digital technologies which had enabled us, working collaboratively yet thousands of miles apart, to piece together—from hundreds of fragmentary and formerly 'lost' pieces of information—a fairly comprehensive account of Dhammaloka's public career as a monk between 1900–1913. This research continues and we have recently discovered, for example, that Dhammaloka was ordained in Rangoon in July 1900 (Turner 2013) and that he spent several months travelling in Australia in 1912. Phibul Choompolpaisal's research (2013) has shown that Dhammaloka's efforts in Siam were surprisingly effective and led to the establishment of a pioneering bilingual school still in existence today. What the present special issue of *Contemporary Buddhism* makes very clear is that the methods which have enabled us to recover Dhammaloka from obscurity have the potential to expand the study of Buddhism much more broadly.

Thousands of newspapers, books, personal documents, realia and images from the nineteenth and early twentieth centuries are now newly available worldwide in digital form, increasingly in a multiplicity of languages and scripts. Individual pieces of digitized material are, of course, often of questionable value as documentary evidence. Dhammaloka, whose own pseudonymous report of his death from *beri-beri* in a Melbourne temperance hotel was widely circulated in the Southeast Asian press in 1912 before he reappeared in Singapore to resume his preaching tours, was particularly well-placed to warn against believing what you read in the papers! However, the more material that becomes available, the greater the chance to check any piece of information against independent sources.

The articles in this issue demonstrate just how much of the conventional narrative about the rise of modern Buddhism has been founded on a limited body of centrally preserved sources. Often, in the pre-digital age, the work required to 'join the dots' between snippets of data was too overwhelming, discouraging the creation of social, plebeian and alternative Buddhist histories of this period. These sources have always been available somewhere (see Yoshinaga 2013 for a remarkable Japanese example), but the technologies that allow for broader and more rapid searches let us build unprecedented connections and value multiple types of evidence in order to write new histories of Buddhism.

The exponential increase in digital sources in a variety of languages makes collaborative research almost an imperative. Any account of Pfoundes, McGovern, Utsuki or M. T. Kirby, for example, relies almost half and half on English and Japanese sources, often hard to interpret even for a native speaker (Bocking 2013; Yoshinaga 2013). With reference to the specific theme of 'Buddhist crossroads', grasping trans-Asian processes and relationships is always likely to require expertise in multiple languages and/or contexts. At the same time, the new wealth of digital data often needs a variety of methodological tools to analyse and interpret adequately; this is another dimension where a single scholar can rarely be expert in all the dimensions needed for such research.

Collaboration raises its own tricky issues of course, especially for early-career faculty, graduate students and others who need to collaborate in order to benefit from multilingual digital resources but may at any point find themselves being judged on what of the research output they can claim as 'their own'. In this respect, scholars in the humanities may have something to learn from colleagues in the material sciences, where publications are routinely issued as multi-authored works, thus avoiding the whole area of the etiquette of acknowledgements. On the other hand, what we have to learn from colleagues in the sciences may also be a hard lesson; that in a team effort the one who really does make a key discovery is not always the one who gets the credit.

Technological issues also raise their head in relation to the problem of organizing and archiving. The new digital research tools enable the rapid generation of vast quantities of data, which readily outstrip the capacities of an individual brain to order or remember. The data is also, often, in a wide variety of formats, making an effective cataloguing system a tall order. Paywalls, copyright issues and institutional access further complicate individual management of digital data.

From the other side, when data collection is primarily a question of digitization by the researcher, as is often the case with obscure religious periodicals for example, the question becomes how best to archive such data for future use and accessibility, not only by the collector but by other researchers. While few will argue that a researcher who has just completed something as labour-intensive as scanning, uploading and cataloguing a whole series of a periodical does *not* have a right to retain it for personal use for a while, most will agree that at some point the researcher should ensure the future survival of the digital material and its widespread availability to others. Increasingly, open-access conditions attached to research grants are taking this decision away from researchers, making it all the more urgent for the individual or team to exploit as quickly as possible all of the data painstakingly gleaned through the effort of retrieval and digitization—an effort which very often involves much travel, time, and diplomacy in obtaining access to obscure repositories.

As we have found time and again in working on Dhammaloka and other pioneer Buddhists, and indeed as every researcher who uses 'primary' documents already knows well, the same raw material may at first glance yield very different insights from those that emerge on subsequent review and in light of further information. It is not just a matter of doing the work on digitized materials 'properly' the first time before releasing them to the world. Generating a reliable assessment and understanding of (usually) decontextualized material texts and images is an intrinsically complex, iterative and therefore lengthy process.

A technological question of a different order is raised by our engagement, through the lens of what twenty first century choices have made available in digital form, with the changing technologies of the late nineteenth and early twentieth centuries. An understanding of shipping routes and the chronology of railway lines, for example, proves important to understanding the strategic importance of some locations for networking. The development of the telegraph and cheap printing underpins the lively ecology of colonial newspapers and small religious and radical periodicals, often reprinting each other's material across great distances, through which we now grasp the activities of many of the pioneer Buddhists. Digitized guide books, street directories, university yearbooks and the like, in a variety of languages, all become important tools. Maps acquire a crucial importance, particularly in Asian cities ravaged first by war and then by breakneck building booms, where the city of 100 years ago may well prefigure the contemporary geography but has often disappeared from view except in maps. Finally, as we move into studies of events in the mid-twentieth century in particular, we will need to explore how other emerging technologies (photographs, wireless, films, audio recording, television) shaped the transmission of Buddhist ideas and Buddhist lives.

Buddhism at a crossroads?

Early versions of the papers collected in this special issue were among those presented at the conference, 'Southeast Asia as a Buddhist Crossroads: Pioneer European Buddhists and Asian Networks 1860–1960' hosted by the Study of Religions department of University College Cork, Ireland, in September 2012. Details of the conference participants and abstracts of papers presented at the conference are available on the conference legacy website (http://buddhistcrossroads.wordpress.com).

This innovative conference brought together scholars from around the world working on very different, and in many cases seemingly unconnected, 'pioneer' Buddhists and new examples of Buddhist connections and interactions spread across a period of almost a century. As it turned out, we discovered through three days of stimulating presentations and fruitful and engaged discussion that we had many research themes and questions in common. The conference generated several new lines of individual and collaborative research which are already under way and will undoubtedly bear fruit in future publications.

The 'Buddhist Crossroads' conference concluded with a lively and thought-provoking workshop session which sought to identify and feed back to the whole conference those themes which participants felt were most significant for future research. Many of the themes highlighted in this Introduction, notably the comments on the role of technologies (whether nineteenth or twenty-first century), the significance of failure and the question of representativity stem from that workshop. Hence, the ideas presented in this Introduction are by no means ours alone and we wish to acknowledge the contribution of all the participants in the conference.

The 'Buddhist Crossroads' conference in Cork was funded by the Dhammakaya International Society of the UK (DISUK) as part of a one-year Postdoctoral Fellowship entitled 'Continuities and Transitions in Early Modern Thai Buddhism'; itself part of a wider project on premodern and modern Thai Buddhism involving the universities of Cork, Oxford and London (King's College). The Postdoctoral Fellowship at University College Cork was held during 2012 by Dr Phibul Choompolpaisal, who played the leading role in publicizing and organizing the September 'Buddhist Crossroads' conference, the initiative which has led directly to this special issue of *Contemporary Buddhism*.

ACKNOWLEDGEMENTS

Laurence Cox would like to thank the Irish Research Council for funding enabling his work on this special issue and ongoing research on U Dhammaloka and early western Buddhists in Asia.

NOTE

1. In addition to the articles collected here see: Blackburn (2012), Jaffe (2004 and 2006), Kirichenko (2012), Cao and Lau (2013), Tweed (2011).

REFERENCES

BLACKBURN, ANNE M. 2010. *Locations of Buddhism: Colonialism and Modernity in Sri Lanka*. Chicago: University of Chicago Press.

BLACKBURN, ANNE M. 2012. *Ceylonese Buddhism in Colonial Singapore: New Ritual Spaces and Specialists, 1895–1935*. Asia Research Institute Working Paper Series. Singapore: Asia Research Institute, National University of Singapore.

BOCKING, BRIAN. 2010. 'A Man of Work and Few Words'? Dhammaloka Beyond Burma. *Contemporary Buddhism* 11 (2): 125–47.

BOCKING, BRIAN. 2013. Flagging up Buddhism: Charles Pfoundes (Omoie Tetzunostzuke) Among the International Congresses and Expositions, 1893–1905. *Contemporary Buddhism* 14 (1): 17–37.

CAO, NANLAI, and SIN WEN LAU. 2013. Reconstituting Boundaries and Connectivity: Religion and Mobility in a Globalising Asia. *The Asia Pacific Journal of Anthropology* 14 (1): 1–7.

CHOOMPOLPAISAL, PHIBUL. 2013. Tai-Burmese-Lao Buddhisms in the 'Modernizing' of Ban Thawai (Bangkok): The Dynamic Interaction between Ethnic Minority Religion and British–Siamese centralization in the Late Nineteenth/Early Twentieth Centuries. *Contemporary Buddhism* 14 (1): 94–115.

COX, LAURENCE. 2010. The Politics of the Buddhist Revival: U Dhammaloka as Social Movement Organizer. *Contemporary Buddhism* 11 (2): 173–227.

COX, LAURENCE. 2013. Rethinking Early Western Buddhists: Beachcombers, 'Going Native' and Dissident Orientalism. *Contemporary Buddhism* 14 (1): 116–133.

DESLIPPE, PHILIP. 2013. Brooklyn Bhikkhu: How Salvatore Cioffi Became the Venerable Lokanatha. *Contemporary Buddhism* 14 (1): 169–186.

FRASCH, TILMAN. 2013. Buddhist Councils in a Time of Transition: Globalism, Modernity and the Preservation of Textual Traditions. *Contemporary Buddhism* 14 (1): 38–51.

GRAMSCI, ANTONIO. 1971. *Selections from the prison notebooks of Antonio Gramsci*. London: Lawrence and Wishart.

HARRIS, ELIZABETH J. 2013. Ananda Metteyya: Controversial Networker, Passionate Critic. *Contemporary Buddhism* 14 (1): 78–93.

JAFFE, RICHARD. 2004. Seeking Sakyamuni: Travel and the Reconstruction of Japanese Buddhism. *Journal of Japanese Studies* 30 (1): 65–96.

JAFFE, RICHARD. 2006. Buddhist Material Culture, 'Indianism,' and the Construction of Pan-Asian Buddhism in Prewar Japan. *Material Religion: The Journal of Objects, Art and Belief* 2 (3): 266–92.

KIRICHENKO, ALEXEY. 2012. *New Spaces for Interaction: Contacts between Burmese and Sinhalese Monks in the Late Nineteenth and Early Twentieth Centuries*. Asia Research Institute Working Paper Series. Singapore: Asia Research Institute, National University of Singapore.

MCDANIEL, JUSTIN. 2011. *The Lovelorn Ghost and the Magical Monk Practicing Buddhism in Modern Thailand*. New York: Columbia University Press.

OBER, DOUGLAS. 2013. 'Like embers hidden in ashes, or jewels encrusted in stone': Rāhul Sāṅkrtyāyan, Dharmānand Kosambī and Buddhist activity in colonial India. *Contemporary Buddhism* 14 (1): 134–148.

SKILTON, ANDREW. 2013. Elective Affinities: The Reconstruction of a Forgotten Episode in the Shared History of Thai and British Buddhism—Kapilavaḍḍho and Wat Paknam. *Contemporary Buddhism* 14 (1): 149–168.

TURNER, ALICIA. 2010. The Irish Pongyi in Colonial Burma: The Confrontations and Challenges of U Dhammaloka. *Contemporary Buddhism* 11 (2): 149–71.

TURNER, ALICIA. 2011. "Across Colonial Contexts with an Irish Ally: U Dhammaloka and His Patrons," paper presented at Association of Asian Studies and International Convention of Asia Scholars joint conference, Honolulu, Hawaii, March 31, 2011.

TURNER, ALICIA. 2013. The Bible, The Bottle And The Knife: Religion as a Mode of Resisting Colonialism for U Dhammaloka. *Contemporary Buddhism* 14 (1): 66–77.

TURNER, ALICIA, LAURENCE COX, and BRIAN BOCKING. 2010. Beachcombing, Going Native and Freethinking: Rewriting the History of Early Western Buddhist Monastics. *Contemporary Buddhism* 11 (2): 125–47.

TWEED, THOMAS. 2011. Theory and Method in the Study of Buddhism: Toward 'Translocative' Analysis. *Journal of Global Buddhism* 12: 17–32.

YOSHINAGA, SHIN'ICHI. 2013. Three Boys on a Great Vehicle: 'Mahayana Buddhism' and a Trans-National Network. *Contemporary Buddhism* 14 (1): 52–65.

FLAGGING UP BUDDHISM: CHARLES PFOUNDES (*OMOIE TETZUNOSTZUKE*) AMONG THE INTERNATIONAL CONGRESSES AND EXPOSITIONS, 1893–1905

Brian Bocking

Charles James William Pfoundes (1840–1907), a young emigrant from Southeast Ireland, spent most of his adult life in Japan, received a Japanese name 'Omoie Tetzunostzuke', first embraced and then turned against Theosophy and, from 1893, was ordained in several Japanese Buddhist traditions. Lacking independent means but educated, intellectually curious, entrepreneurial, fluent in Japanese and with a keen interest in Asian culture, Pfoundes subsisted as a cultural intermediary, explaining Japan and Asia to both Japanese and foreign audiences and actively seeking involvement in global expositions and congresses, in Asia and beyond. Drawing on a previously unstudied collection of Pfoundes' personal documents, this paper first outlines Pfoundes' unusual career and then focuses on his engagement, in the last 15 years of his life, in actual or proposed international congresses and expositions in London, Chicago, Japan, Hanoi, St Louis and Oregon. The paper thereby draws attention, through the forgotten figure of Charles Pfoundes, to the distinctive nineteenth century phenomenon of great international expositions and their associated congresses, viewing these complicated events as another kind of crossroads; innovative nodes and material stimuli to the kinds of travel, cultural communication and interaction which, like monastic, trade, political and ethnic networks, helped to exchange and promote modern representations of Buddhism.

In December 1902, the first Congress of Orientalists ever to be held in the East was convened in Hanoi, French Indo-China, in conjunction with a major trade exposition (Premier Congrès International Des Études D'extrême-Orient 1902; Schneider 1903). During a post-conference excursion on Sunday 9 December, the Congress delegates, most of whom were distinguished scholars from Europe and Japan, took a short train ride and then walked towards the famous Lim Pagoda 'preceded', as reported some weeks later in *The Times of India*, 'by the flag of the Irish Buddhist, which represented rays of light proceeding from the mystic svastica in the centre'.[1]

We know that just over a year later, on 17 January 1904, another 'Irish Buddhist', the Burmese-ordained monk, U Dhammaloka, would unfurl Colonel Olcott's many-striped Buddhist flag aloft the new 'Buddhist Mission' opened by Dhammaloka in Havelock Road, Singapore, but the Hanoi excursion of 1902 featured neither Olcott's flag nor the plebeian monk U Dhammaloka (though Dhammaloka was not very far away from Hanoi in December 1902, being himself *en route* from Tokyo via Kobe and Hong Kong to Singapore).[2] Instead, 'the Irish Buddhist' heading the procession of savants was a well-educated 62 year old with the unusual name of Charles Pfoundes. Pfoundes was present at the Hanoi Congress as one of 54 individual '*adhérents*', not as an official national or learned society delegate (Schneider 1903, 51), but he saw himself as representing a consortium of mainstream Buddhist sects in Japan, for it was a flag of modern Japanese Buddhism that he was carrying[3] and the *Hong Kong Daily Press* reported that Pfoundes would represent at the Congress 'the chief monasteries of the Tendai, Shingon, Zen, and Jodo sects and also Japanese art'. [4] For Pfoundes, managing to position himself in the role of Buddhist leader at the head of a procession of genuinely eminent orientalist scholars must have been one of the high points in a life marked often by disappointment and frustration. Pfoundes' enjoyment of the congress is evident in the conclusion to a report on the Hanoi visit that he sent the following month to *The Open Court* in Chicago:

> ... I visited a number of the temples, and the bonzes performed ceremonies and read the Buddhist scriptures. I took with me some of the vestments given me by the Japanese Cathedrals (Dai Hon Zan). Thus there were opportunities for my seeing the natives. Early every morning I went to the markets—of which there are a number—and purchased fruits and flowers. The cafes not being opened until late, I had a morning meal of fruit, bread, and light wine; then took the electric tram and visited the temples, returning in time for the Congress meetings. The exhibits at the Exhibition illustrated what is being done, and the past efforts as well as future projects to exploit the Colonies. It was altogether a delightful trip. (C. Pfoundes, January 8, 1903, Kobe, Japan)[5]

An outline of Pfoundes' life

Charles Pfoundes was born Charles James William Pounds in 1840 in or near Waterford, a coastal town in the South East of Ireland, which was then part of the UK.[6] He was the second son of Caroline Elam, an Irish-born descendant of Yorkshire Quakers who is remembered now in Australia as an obscure but accomplished watercolourist, and her husband James Baker Pounds, an Irish Protestant apothecary and entrepreneur who went bankrupt around the time of the great famine (1845–1846) and later emigrated to Australia where he became a respected coroner and magistrate in Victoria. [7] Charles had very little contact with his family after the age of 14 years. He sailed, apparently alone, to Australia in 1854 on the *Great Britain*,[8] almost immediately joined the colonial navy and by the early

1860s was captaining a Siamese ship. He changed his surname to the near-unique and more interesting-sounding 'Pfoundes' (usually pronounced 'Founds') in his late twenties, by which time he was resident in Japan.[9]

The 'other' pioneer Irish Buddhist, U Dhammaloka, was a celebrity in South-East Asia between 1900–1913 but who Dhammaloka 'really' was and what he had been up to in his 45-odd years of (presumably) secular life before catching the public eye as a monk in Rangoon remains entirely obscure.[10] Pfoundes' whole life, by contrast, is relatively well documented, not only because Pfoundes had evidently received a good school-level education which later enabled him to produce written works worthy of academic and other publication, but also because he wrote and spoke prolifically, often about his own activities. The present article draws in particular on a collection of previously unstudied papers of Pfoundes', held in the archives of the Oregon Historical Society and comprising more than 40 pages of typed, printed and handwritten items sent during 1902–1903 by Pfoundes in Kobe to the organisers of the forthcoming (1905) Lewis and Clark Centennial Exposition in Portland, Oregon. Since Pfoundes was attempting to establish his *bona fides* with the organising committee, with a view to being appointed organiser of a Congress of Orientalists at the Exposition, the cache of correspondence largely rehearses Pfoundes' accomplishments and amounts to a lengthy curriculum vitae richly documented with supporting explanations, flyers, booklets and advertisements. Allowing for a certain amount of exaggeration and omission, this new material has proved extraordinarily helpful in filling in a number of gaps in Pfoundes' history and helping to clarify his thinking on several topics.

Pfoundes was in Japan very early indeed. He arrived aged 23 in 1863, five years ahead of the transformative 'Meiji Restoration' of 1868 and during a period of considerable local and international tension and civil disorder. Pfoundes had already travelled widely in the Far East as a naval seaman and he quickly learned Japanese, so that over the 12 years from 1863–1875 he was able to assist, in various ways, the British, US and other foreign legations, as well as the Japanese authorities. He imported and exported foreign goods and in 1870–1871 accompanied some high-ranking Japanese government and business figures to Europe (including a visit to the Pope) and the USA.[11] From 1871–1876, Pfoundes played a significant role in the emerging Japanese merchant shipping industry, writing later that he was 'appointed to assist the semi-official Directors of the first Japanese Mail and Transport Steam Ship service, in organization and super-intendence, up to 1876'.[12] By the age of 35, after 12 years in Japan, Pfoundes had also acquired a remarkably wide knowledge of Japanese history, art, culture, customs and folklore; a knowledge which, for the rest of his life, he showed himself keen to share with anyone who would listen.

In 1876, Pfoundes left Japan for Philadelphia and New York where, in June 1876, he presided over a sale of 'Japanese art treasures', many from his own collection, and lectured in Boston and elsewhere. The sale realized a considerable sum, though apparently insufficient to give him financial independence in London where he evidently planned to settle.[13] As it happens, the Theosophical Society had been founded in New York by Blavatsky and Olcott only a few months earlier, in November 1875, and was holding regular meetings. It is quite probable that Pfoundes became aware of the Theosophical Society at this very early stage of its development; he subsequently contributed several articles to Theosophical journals, reflecting his general interest in Buddhism, spiritualism and esoteric matters. However, contacts between the Theosophists and modernising Buddhists in Japan were, according to Yoshinaga (2009), initiated only much later and independently of Pfoundes, through contacts in 1887 between William Q. Judge of the American Theosophical Society and Matsuyama Matsutarō, and between Colonel Olcott and Anagarika Dharmapala in Ceylon and Hirai Kinza.[14]

Between 1876–1878 Pfoundes travelled widely in Western and Eastern Europe.[15] We know that in 1877 he was in Ireland on at least two occasions, trying to extract from his mother Caroline—with threats—various personal possessions and some papers which he believed would help him secure a civil service post in London. Mrs Pounds took him to court where on 2 November 1877, he was bound over to keep the peace.[16] Four months later in March 1878, at Liverpool Registry Office, Pfoundes married 22 year old Rosa Alice Hill, one of the daughters of Lewis Hill, the governor of Sandwich gaol in Kent. From 1879 onwards, Pfoundes and his new wife lived in London where throughout the 1880s Pfoundes held a minor position as a scribe in the Admiralty and outside working hours threw himself into the activities of many of the learned and professional societies of the capital, delivering a host of public lectures on topics ranging from Japanese art, literature and folklore to first aid, Buddhism, respect for Oriental cultures, spiritualism, [anti-] Theosophy, vegetarianism and colonial policy, and participating in discussions of lectures given by others.[17]

Pfoundes was an indefatigable public speaker. A booklet from the 1890s, printed by Pfoundes to advertise his services, lists no fewer than 170 *topics* on which he was prepared to speak! Newspaper reports and learned society annals of the time convey the flavour of dozens of his lectures. Published works by Pfoundes which have come down to us are only slightly less ambitious in their scope. The earliest pieces, in the 1860s and 1870s, comprised occasional columns on Japanese art, literature, folklore and customs for the *Japan Mail*, an English-language newspaper published in Yokohama. In 1875 these items on Japanese culture and customs were collected and published as *Fuso-mimi-bukuro: A Budget of Japanese Notes*, a work similar in conception to Basil Hall Chamberlain's later *Things Japanese* which, from 1890, effectively superseded Pfoundes' book. In the 1870s, Pfoundes was also publishing trenchant criticisms of the behaviour of his Japanese and foreign compatriots engaged (like him) in the scramble for wealth and position in the new Japan in a series of substantial letters written to the *Japan Herald* under a bewildering variety of pen names.[18]

While still in Japan, Pfoundes became a founder member of the London-based Folklore Society,[19] contributing some Japanese folk tales to the very first (1878) issue of the society's journal. Pfoundes' broad familiarity with Japanese artistic and religious objects is well reflected in his essays and entries in the catalogue *Japanese Art Treasures* (1876), published in New York for the sale of 627 lots belonging to Pfoundes and the Japanese government.[20] From 1880 onwards he published in a variety of outlets, from lectures reproduced in learned journals such as the *Transactions of the Royal Society of Literature* to accounts of his intrepid early exploits in Japan and China for the children's adventure magazine *Young Folks Paper*.[21] In the late 1880s and early 1890s, Pfoundes had articles on esoteric thought and Buddhism accepted by Theosophical journals such as *Le Lotus, Lucifer, The Lamp* and *Theosophical Siftings*, presumably with some publishing delay since by the time the articles appeared Pfoundes was actively denouncing Theosophy in his London lectures. Several letters and articles from Pfoundes in London warning against Theosophy were published in Japanese Buddhist magazines in the same period (Akai 2009). Back in Japan, from 1893 onwards, Pfoundes wrote a number of articles on Japanese religions and Buddhism for Paul Carus' *The Open Court* in Chicago, including a remarkably even-handed 1895 assessment of the relative prospects of Christianity and Buddhism in Japan and his 1903 account of the Hanoi congress (as quoted above).[22]

In London, in the early 1890s, Pfoundes was living alongside Ramsay Macdonald and others in a commune of the socially progressive and spiritually-oriented 'Fellowship of the New Life' led by Edith Lees, later consort of the sexologist Havelock Ellis (Cox 2013). About this time Pfoundes became the London representative of the modern Jōdo Shinshū-backed Japanese Buddhist missionary society the *Kaigai senkyōkai*, a role in which he reportedly warned the young scholar Takakusu Junjirō away from the London Theosophists and hence towards Max Müller (Akai, 2009, 190); a significant Weberian moment in the history of Japanese Buddhology, if so. The other activities, if there were any, of Pfoundes' London Japanese Buddhist outpost remain undocumented; perhaps an unwritten—and very early—chapter in the history of Buddhism in the UK. However, by 1893, things were not going well for Pfoundes in London. His marriage had failed,[23] in 1893 he lost his post at the Admiralty (later suggesting that he had retired, for his health)[24] and with a passage as far as Hong Kong provided by the British government, he returned alone to Japan in the same year. There he remained, working in a hectic variety of roles—as shipping agent, interpreter, licensed travel guide, cultural and business intermediary[25] and self-appointed 'senior resident' of Kobe (Figure 1)—until his death of heart failure in 1907, at the age of 67.[26]

It was during his final period of residence in Japan, from 1893 onwards, that Pfoundes was ordained in various mainstream Buddhist sects (certainly Shugendō/Shingon and Tendai; probably Zen and Jōdo Shinshū)[27] and had a role, at least initially, as spokesman for Buddhism against Christianity. In lectures delivered during 1893 and published in the same year by his Buddhist sponsors, Pfoundes criticized Christian missionaries for looking down on both Buddhism and Japan (Thelle, 1987, 109).[28] After 1893, the Chicago World's Parliament of Religions created a new atmosphere of religious dialogue in Japan, the era of 'White

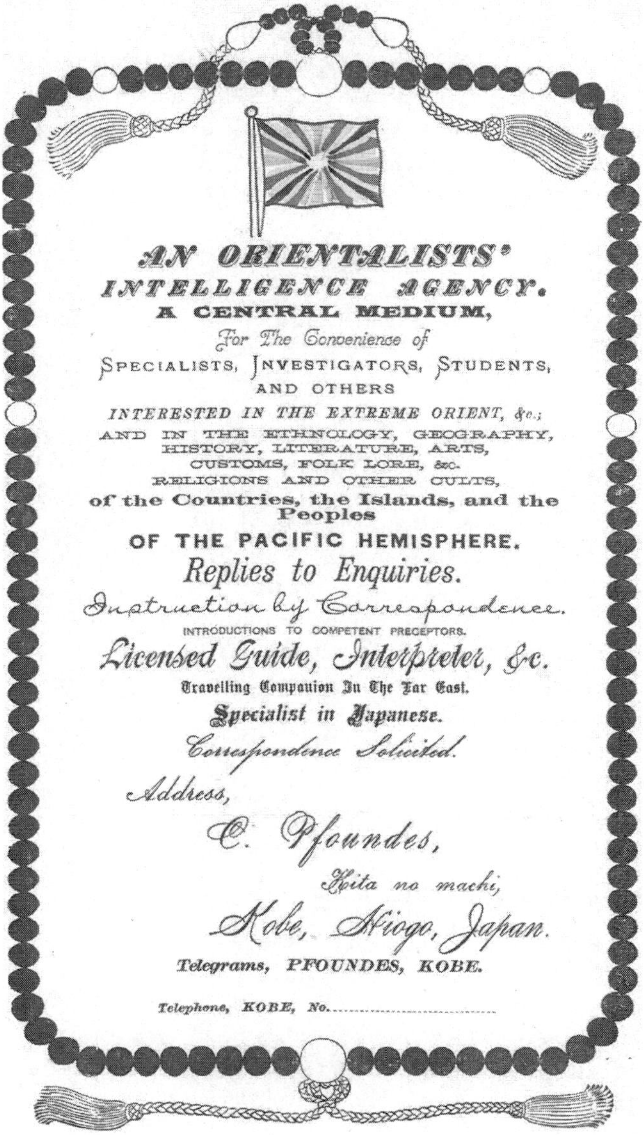

FIGURE 1

One of several handbills produced by Pfoundes in Kobe to advertise his services. This example with hand-coloured flag and Buddhist rosary border, c. 1902. Lewis and Clark Centennial Exposition records, MSS 1609, Oregon Historical Society Research Library.

Buddhist' champions had passed with Olcott and Japanese Buddhists soon found Pfoundes difficult to deal with (Yoshinaga, 2009, 122, 126; Pfoundes reportedly pointed a gun at one Buddhist colleague[29]). However, Pfoundes did not leave Japan, as Thelle and other commentators have assumed. He worked incessantly and in 1899 even attempted, albeit unsuccessfully, to become a Japanese citizen.[30] As we have seen, he was in Hanoi in 1902 purportedly representing the major Japanese Buddhist sects. Photographs published in the *East of Asia Magazine* (Pfoundes 1905) show him taking part in a Shugendō fire ritual to benefit the nation in its 1904–1905 war with Russia.[31] It is evident that he died in 1907 a Japanese Buddhist.

Pfoundes' Buddhist credentials were noticed only posthumously by the *Buddhist Review* in London after an exhibition of Japanese temple pictures, catalogued by Pfoundes for their owner some years earlier, was shown at Fishmongers' Hall, London, in 1911. *The Times* reported that:

> The pictures were collected by Mr. Ambrose De'ath during his wanderings in Japan, where he lived for 38 years. [. . .] The descriptions and particulars were collected and compiled by the late Mr. C. J. W. Pfounds (*sic*), assisted by a number of priests and laymen versed in Buddhist lore. Mr Pfounds went to Japan in the early '60s and gave up his whole time to the study of the language. He afterwards occupied several important positions. Becoming a convert to Buddhism, he took up his abode at the principal temple in Matsue, in the province of Izumo, residing with the priests. Continuing his studies, he passed his examination and was duly admitted to orders as a novice, and was attached to the temple, taking part in the performance of the religious ceremonies. (*The Times*, May 23)

Pfoundes among the international expositions and congresses

Large-scale expositions and their associated congresses were, by the end of the nineteenth century, a major contributor to the globalization of cultural ideas and practices. While showcasing new technologies and products from the industrializing nations, the expositions commanded such impressive resources and attracted such a large proportion of the local population as visitors[32] that they were able to project a coherent and convincing vision of a modernising and secularising world (Burris, 2001, xiv).

In *Exhibiting Religion: Colonialism and Spectacle at International Expositions 1851–1893*, John P. Burris argues that these large-scale international events were particularly important in the development of the field of *religion*. He says this is

> because for the vast majority of those writing about the expositions at the time of their occurrence, religion was perceived as both the essence of cultural structures and the most plausible point of departure for intercultural comparisons. The events thus provided ideal settings in which religion, as the

> most basic source matter for that field, could come into clearer focus than ever before. (Burris, 2001, xiv)

Burris goes on to emphasize that such events:

> were historically significant because they were of an *international* character and were unprecedented as such. The specific character of the modern 'nation'—never easy to define—came into sharp focus at the expositions as many emerging nations found themselves in close proximity to one another. Further, beyond being international, the expositions were also *intercultural* at a time when concepts of 'culture' had scarcely begun to make inroads. The idea of interculturalism—as an addition to, and in tandem with, internationalism—appeared in embryonic form within the international exposition tradition. The application of the term 'culture' was never precise at the expositions, but it was regularly used to distinguish 'nations' and full-blown 'civilizations' from social entities that were seen as being somehow less than that. With all the world's peoples represented within the single setting of [e.g.] the Great Exhibition, these long-developing and previously vague categorizations of the world's many peoples began to emerge in crisp detail as politically charged global hierarchies. (Burris, 2001, 3)

In Chicago, in 1893, such a hierarchy was epitomized in the relationship between the 'White City', built temporarily for the Chicago Columbian Exposition to house the fruits of modern industrial progress, and the mile-long 'midway' corridor stretching away from the White City, along the length of which the lesser cultures were exhibited, more or less[33] in order of diminishing evolutionary status according to contemporary anthropological thinking (Burris, 2001, 112–13). First were some superseded forms of European culture (including exhibits of ancient Irish castles and a German village of 400 years ago) and then human and cultural exhibits representing various non-White, non-Christian races and cultures in their alleged present condition. Native Americans and Dahomeans (representing also African Americans) were exhibited at the farthest end.[34] To the crowds who attended these events, colonial Euro-American ideas of social and cultural evolution which might be grasped only imperfectly through texts and speeches took a visceral, physical and easily comprehensible form in which the very location of booths exhibiting the 'lower' races and cultures demonstrated in a most literal way their distance from 'us'.

This 'top down' hierarchical vision of the world could also of course be challenged in minor but important ways. Subaltern ideas which defied the dominant discourse and yet managed to find an airing through the exposition might thereby exercise an unprecedented influence. Thus the 1893 'World's Parliament of Religions' held during the Columbian Exposition and originally conceived by its American planners as an attempt to subsume the world's faiths under a liberal Protestant Christian conception of religious unity; 'the Fatherhood of God and the Brotherhood of Man'[35] is now best remembered for the platform it unexpectedly provided for two charismatic representatives of 'Eastern' religions: Swami Vivekananda and Anagarika Dharmapala.

The World's Parliament of Religions was only one among many short-term cultural events forming the 'Auxiliary Congress' strand of the gigantic Columbian Exposition. The World's Parliament could not have happened, and Vivekananda's and Dharmapala's impact would not have been felt, without the huge impetus of the Exposition proper which drew the crowds and thus the attention of the press (Seager 1995; Burris 2001). The Exposition alone provided sufficient material cause for the World's Parliament organizers to summon to Chicago representatives from many diverse religions and cultures to take part in 'Auxiliary' proceedings. It seems that Pfoundes (who had left Japan back in 1876 tasked with setting up a Japanese exhibit at the Philadelphia Exposition) grasped the potential of such global expositions and conferences to provide a challenge to official hierarchies and a boost to minority opinions, not least his own, from around the globe. From 1892 onwards, he participated personally in a number of congresses and expositions, and actively sought to be involved in more, including planning at least one exposition on his own initiative which he hoped would take place in Japan.

In 1892, shortly before his final return from the United Kingdom to Japan, Pfoundes took part in the ninth International Congress of Orientalists, held at the University of London. Being one of an established series of congresses and in London, this Orientalist Congress did not need the support of an exposition to attract sufficient international participants. It seems to have given Pfoundes a taste for such events. He presented a paper which, according to a contemporary report, pointed out

> the gross errors made by 'people who called themselves Esoteric Buddhists, and professed the hotch-potch mis-named theosophy'. The lives and ideas of many of the Buddhistic sects, [Pfoundes] declared, compared favourably with those of people much nearer home.[36]

Pfoundes had been in contact from 1891 onwards with the organisers of the Columbian Exposition in Chicago and he was, as he later put it, 'appointed a member of the Advisory Council of the Congress Auxiliary & Parliament of the Worlds' (sic) Religions'.[37] Pfoundes did not however attend the Chicago exposition in person.

From September 1902, back in Japan, Pfoundes attempted to arrange his own follow-up to the Chicago Exposition of 1893 with grand plans for a two-centre 1903 event in Osaka and Kyoto including an 'International Parliament of Religions'. In a letter of 6th September 1902 sent to the Lewis and Clark Centennial Committee, Pfoundes claims that 'preparations for the forthcoming Japanese National Exposition at Osaka next year are well in hand'.[38] Pfoundes was most probably working solo on his Osaka-Kyoto proposal, but he was not the only one in Japan to conceive a follow-up to Chicago. It is suggested elsewhere[39] that news of the attempt by Okakura Kakuzō (Tenshin) to organize a repeat of the Chicago World's Parliament of Religions in Tokyo, with Vivekananda as guest of honour, may have attracted U Dhammaloka and Swami Rama Tirtha to Japan in 1902. Pfoundes' similar proposal was circulated worldwide, although Dhammaloka was already in Japan by the time it was issued. In England, for example, the *Gloucester Citizen* newspaper of 21 October 1902 (p. 3) reported on Pfoundes' plans as follows:[40]

> A JAPANESE EXHIBITION
> Mr C Pfoundes, who was an advisory member of the Chicago Centennial Congress, writes me that he is endeavouring to arrange a similar event to take place next year at Osaka and Kioto, in Japan. Influential officials are cordially approving and aiding in the necessary preliminaries. A large assembly hall, in a central locality, is now nearly completed in Osaka, which will be available; and there will be facilities for an International Parliament of Religions, an Orientalists' Congress, and conferences on scientific, artistic, literary and social matters.

At this point the editor breaks off to relate this somewhat obscure news to a more local and pressing concern, the bitter British parliamentary controversy over the kind of religious instruction to be provided in state-funded schools:

> What a pity we cannot refer this troublesome Education Bill to the Parliament of Religions at Osaka!

In December 1902, as we have seen, Pfoundes participated in the Congress of Orientalists in Hanoi, organised by the French in conjunction with a major industrial and scientific exposition. In his January 1903 report on the congress to *The Open Court*, Pfoundes professes himself amazed by the remarkable progress that has taken place in French Indo-China since his previous experience of the country 40 years before, when, as captain of a Siamese vessel, he was hesitant even to draw near the shore. He says:

> Everything I saw and learned came as a surprise to me. Considering the difficulties encountered during the past twenty years, since the French determined to force open the Red River, and that it has only been quite recently determined upon to make Hanoi the seat of government, it is simply astonishing what has been achieved. A magnificent capital for the Franco-Indo-China Colonial Empire in the extreme Orient has been raised up; and no half measures. Everything is 'up to date.' Electric trams to the suburbs, and on the principle (*sic*) thoroughfares. Electric lighting, water works, sanitation, drainage, wide boulevards well macadamised (steam rollers used). Shade trees along the sidewalks. Clean and tidy everywhere. No unsavory smells or unpleasant sights. All natives well clad and clean, evidently prospering, contented and happy under the regime of the conquering race.[41]

The Proceedings of the Hanoi congress, published in French by the organisers in 1903, show that the eminent scholars who formed the official Japanese delegation (J. Takakusu, B. Nanjio, R. Fujishima, E. Baelz and K. Florenz) devoted their papers entirely to textual, literary, archaeological and historical scholarship, as was expected of orientalists at the time. The brief account supplied of Pfoundes' lecture, delivered on the morning of Wednesday 5 December, indicates a rather different type of presentation:

> On the outward forms of religion in Japanese Buddhism, by Mr. C Pfoundes.
>
> Mr. Pfoundes, who has resided in Japan for many years, has lived extensively in Japanese environments and has succeeded in affiliating himself to several Buddhist sects. He has passed through various grades of the religious hierarchy and is at present entitled to wear certain insignia restricted to the dignitaries of the orders. It is the details of these privileges that Mr Pfoundes presents to the Congress, indicating both the immediate purpose and the esoteric meaning of the tiaras, rosaries and scapulars which he wears by turns.[42]

Throughout 1902–1903 Pfoundes tried hard, though he ultimately failed, to secure an invitation to host his own 'Congress of Orientalists' at the forthcoming St Louis' World's Fair of 1904. An issue of the St Louis *World's Fair Bulletin* of March 1903 carried an item, most of which was evidently supplied by Pfoundes himself (alongside, as it happens, a picture of the top-hatted members of the official 'Japanese Commission').

> 'Congress of Orientalists'
> Capt. C. Pfoundes, a resident of Kobe, Japan, and an Orientalist of more than forty years' standing, is taking a deep interest in the assembling of a Congress of Orientalists at the World's Fair in St. Louis. He believes that both Americas were peopled from the Pacific coast of Asia, and that a proper study of the archaic writings and civilizations of the Islands on the Pacific coast of Asia will eventually lead to the deciphering of the inscriptions of the prehistoric cities of Central America, and explain the monuments of a prehistoric American civilization in connection with Chinese and Japanese traditions of trans-Pacific voyages. To this end he is forming 'The Orientalists International Union of the Pacific Hemisphere,' with a special view to studies that may throw light on the ethnographical and other affinities traceable from the Asiatic to the American coasts. In a recent letter from Kobe to the Secretary of the Louisiana Purchase Exposition, Capt. Pfoundes expresses confidence that the Union will soon include the leading Orientalists of the world in its membership, and be able to assist the Exposition's Director of Congresses in organizing a successful Congress of Orientalists at the World's Fair in 1904. (p. 34)

During the Spring and Summer of 1903, Pfoundes engaged in extensive if largely one-way correspondence with the organisers of the 1905 Lewis and Clark Centennial Exposition in Portland, Oregon, specifically the American Pacific Exposition and Oriental Fair department. Amongst other proposals we find once again Pfoundes' idea for a congress of 'The Orientalists' International Union of the Pacific Hemisphere' to further his theory that both Americas were peopled from the Pacific coast of Asia. Pfoundes had approached many scholars around the world and claimed that the Earl of Mexborough and others had signed up to his new 'International Union', but his grandiose congress plans never materialised.

Conclusions

Yoshinaga has elsewhere (2009, 126) described Charles Pfoundes as 'a problematic person'. Pfoundes was indeed a 'difficult' character, a man with few if any friends. He seems to have been choleric with an occasional impulse to violence; nowadays we might identify anger management problems stemming from a troubled childhood. He constantly sought peer approval and was aware that many of his social superiors found him pedantic and even ridiculous. He was at various times sued for (and sued others for) libel, and was at least once charged with assault.[43] However, we might also pause to acknowledge the manifold pressures on Pfoundes as a man who did not quite 'belong', either in Europe or Japan, during a period of radical social change. He worked immensely hard throughout his life, evidently obliged to earn his own living right up to the end (he was working as a Japanese court interpreter in the week before he died). Yet he also toiled well beyond the call of duty to fulfil a seemingly self-imposed and often lonely mission; that of elevating European regard for modern East Asian civilization. Pfoundes' admiration for the nobler aspects of East Asian life and culture, which he found particularly in Japanese manners, art, literature and Buddhism, distanced him from most of his European acquaintances. Pfoundes, in turn, deplored their arrogance and ignorance in assuming the cultural, religious and moral superiority of the West.

Pfoundes is undoubtedly of interest to students of Buddhist modernism as a pioneer Western Buddhist and he deserves recognition in at least two major respects. Firstly, he was the earliest Irish Japanologist of any note, his studies in Japan predating those of the famous Irish/Greek author and scholar Lafcadio Hearn by more than two decades.[44] Pfoundes may have been regarded by contemporary university-educated Japanologists, including Ernest Satow, as an intellectual inferior[45] but Pfoundes was an indefatigable (some might say obsessive) researcher whose interests extended to every aspect of Japanese life and beyond Japan to the larger Asian and global geopolitical context. Secondly, Pfoundes deserves acknowledgement for his creative personal engagement with Japanese Buddhism in later life and his efforts to propagate, not uncritically, knowledge and appreciation of modern Japanese Buddhism as a lived practice; this *inter alia* meant he could distinguish clearly between Japanese Esoteric Buddhism and Theosophy. In this respect, as well as in his individual dealings with Japanese Buddhists, Pfoundes made a distinctive contribution to the complex history of the nineteenth century Buddhist revival in Asia even if, as with other pioneers dealt with in this issue of *Contemporary Buddhism*, his 'failed' projects outnumbered his moments of apparent success.

It might also be argued that Pfoundes was in some respects ahead of his time in the study of religions. The 1902 Hanoi congress was the first time a Congress of Orientalists had met in Asia and the papers presented there, whether by European or Japanese scholars, were almost entirely as they would have been in Europe: textual-historical studies concerning literature, scriptures and archaeology. Pfoundes reportedly argued in his paper that as a Buddhist initiate he had access to the inner mysteries of Buddhism 'unknown to scholars who studied the subject from the outside'[46] and, as we have seen from the official account, he used the occasion to don some of his own ceremonial vestments, thereby drawing attention to his complete familiarity with the *habitus* of Japanese Buddhism and confronting the delegates with the incontrovertible example of a European esoteric Japanese Buddhist priest. Whilst Pfoundes' claim to inner knowledge raises many methodological questions for us today, his performance surely deserves recognition as a very early 'participant observer' intervention in the overwhelmingly philological-historical approach that characterized Western and Japanese academic approaches to Asian religions right up to the late twentieth century.

Pfoundes' keen interest in the great congresses and expositions moreover alerts us to the fact that these nineteenth century innovations were yet another kind of emerging transnational network which had the potential to attract, accommodate and disseminate competing interpretations and understandings of Buddhism, or Buddhisms, or however we wish to characterize that whose meaning was being negotiated. In Pfoundes' time, the organization of these colossal and costly events was still very much a Euro-American monopoly and the expositions served overwhelmingly to confirm the West's sense of cultural and technological superiority. As Seager (1995, 155, 158) shows in his analysis of the 1893 World's Parliament, Vivekananda's and Dharmapala's success in Chicago was far more significant for Asian than for American thinking at the time. In 1902, even Japan could not aspire to mount its own exposition and the Hanoi exposition and congress was run from Paris. Yet in his approach to the organisers of the forthcoming 1905 Lewis and Clark Exposition in Portland, Pfoundes wrote that his only objective in starting his new 'International Union of Orientalists', was 'inducing the Japanese to be as enterprising as my French friends at Hanoi . . .'[47] Pfoundes' attempts not only to engage with the Euro-American expositions but to initiate equivalent Japanese-organized congresses and gatherings in Osaka and Kyoto, rather than in the West, deserves to be noticed, for a Japan-based 'International Parliament of Religions' would surely have framed the relationship between cultures and religions from a Buddhist and Asian, rather than Christian and Western, point of view.[48]

Does it matter that in many cases Pfoundes' ambitious plans came to nothing? He was only one among probably thousands of would-be individual participants in the great international, intercultural expositions who submitted ambitious but ultimately unrealized proposals to the organizing committees. Like other 'pioneer' figures whose lives are explored in this issue of *Contemporary*

Buddhism, Pfoundes' failures were the hallmark of real effort and activity, not of inaction or lack of ambition. Much more could be said of Pfoundes, but in the spirit of this special issue of *Contemporary Buddhism* which recognizes that much of the work on Western Buddhist pioneers is at an early stage, the paper will conclude by highlighting just two themes suggested by Pfoundes' activities that might stimulate further research in other contexts.

Firstly, as we have noted, giant international expositions and their associated global congresses were a distinctive late nineteenth century phenomenon which depended for their existence on the extraordinary advances in global travel, trade and communication that characterized the period. Such huge and complex events constituted innovative kinds of 'crossroads', generating new nodes of engagement and communication. They provided locations in which notions of 'the world's religions' played a key role in the popular and academic construction of cultural hierarchies. They also provided material stimuli to global travel and intercultural encounter. Like monastic, trade, political and ethnic networks, and along with expanding steamship lines, railways, telegraph routes and international postal services, the global expositions and congresses promised novel opportunities for modern representations of Buddhism to gain recognition worldwide. In Hanoi, Pfoundes seized the opportunity of his participation in the congress to 'fly the flag' for Japanese Buddhism, a tradition which he represented as modern, ecumenical and patriotic, yet still holding the key to secret knowledge. He did this quite literally by carrying his flag at the head of the scholars' procession to the temple and he did it metaphorically in his conference session by presenting himself as an initiated European Buddhist and arguing that the deeper meaning of Buddhism was thereby available to him, but unavailable to those studying 'from the outside' (implying from a non-Buddhist, European perspective). Pfoundes' attempts to involve himself in the Chicago, St Louis and Lewis and Clark expositions, his efforts to generate support for a similar Osaka-Kyoto event and his actual involvement in the 1902 Hanoi congress raise the question of whether and how other forgotten pioneer Buddhists (not only the well-known figures present in Chicago in 1893) used, or planned to use, the opportunities provided by the increasing number and variety of international congresses and expositions of the nineteenth and early twentieth centuries to further 'Buddhist' causes. In this connection, we might again recall that Dhammaloka came to Tokyo in 1902, almost certainly in the expectation of a reprise of the Chicago World's Parliament (Bocking 2010).[49]

Secondly, there is the question of Buddhist flags. This is a topic in the history of modernist Buddhism that has not so far attracted much serious study,[50] yet the two best-known 'Irish Buddhists' of the period, U Dhammaloka and Charles Pfoundes, both made a point of flying Buddhist flags, one designed by an American, the other—unless Pfoundes invented it—by a Japanese. Exactly whose flag was Pfoundes carrying at the Hanoi Congress? By this gesture, was he representing several major sects of Japanese Buddhism and what did Buddhist flag-flying signify, whether in Japan or in Hanoi, or, for that matter, at

Dhammaloka's 'Buddhist Mission' in Singapore? Apart from Olcott, the production of Buddhist flags seems to have been largely a Japanese preoccupation in this period, but the practice has since spread. What does it mean, at specific times and in specific places, for a conception, sect or tradition of Buddhism to promulgate its own *flag*?

ACKNOWLEDGEMENTS

The initial version of this paper was presented at the Conference *SE Asia as a Crossroads for Buddhist Exchange: Pioneer European Buddhists and Asian Buddhist Networks 1860–1960* hosted by the Study of Religions Department, University College Cork, Ireland, 13–15 September 2012 and funded by the Dhammakaya International Society of the United Kingdom as part of the 2012 postdoctoral fellowship 'Continuities and Transitions in early Modern Thai Buddhism'. I am grateful to my fellow Pfoundes researchers Yoshinaga Shin'ichi and Laurence Cox who have so generously shared their findings in our ongoing and expanding research on pioneer Western Buddhists. Cox's account of Pfoundes in his *Buddhism and Ireland* (Equinox 2013) was completed before this article was begun, as of course were the 2009 articles by Yoshinaga and Akai. Thanks also to Fiona Fitzsimons of Eneclann for research into Pfoundes' family background, to Gaynor Sekimori (School of Oriental and African Studies) for insights into Pfoundes' Shugendō connections and to Jennifer Keyser of the Oregon Historical Society for help with the Lewis and Clark Exposition papers.

NOTES

1. Congress of Orientalists: The Hanoi Meeting. *Times of India*, 19 January 1903, p. 6, from the paper presented to the Bombay branch of the Royal Asiatic Society by Professor Macmillan two days earlier (Macmillan 1904).
2. Dhammaloka had broadcast his intention of heading from Hong Kong North, travelling temple by temple to Peking (which he may have reached) and thence Lhasa (which he did not). Kobe. *London and China Telegraph*, March 2, 1903, 162.
3. I have not yet found a flag of the period with exactly this combination of elements. The swastika is of course ubiquitous as a sign of Japanese Buddhism and the rising sun flag was, by 1902, well-recognised as the emblem of the Japanese navy. Today's Tibetan 'snow lion' flag (accessed January 27, 2013. http://www.artelino.eu/en/articles/tibetan-mythology/179-tibet-snow-lion.html) designed in the same year, 1902, and perhaps by the same Japanese priest Aoki Bunkyō (Shimatsu, 2008, 92), has the Japanese sun's rays, while a circular Buddhist motif with swastika and rays can evidently be found in Vietnam today. See, for example, the chance image from Saigon in a comment by 'Kasalt' headed 'the swastika in Buddhism' responding to Swami B.G. Narasingha's 'The

Swastika and the Cross' (accessed January 27, 2013. http://www.davidicke.com/forum/showthread.php?t = 31635).

4. H.K. Daily Press. November 18, 1902. C. PFOUNDES. Capt. C. Pfoundes of Japan passed through H.K. yesterday on his way to the Hanoi Exposition, where he will represent the chief monasteries of the Tendai, Shingon, Zen, and Jodo sects and also Japanese art (Papers of Harold S. Williams, MS 6681, National Library of Australia).

5. The French Colonies in China. *The Open Court* 1903 (3): 175–176.

6. Charles' age is given as 38 years in his Liverpool marriage certificate of March 1878 and 40 in the 1881 UK census. His elder brother [Joseph] Elam Pounds was born in 1838 in Mothill (=Mothel?), Co. Waterford, according to his Australian marriage certificate. A younger brother, George St Ledger Pounds, b. 1843, died at 6 months.

7. Caroline's father, Lt. Joseph Elam (d. 1829), was emphatically not a Quaker; for the long Elam ancestry see Neill (1995). James Baker Pounds can be traced in New Ross, Wexford (late 1830s to 1850s) and in Australia from the mid-1850s to his death in 1884. According to an 1871 court report of Caroline Pounds' testimony ('Strange Case', *Freeman's Journal*, November 3, 1877), Charles' parents separated when he was about 6 years old, Charles emigrating with his father and Caroline abandoned in Ireland. However, Caroline seems to have been in Australia in the late 1840s. Her Australian flower and bird paintings, one reportedly dated 1846, were discovered in the early 1980s in Geelong, Victoria, in the attic of the family home of Lilias Ibbotson, second wife of Charles' elder brother Elam. Butler (1999) writes: 'By 1846, according to an inscription by the artist on one of her watercolours of native Australia plants, the family had arrived in Sydney'. Such inconsistencies in the records suggest the Pounds might have travelled briefly to Sydney around 1846 and the couple separated on return to Ireland, Charles emigrating to Melbourne in 1854 on the SS Great Britain (President's Office Correspondence), Elam in October 1855 (on the *Shackamaxon*) and their father James c. 1856, while Caroline remained in Ireland until her death in 1898.

8. President's Office Correspondence.

9. The name 'Pfoundes' appears (at least to me) to be a clever play on the English name Pounds and his Japanese name 'Omoie Tetzunostzuke' (*Omoi Tetsunosuke* 重鉄之助) literally 'weight assisted by iron' reportedly bestowed on Pounds in the 1860s. In *The Far East* 1 (11), 1908 (after Pfoundes' death), Adachi Konnosuke says: 'His name I believe was Pound, and we gave him a Japanese name of Omoi Tetsunosuke (which being interpreted means "heavy iron") which we thought came as near as possible to his original name' (Gaynor Sekimori, pers. comm.). 'Pounds' in *katakana* ﾌｵﾝﾃﾞｽ is 'PfuONDESu', and pounds = *libra* = weight. If we add *fe*, the chemical element for iron, to 'Pounds' this yields 'Pfoundes'; pounds plus iron. Incidentally Pfoundes was never called 'Condor'. The newspaper headline 'Well done Condor' quoted in a January 1899 letter to Satow (Ruxton, 2005, 384) is Pfoundes' own salute to HMS *Condor*, the gunboat heroically captained at Alexandria in 1882 by Charles, Lord Beresford who, Pfoundes hoped, was about to visit Kobe from Hong Kong.

10. Probably not for long: Laurence Cox, Mihirini Sirisena and Rachelann Pisani are currently (2012–2013) engaged in an Irish Research Council-funded project to identify Dhammaloka's pre-monastic identity and whereabouts and hence the course of his political and intellectual formation.
11. Including Count Mutsu Munemitsu (Von Siebold 2000). For China and Japan. *Daily Alta California*, 23 (7679), 1 April 1871. President's Office Correspondence.
12. President's Office Correspondence. In the Yedo Hong List and Directory (*Japan Gazette* 1874), p. 45, top of the list of foreigners working for the National Mail Steam Ship Company of Japan is 'Pfoundes, C., Director's Office'.
13. A report of the sale with prices obtained appeared in the *New York Times*: Japanese Art Treasures (1876), June 7; The Pfoundes Collection—Remarkable Display of China and Bronzes—Characteristics of Japanese Art.
14. On Hirai, who started as an anti-Christian nationalist and became a Unitarian after participating in the World's Parliament of Religions in Chicago see Nozaki (2009, 157ff). On Matsuyama, an English teacher in Kyoto, see Yoshinaga (2009, 124–5).
15. President's Office Correspondence.
16. A Strange Case (1877) *Freeman's Journal*, November 3.
17. Numerous notices and reports of these events have survived but a full analysis will have to wait for another occasion.
18. Pseudonyms include Censor, ABC, E. Non Fumari, Amateur, Mercator, Argus, Nemesis, A Proselyte, Damocle's (*sic*) Sword, Scrutator, Argus and Reformer. Pfoundes' collected letters, with two other letters from 'Merchant' (Pfoundes 1874), were prefaced by this instruction from Pfoundes: Dear Sir,—Please reprint all my contributions to your paper, without exception, from the beginning. And oblige, Yours truly, C. J. Pfoundes, 17 August 1874.
19. He is listed on p. vi of the Folk-Lore Society's 'List of Members', prefacing *The Folk-Lore Record*, Part I, 1878, as 'C Pfoundes Esq., Tokio, Japan'. Pfoundes' versions of 11 Japanese folk tales appear on pp. 118–135.
20. In the President's Office Correspondence, Pfoundes explains in great detail how he arranged the sale.
21. See Pfoundes (1882) (paper in London read May 25, 1881), and Pfoundes (1886, 390).
22. Why Buddhism? *The Open Court: A Weekly Journal Devoted to the Religion of Science* No. 415 (Vol. IX–32), Chicago, August 8, 1895: 4594–4597; The French Colonies in China. *The Open Court* 1903: 175–176.
23. Rosa Alice Pfoundes remained for some years in London working as a civil servant and long outlived Pfoundes; she died in 1936 at the age of 80 in Worthing, Sussex and is buried there in a pauper's grave.
24. President's Office Correspondence.
25. The Oregon papers (President's Office Correspondence) naturally highlight Pfoundes' role as a diplomatic or business intermediary for Americans.

26. Returning to Japan in 1893 after 17 years absence, Pfoundes claimed on arrival in Matsue to be 62 (Okazaki Hideki, pers. comm.), presumably this was to add credence to his claim that he had taken normal retirement from the Admiralty. In fact he was 53, so his subsequent self-proclaimed status as 'senior resident' of the Kobe foreign community (see Richard Gordon Smith, *Travels in the Land of the Gods* p. 149, cited in Rogala, 2000, 192) relied on his compatriots thinking he was far older than he was. The British consul obligingly estimated his age at death as 79 years.
27. The Buddhist journal *Hansei Zasshi* 8 (7), July 1893, reports Pfoundes' Tendai ordination at Mt Hiei on July 17, 1893. A photo of Pfoundes taking part in a Shugendō firewalking ritual c. 1904 and another of him in eclectic Zen/Shingon attire appeared in *East of Asia Magazine* (Pfoundes 1905). The *Hong Kong Daily Press*, 18 Nov 1902 reports what is presumably Pfoundes' own claim that in Hanoi he would represent the 'Tendai, Shingon, Zen, and Jodo sects'; the Hanoi Congress *Compte Rendu* reported that 'he has succeeded in affiliating himself to several Buddhist sects'.
28. Thelle 1987, 109n cites: Uchiyama Torasuke, ed. 1893. *Pfoundes, Bukkyō enzetsushū*, [*C. Pfoundes: A Collection of Buddhist Lectures*]. Kyoto: Kōbundō.
29. Yoshinaga Shin'ichi, pers. comm.
30. Satow refused to help, writing to Hall that 'it is a piece of impudence for a B[ritish] S[ubject] to ask a British official to help him to get rid of his allegiance to the Queen' (Ruxton, 2005, 390, 393).
31. Pfoundes (1905).
32. For example, Burris (2001) reports that 20% of the English population visited London's Great Exhibition of 1851 and 27 million of a total US population of 66 million attended the 1893 Columbian exposition in Chicago.
33. Burris (2001, 112–113) points out that commercial priorities meant several cultures were in fact 'out of place' in what has usually been characterized as 'an evolution-minded "sliding scale of humanity"'.
34. India and Japan secured a place in the White City (Burris, 2001, 113–115).
35. The original aim 'to unite all religion against irreligion' was revised by 1892 to seeking 'an accurate and authoritative account of the present condition and outlook of Religion among the leading nations of the world' while considering 'the impregnable foundations of Theism', but most participants retained the universalist aspiration (Seager, 1995, 48–49).
36. The Oriental Congress (1892) *The Colonies and India* [newspaper], September 17, 16.
37. President's Office Correspondence, letter dated March 25, 1903. A Japanese Exhibition, *Gloucester Citizen*, October 21, 1902, 3. Pfoundes is listed by Barrows (1893, 46) as one of about 3000 advisors to the Parliament.
38. President's Office Correspondence.
39. Bocking, 2010, 236–237.
40. The President's Office Correspondence has the full undated circular letter, probably September 1902.
41. The French Colonies in China, *The Open Court* 1903 (3): 175.

42. My translation from the French in Schneider (1903, 51). See the very similar account of Pfoundes' talk in Macmillan (1904, 501–502): he refers to 'vestments, scarfs and rosaries'. Curiously, Pfoundes' own 'Bulletin No.1' circulated to Orientalists worldwide following the Hanoi congress (and which claims that a number of scholars and diplomats have already joined his new 'Orientalists' International Union') gives the title of his Hanoi paper as 'The Iconography and the Buddhist Art, Pinctic and Glyptic, of Japan, &c.' (President's Office Correspondence, probably early 1903).
43. A Strange Case, *Freeman's Journal*, November 3, 1877.
44. Much later, in Matsue in 1893, Pfoundes missed encountering Lafcadio Hearn, who had left there in 1891 for Kumamoto.
45. Satow looked down on Pfoundes, in 1899 describing him as a 'mountebank' and 20 years earlier dismissing his writings as 'utterly valueless' and deriding his plans for a 'Nippon Institute' in London (Ruxton, 2008, 127). However, Pfoundes' 1875 collection *Fuso-mimi-bukuro: A Budget of Japanese Notes*, which appeared 15 years before Chamberlain's admittedly more erudite *Things Japanese* had an appreciative readership: Reed (1880), for example, took many of his examples from Pfoundes.
46. Congress of Orientalists: The Hanoi Meeting (1903) *Times of India*, January 19, 6.
47. President's Office Correspondence.
48. On his return from Tokyo to Siam in 1903, U Dhammaloka was inspired by his Japanese experience (specifically, the 1902 launch of the International Young Men's Buddhist Association (IYMBA) but more broadly by the unrealized prospect of a Japanese World's Parliament of Religions), to plan for a large international Buddhist congress in Bangkok (Proposed Buddhist Congress, *Bangkok Times Weekly Mail*, June 23, 1903, 15).
49. We have no evidence that Pfoundes and Dhammaloka met, though it is entirely possible they did in 1902. Both were in Japan in the autumn but Pfoundes was probably in Kobe rather than present at the September launch of the IYMBA in Tokyo.
50. Kate Crosby has drawn my attention to the following work in Khmer: Sok, Buntheoun (2000, BE); *Browat Tong Preah Putthasasna* [The History of the Buddhist Flag].

REFERENCES

AKAI, T. 2009. Theosophical Accounts in Japanese Buddhist Publications of the Late Nineteenth Century: An Introduction and Select Bibliography. *Japanese Religions* 34 (2): 187–208.

BARROWS, J. H., ed. 1893. *An Illustrated and Popular Story of the World's First Parliament of Religions, Held in Chicago in Connection with the Columbian Exposition of 1893.* Vol.1. Chicago: The Parliament Publishing Company.

BOCKING, B. 2010. 'A Man of Work and Few Words?' Dhammaloka Beyond Burma. *Contemporary Buddhism* 11 (2): 125–47.

BURRIS, J. P. 2001. *Exhibiting Religion: Colonialism and Spectacle at International Expositions 1851–1893*. Charlottesville, VA: University Press of Virginia.

BUTLER, P. 1999. *Irish Botanical Illustrators & Flower Painters*. Woodbridge, UK: Antique Collectors' Club Ltd.

COX, L. 2013. *Buddhism and Ireland: From the Celts to the Counter-Culture and Beyond*. London: Equinox.

JAPAN GAZETTE. 1874. *The 'Japan Gazette' Hong List and Directory for 1874*. Yokohama: Offices of The 'Japan Gazette'.

JAPANESE ART TREASURES. 1876. Prop. C. Pfoundes and Others. New York: Field, Morris & Fenner Co.

MACMILLAN, P. 1904. The Oriental Congress at Hanoi. *Journal of the Bombay Branch of the Royal Asiatic Society* XXI: 499–504, Bombay: Society's Library; London: Kegan Paul, Trench, Trübner & Co.

NEILL, N. 1995. *The Elam Family: Quaker Merchants of England and America*. Doncaster, UK: N.C. Neill.

NOZAKI, K. 2009. Hirai Kinza and Unitarianism. *Japanese Religions* 34 (2): 155–70.

PAPERS OF HAROLD S. WILLIAMS. 1867–2000. MS6681. Canberra: National Library of Australia.

PFOUNDES, C. J. 1874. *Letters Which Have Appeared in the 'Japan Daily Herald'*. Yokohama: Japan Daily Herald.

PFOUNDES, C. 1882. The Popular Literature of Old Japan. *Transactions of the Royal Society of Literature of the United Kingdom*. 2nd series, Vol. 12, 591–623. London: John Murray.

PFOUNDES, C. 1886. An Excursion in Japan. *Young Folks Paper* 28 (812): 390. Columbia, SC: University of South Carolina, Irvin Department of Rare Books and Special Collections.

PFOUNDES, C. 1905. The Fire Ordeal: An Esoteric Ceremony in Kobe. Described by C. Pfoundes, An Adept of the Order. *East of Asia Magazine* IV: 310–7.

PREMIER CONGRÈS INTERNATIONAL DES ÉTUDES D'EXTRÊME-ORIENT, tenu a Hanoi du 3 au 8 Décembre 1903. 1902. Hanoi: Imprimerie Typo-Lithographique F.-H. Schneider.

PRESIDENT'S OFFICE CORRESPONDENCE. Mss 1609, Lewis and Clark Centennial Exposition Records. Oregon Historical Society Research Library.

REED, E. J. 1880. *Japan: Its History, Traditions, and Religions: With the Narrative of a Visit in 1879*. London: Murray.

ROGALA, J. 2000. *A Collector's Guide to Books on Japan in English: An Annotated List of over 2500 Titles with Subject Index*. Abingdon, UK: Routledge.

RUXTON, I. 2005. The *Correspondence of Sir Ernest Satow, British Minister in Japan, 1895–1900—Volume One*, Lulu.com

RUXTON, I. 2008. *Sir Ernest Satow's Private Letters to W.G. Aston and F.V. Dickins: The Correspondence of a Pioneer Japanologist from 1870 to 1918*, Lulu.com

SEAGER, R. H. 1995. *The World's Parliament of Religions: The East/West Encounter, Chicago, 1893*. Bloomington: Indiana University Press.

SCHNEIDER, F. -H. 1903. *Premier Congrès International des Études d'Extrême-Orient: Compte Rendu Analytique des Séances*. Hanoi: Imprimer-Éditeur.

SHIMATSU, Y. 2008. A Hidden History: 'Free Tibet, the Lost Crusade of Buddhist Japan'. *Japanese Religions* 33 (1–2): 91–5.

THELLE, N. 1987. *Buddhism and Christianity in Japan: From Conflict to Dialogue, 1854–1899*. Honolulu: University of Hawaii Press.

VON SIEBOLD, A. FREIHERR. 2000. Korrespondenz Alexander von Siebolds. In *den Archiven des Japanischen Aussenministeriums und der Tōkyō-Universität 1859–1895*, edited by Vera Schmidt. Wiesbaden: Otto Harrassowitz Verlag.

YOSHINAGA, S. 2009. Theosophy and Buddhist Reformers in the Middle of the Meiji Period: An Introduction. *Japanese Religions* 34 (2): 119–31.

BUDDHIST COUNCILS IN A TIME OF TRANSITION: GLOBALISM, MODERNITY AND THE PRESERVATION OF TEXTUAL TRADITIONS

Tilman Frasch

This article looks at what is genuinely new in the Buddhist transnationalism of the modern period. It examines the history of Buddhist councils and synods from the early gatherings after the demise of the Buddha to the Buddhist World Council in the twentieth century. These often international events followed a role-model, defined by the first three councils, of creating and handing down an authoritative version of the Buddha's teachings (dhamma) while they could also lead to a 'purification' of the monks' order (sangha) if monks sticking to divergent textual traditions were expelled from the sangha. Despite their importance, however, councils have received rather little attention in scholarly literature. This article takes a fresh look at Buddhist synods with a focus on those convened since the mid-nineteenth century. It explores how the latter sought to comply with inherited forms and functions, while at the same time becoming innovative in order to adapt Buddhism to its modern environment.

Introduction

The fundamental change taking place during the nineteenth century, which can be succinctly described by the terms 'modernization' and 'globalization', did not leave the Buddhist communities of Asia untouched. Confronted with Christian missionary efforts and the rising self-awareness of other religious communities, Buddhists too began to see transnational cooperation as a way of defending their religion. They used modern technologies such as the telegraph, postal services and steamships and, ultimately, cooperated in transnational institutions such as the Mahabodhi Society (founded in 1891 CE) or the World Fellowship of Buddhists (1950). However, this becoming modern and going global of Buddhists across Asia which began in the second half of the nineteenth century, notably among Theravada communities around the Bay of Bengal, should not detract attention from the fact that Buddhism had been a transnational religion almost from its earliest days. During the third century BCE, under the Mauryan king Asoka, the

Buddha's teachings were spread to Sri Lanka, Asia Minor, Central Asia, China, and very likely to Southeast Asia ('Suvannabhumi') as well. This dissemination was followed by centuries of continuous though intermittent contacts which intensified notably in the first centuries CE, when the emerging Theravada tradition spread from Sri Lanka to the Southeast Asian mainland. Thereafter, and until the nineteenth century, members of the Theravada communities on both sides of the Bay came together on numerous occasions to exchange texts, visit sacred monuments and validate their ordination lineages. Given the existence of this closely tied and durable network of interaction, we have to reconsider the Buddhist transnationalism of the modern period to determine what was really new or pioneering and where cooperation merely continued on established paths. To this end, the focus in this paper will be on the one institutionalized form of interaction, the Buddhist synods.[1]

The major function of Buddhist synods was determined by the first three of them to be held after the decease (*parinibbana*) of Gotama Buddha, when the monks sat together to agree upon a common and authoritative version of the *dhamma*, the body of the Buddha's teachings and laid down some principles for the organization of the monks' order (*sangha*). The latter point was allegedly the main subject of the third council, which established the relationship between ruler and *sangha* and provided a blueprint for the expulsion of non-conformist monks from the order. For these reasons, the early synods have been intensively studied and sometimes controversially discussed by Indologists and historians of ancient India alike.[2] In striking contrast, the later synods have received much less attention. Of the three synods to convene between 1860–1950, only the last one, the Sixth World Council held at Rangoon from 1954–1956, has found mention in scholarly literature, not least because it was highly publicized by the media of the day. The other two synods that took place during this period, one sponsored by the Burmese king Mindon Min in 1871–1874 at Mandalay (the fifth synod according to the Burmese computation) and the other by the Thai king Chulalongkorn at Bangkok in 1888 (the tenth according to the Thai tradition), are hardly ever mentioned in a more than casual manner and references to them in scholarly literature appear to be beset with misinformation. Against that background, this article will review the early synodic process and then locate the synods of the nineteenth and twentieth centuries in the historical context of Buddhist transnationalism before looking more closely at their reasons and outcomes. It will be argued that although all three of these modern synods had certain pioneering or innovative elements to them, only the Rangoon World Council of the 1950s can be regarded as truly global event, both for the composition of its participants and its outreach.

Transnationalism and the Buddhist ecumene

Following the Buddha's order that the *sangha* collectively would be responsible for the upholding of his *dhamma*, leading monks assembled at Rajgir following his decease for a joint recitation which resulted in an authoritative version of the textual foundation of the new religion. Texts were moreover arranged in groups to facilitate memorization. As the *dhamma* spread from the Buddha's 'homeland' in Northern India across the Indian subcontinent and beyond, further monasteries and chapters of the *sangha* emerged, necessitating another synod. Besides reconfirming textual versions, the Second Council at Vesali was mainly concerned with the interpretation of certain rules relating to monks. However, the problem of 'dissenting' monks who violated Vinaya rules or altered the wording of the canon continued, so a third synod was convened at Pataliputra, supposedly sponsored by the Mauryan king Asoka. It is not clear what precisely happened in this meeting, but it seemingly ended with a 'purification' of the *sangha*; that is, the expulsion from the order of monks who were seen to hold wrong beliefs. The synod thus set a model for the relationship between the *sangha,* which was responsible for the preservation of the texts, and the king, whose authority made the elimination of dissidents effective.[3]

The transmission of the *dhamma* to Sri Lanka had considerable consequences for the future state of the order as it ultimately resulted in the emergence of the Theravada tradition, which took its final shape before the fifth century CE. On the one hand, it seems that the formation of the Theravada was linked to sectarian quarrels between the two major monasteries at Anuradhapura: the Mahavihara and the Abhayagirivihara. Against the latter, which seems to have been more cosmopolitan in terms of welcoming monks from abroad and collecting Buddhist scriptures of uncertain provenance and status, the monks at the Mahavihara took a more orthodox, almost fundamentalist stance. They insisted that only they represented the uninterrupted ordination lineage going straight back to the Buddha, that they had retained the best textual tradition of the canon and, therefore, that they should be regarded as superior to any other monastic tradition and lineage on the island. The struggle for superiority between the two monasteries eventually became a competition for material resources as well, which almost led to the extinction of the Mahavihara when King Mahasena embargoed the monastery in the third century CE.[4]

On the other hand, the formation of the Theravada tradition was also linked to notions of religious decline and revival by way of a messianic figure. Even in his last words, the Buddha maintained that everything was subject to decline, including his own religion. However, as this world was a 'blessed aeon' (*bhadda-kappa*), another Buddha was prophesied to appear in a future time and restore the *dhamma* and the *sangha*. The length of the interval between the fourth Buddha (Gotama) and the fifth Buddha (Metteya) however, remained undetermined, though a widely-held belief claimed that Metteya would appear 1000 years after his predecessor. The questions of how long the interval would last and from which date the computation should start became a major issue in fourth and fifth century Sri Lanka. Monks at the island's foremost monastery, the Mahavihara, came to the conclusion that Gotama had entered the state of *parinibbana* in 544 BCE, thus claiming that Metteya could be expected around the year 456 CE.[5]

Indeed, as the Sinhalese chronicles report, messianic (or rather Metteyanic) expectations were prevalent in the capital of the island, Anuradhapura, around the middle of the fifth century CE. However, as we know, Metteya failed to appear and Buddhaghosa, the most prominent and learned monk at the Mahavihara, came up with a new calculation in which he argued that it would take not one but five millennia, each one showing increasing signs of decline, until the appearance of Metteya. This was a clever argument as it explained why Metteya had failed to appear, projected his advent into a very distant future and at the same time acknowledged the efforts of the *sangha* (and especially the Sinhalese *sangha*) to avert decline by keeping the *dhamma* intact and the *sangha* free from unworthy monks. This implied the notion that synods were a crucial instrument for both aims.

Curiously, the Sinhalese Mahavihara-Theravada tradition as encapsulated in its chronicles beginning with the fourth to fifth century CE *Dipavamsa* appears to be rather uncomfortable with identifying or acknowledging the significance of synods. The clearest example for this is the meeting that took place at the end of the first century BCE in a remote cave in the hills of central Lanka, as a result of which the Pitakas, transmitted orally until then, were written down for the first time.[6] Virtually glossed over in the chronicles and ignored by Buddhaghosa, the proceedings of this synod and its importance were highlighted for the first time only in much later historical treatises from Southeast Asia, such as the thirteenth to fourteenth century *Saddhammasangaha*.[7]

In the centuries between c. 800 and 1300 CE, Buddhism underwent a major transformation that elsewhere I have called the 'great translocation'.[8] The term serves to describe the almost complete disappearance of Buddhist institutions and communities from their Indian homeland and simultaneous rise on the Southeast Asian mainland, where Theravada became the preferred religion of the people. In the middle of this period Sri Lanka, the fountain of Theravada, experienced a serious crisis when the island was conquered by the South Indian Cholas, who destroyed Anuradhapura and plundered the city's religious institutions. As the restoration of Anuradhapura proved as impossible as the establishment of the new capital Polonnaruwa, the island's political and religious centre had to be transferred from the northern plains to the West of the island (and ultimately to Kandy). After 1200 CE, Pagan in central Burma replaced, to a degree, Anuradhapura and Polonnaruwa as a centre of Theravada Buddhism, both in the magnificence of its monuments and as a refuge for Buddhists from all over Asia.[9]

Despite these political and religious disruptions, Sri Lanka regained its reputation as the leading Theravada nation as more Theravada communities emerging on the Southeast Asian mainland linked themselves to the Sinhalese tradition by importing scriptures and ordination lineages from Sri Lanka. Theravada communities began to intensify their cooperation and exchange at the beginning of the fifteenth century. This formation of a Buddhist ecumene again has to be seen in light of Buddhist millenarian thinking. The second millennium of the Buddhist calendar was to end in 1456 CE, bringing the question of decline and its prevention once again to the foreground. As Buddhaghosa had argued at the end of the previous millennium, the religion was subject to decline in five stages of 1000 years each, and each time the signs of decline would become more obvious, until the future Buddha Metteya restored the original teachings. However, rather than accepting decline as an inevitability, Buddhist rulers, monks and laymen began to think of measures to prevent it. Their activities included visits to the original sites of Buddhism in India and Sri Lanka, as well as formal meetings with Buddhist communities from various countries, on which occasions ordination lineages were reconfirmed and the scriptures were recited jointly.

Three such councils or synods were held in the course of the fifteenth century, the first of them taking place around 1420 CE in the then Sri Lankan capital Kotte, near Colombo. It concluded the visit of a large party of monks from Thailand, Cambodia and Lower Burma who had gone to Lanka to study the scriptures with Sinhalese monks and finally underwent re-ordination with the rites and words of the Sinhalese tradition.[10] After their return, members of the delegation went to their respective homelands to disseminate the 'pure' *dhamma* as they had learnt it and presided over re-ordinations in the Sinhalese fashion themselves. Again, it is curious to note that the synod of Kotte, which qualifies as a 'world council' regarding the composition of its participants and subsequent outreach, was not recognized as such in the Buddhist annals; in fact, there are only very few references to it in the various local Buddhist chronicles of Southeast Asia.[11]

The other two synods of the fifteenth century, in contrast, became recognized. They convened almost simultaneously at Pegu (Burma) and Chiang Mai (Thailand) in the 1470s and followed a largely similar pattern that included references to Bodhgaya, a visit to Sri Lanka for study and re-ordination and an ordination ceremony at home. The convocation sponsored by King Dhammaceti of Pegu, who ordered its proceedings to be recorded in marble inscriptions, later became part of the national history of Burma, while the synod of Chiang Mai was considered as the eighth council of the Thai tradition.[12]

The following centuries witnessed further contacts between Buddhist communities on either side of the Bay of Bengal, mainly involving Sri Lankan Buddhists reforming their *sangha* with help from Burma and Thailand.[13] Among them, the two exchanges with Burma in 1800–1802 and 1863–1865, which resulted in the founding of two reformist fraternities, the Amarapura Nikaya and Ramanya Nikaya, are particularly interesting as they show the increasing degree to which laymen, rather than kings and monks alone, had become involved in reinvigorating and sustaining Buddhist networks. These contacts laid the foundations for the modernization and internationalization of Asian Buddhism that took place in the second half of the nineteenth century.

Synods and Buddhist modernity

The gathering that became the fifth synod, according to the Burmese and later 'official' computation, convened at Mandalay between 1871 and 1874 but despite its official status little is known about its background or proceedings, making way for a number of misconceptions and misrepresentations. The sponsor of this synod, King Mindon Min (1853–1878) had come to the throne in the aftermath of the Second Anglo-Burmese War by deposing his elder brother Pagan Min in a coup d'état meant to appease the British invaders of the country. The war did indeed come to an end but the British retained the areas of Lower Burma they had occupied. In consequence of the defeat, Mindon Min started to reorganize and modernize his kingdom,[14] beginning with the construction of a new capital at Mandalay which was laid out in 1857 and inaugurated in 1860.[15] While constructions were underway, the king ordered a complete copy of the Buddhist canon to be made. This was the fashion among all Burmese kings, but Mindon Min deviated from the custom insofar as his copy was cut in stone rather than being written on palm leaves. The stone library, copying of which lasted from October 1859 to May 1868, was set up in the compound of the Mahalokamarajina (aka Kuthodaw) stupa next to the city wall. The stupa enshrined a copy of a tooth relic the king had received from Sri Lanka in 1859.[16] Planning for the synod did not begin until July 1870—two years after the copying had been completed—following a royal decree.

> The king believes that he owes his kingship to the merit of various good deeds in the past and he wants to continue this accumulation of merit by supporting the Buddha's religion; he considers that to have a Buddhist synod would be best in that line; (...); send a request to the Supreme Leader of the Extension and Propagation of the Buddha's religion to assemble monks (...) and recite the scriptures on all four full moon days of each month in that year (...).[17]

The synod lasted from April until September 1871 and was attended by 2400 monks, none of whom apparently came from outside Burma.[18] It was presided over by the chief monks of the Sudhamma Nikaya (the relatively recent reform fraternity backed by the king) and concluded with another royal order to celebrate the event all over the kingdom.[19]

It seems important here to stress again the sequence of events: the king had the Buddhist scriptures copied on stone before the monks attending the synod could recite and, at best, approve the new authoritative recension. This sequence of events, which seems to run against the natural order of things—where one would expect a joint recitation to precede the writing down, the more so when the material used is stone—has caused much confusion in scholarly literature, where the sequence can be found misrepresented all over the place.[20] Another point worth repeating is the fact that the official account of the synod does not indicate that any monks from outside Burma participated in its proceedings, even though contacts with Sri Lanka had been reinforced during the years immediately preceding the meeting. For instance, the copy of the tooth relic received in 1859 had been enshrined in the stupa located at the centre of the stone library, and two delegations of monks and laymen from Sri Lanka had visited the new Burmese capital in 1861 and 1863. The latter then established a new fraternity built on a Burmese ordination lineage, the Ramanya Nikaya, in 1863.[21] Still, Sinhalese monks seemingly did not participate and there is also no obvious record that monks from Lower Burma were present at the synod.

For this latter problem, the specific circumstances of the early phase of Mindon Min's reign will have to be taken into account. The British annexation of Lower Burma meant that the *sangha* there, already facing much competition from Christian missionary organizations in the field of education, was removed from the control of the king and the board of leading monks residing in Upper Burma. Certain forms of disintegration and decline were an inevitable consequence, even though monks in Lower Burma did attempt to adapt to the new situation. Bechert's perception of the synod as a royal attempt to reunite the various fraternities seems to be close to the point.[22] King Mindon Min's vision may have reached even further. The king never accepted the annexation of Lower Burma and rejected a peace treaty at the end of the war, which indicates that he clung to the idea of reuniting the two parts at some point. The building of the new capital, one that equalled British-designed Rangoon in size and splendour, was another expression of this pan-Burman vision and the synod also shows the King's intent to extend his patronage over the *sangha* of the whole of Burma by providing it with an unalterable, permanent textual basis.

The codification of the scriptures on stone is not the only 'publication project' of Pali texts remaining from the nineteenth century. In 1879, the newly-established Pali Text Society (PTS) published the first volume of the *Vinaya Pitaka*, edited by Hermann Oldenberg, who also edited and translated the Sinhalese chronicle, *Dipavamsa*, in the same year. By the end of the nineteenth century, the PTS had begun to edit all major text collections of the Pali canon, together with their commentaries. While this work was underway, the Thai King Chulalongkorn (Rama IV) invited leading monks and scholars of Siam to his capital, Bangkok, to recite and edit the Buddhist canon again. Altogether 48 monks and 32 laymen were eventually involved in this synod, which became the tenth in the Thai tradition.[23] The authorized version produced by the gathering was then typeset and printed in Thai script, resulting in 39 volumes all paid for by the king.[24] The introduction attached to all volumes illuminates the king's motivation for the enterprise: with both Sri Lanka and Burma having become subject to colonial rule, the role of defender of the faith had now fallen to the Thai king, and fulfilling that role required him to preserve the true and correct wording of the *dhamma*.[25] At the same time, the king acknowledged that Buddhists could no longer ignore the advent of modernity. It was not only the fact that the king sponsored the first ever printing of the Buddhist scriptures in vernacular letters, but also the way the texts were edited. Rather than relying on the collective memory of participants at a synod, the texts were critically edited by a joint committee of monks and scholars and the printed version gives variant readings from Sinhalese and Burmese manuscripts and from the editions produced by the PTS.[26] Despite this innovative approach, the outreach and, therefore, global significance of the royal edition remained limited, being overshadowed by the work of the PTS and not least marred by the fact that printing was stopped without completing the whole canon.[27]

The final synod to come under scrutiny here, the Sixth Buddhist Council held at Rangoon from 1954–1956, took place in a completely different political and intellectual climate. The former colonies of Sri Lanka and Burma had regained independence and begun to set the relationship between religion and the state on a new footing, while Buddhism had, in the meantime, acquired certain features that made it a truly transnational power, comparable to other global religions such as Christianity or Islam. Institutionally, the Mahabodhi Society (formed in 1891) and the Colombo-based World Fellowship of Buddhists (1950) organized the connections among Buddhist communities by way of publications and meetings. These institutions, which were working alongside national institutions and associations often backed by their governments, acted as powerful promoters and disseminators of the *dhamma* in the East and in the West.

The Burma that U Nu was governing—partly accidentally, after general Aung San and six cabinet members of the interim government had been assassinated in July 1947, leaving U Nu as the only person of political stature and skills—had been a major theatre of war during World War II, leaving the country's infrastructure and economy in tatters. Moreover, the country was torn apart by ethno-political conflict, with much of the territory in the hands of rebel armies of varying denominations. During the first years after independence, from 1948 until the mid-1950s, the authority of the union government was limited to the capital and a handful of garrison towns across the country. Gradually, the army succeeded in overcoming rebel resistance to create larger and more coherent patches of territory that offered political and economic stability. As the economic reconstruction of the country progressed, not least with the help of foreign aid, U Nu embarked upon a far-reaching programme of nation-building in which Buddhism was to play an important role. In the hands of U Nu, Buddhism became the basic ingredient of state ideology, providing moral guidance and a platform for social coherence that transcended competing ideologies, especially communism. A devout Buddhist himself, U Nu used every opportunity to emphasize the consoling, pacifying and unifying powers the Buddha's teachings were supposed to offer.[28] For this reason, he was all too eager to organize a Buddhist world council and support it with a substantial part of the state's resources. In 1951, when the decision to hold the synod was made public, one crore kyats (ten million) were set apart for the necessary buildings alone. A sum that had more than tripled by the time the convocation hall (Mahapasana Guha) and the adjacent World Peace Pagoda were inaugurated three years later.[29]

The date of the synod was not accidental, of course. Its concluding session in May 1956 coincided with the anniversary—2500 years—of Gotama Buddha's *parinibbana* and, thus, the halfway point of the 5000 year period thought to separate the historical Buddha from his successor Metteya. Similar to the synods in the fifteenth century, the Sixth Council was embedded in millenarian thinking and Metteyanic expectations. Originally linked to the Theravada tradition, these expectations were now shared by most Buddhists, as the list of participants suggests. Besides monks from Sri Lanka, Thailand, Laos and Cambodia, delegations from Japan, China and even Tibet (which, by the time the synod commenced, had been annexed by China) came to Rangoon to attend the sessions. In a very customary fashion, the objective of the synod was to produce yet another authoritative recension of the Buddhist canon, this time using the versions from the stone library at Mandalay as its basis.[30] In total, 2500 monks were invited to participate in the recitations. They worked in five panels of 500 monks each, presided over by leading monks from Burma (who chaired two groups), Sri Lanka, Thailand, and Laos and Cambodia jointly. Once approved, the texts were to be printed by the Burmese Department of Religious Affairs. The printing of the Chatthasanghayana edition, as it came to be known, took several decades and amounted to 117 volumes, including commentaries and sub-commentaries.[31]

Apart from the Sixth Council itself, the Buddha Jayanti celebrations during the mid-1950s inspired a host of other activities elsewhere in the Buddhist world, most notably in Sri Lanka.[32] More importantly, the 1954–1956 synod also provided a fresh stimulus for attempts to spread the *dhamma* across Asia, especially to countries where the religion had already flourished at one point. In India, the public conversion of B. R. Ambedkar and a large group of followers made Buddhism the religion of India's Untouchables,[33] while attempts to re-introduce the Theravada tradition to Nepal and Indonesia were less successful or indeed complete failures.[34]

Conclusion

Although the history of the Buddhist synods, especially in the later period, remains to be written, two preliminary observations can be presented here. The first observation concerns the function of Buddhist synods, which were held not least to produce and retain an agreed, authoritative version of the *dhamma*, the corpus of the Buddha's teachings. In this, the synods did not change, from the first synod convened after the Buddha's decease down to those taking place in the nineteenth and twentieth century, no matter the cultural and social context in which they were held. What was different, however, was the importance attributed to them in various traditions: the Sinhalese Mahaviharins basically stopped counting after the religion had been firmly established on the island, while the Thais included minor and even unrecognized synods in their accounts. The Burmese remained somewhere in the middle, but display a good grasp of important events by including the 'forgotten' synod of the first century BCE, when the Buddhist canon was allegedly written down for the first time, in their count.

This leads to the second observation, which concerns innovations. The three synods surveyed were all, at least to a degree, pioneering. King Mindon Min's decision to have the scriptures recorded in stone was in line with the custom, established at the previous synod (of the Burmese tradition) in Pegu, that an authorized version was to be fixed in writing. Using marble for this purpose was a novelty and, at the same time, a powerful statement that the true wording of the teachings would not get lost and could not become obscured anymore. It seems that this claim was well understood in neighbouring Thailand, where the ruler sponsored the first printed version of the canon in a vernacular script only few years after the stone library had been completed. The Sixth (1954–1955) Council in turn marked the culmination of a Buddhist transnationalism that had been forming since the end of the nineteenth century. In that respect, it was less pioneering than simply bringing together what had been in the making for a while. However, what it achieved for the first time was to bring together monks not only from the various Theravada traditions but also from other Buddhist schools. In this sense, it was the first true world council of Buddhists. The only synod that could make a similar claim, at least as far as the Theravada world is concerned, was the meeting held at Kotte in the 1420s, but this synod—ironically—is not even acknowledged in any Theravada tradition.

ACKNOWLEDGEMENTS

This paper emerged from the conference: Southeast Asia as a Crossroads for Buddhist Exchange, sponsored by the Dhammakaya International Society, UK, and University College Cork, Republic of Ireland. The author is grateful to acknowledge the support he received from these institutions to attend the conference.

NOTES

1. Although the term 'council' appears to be more common, 'synod' will be used here to denote the meetings as, later on, permanent boards of monks also came to be called councils. The Pali equivalent of a synod would be *sanghayana* or *sangiti*.
2. Frauwallner (1952); Bareau (1955); Alsdorf (1959); Bechert (1961); Hallisey (1991). For an overview of the discussions, see Prebish (1974).
3. Alsdorf (1959); Bechert (1961); Norman (1983).
4. Frasch (1998a, 2000). For a general history of Theravada Buddhism, see Gombrich (2006).
5. Frasch (2000, 2011).
6. For the context of this synod, see Norman (1983, 10–11) and Bechert (1992). For the role of the canon, see Collins (1990).
7. In his *Samantapasadika* (Jayawickrama 1962, 91–93), Buddhaghosa stops with the rehearsal of the Vinaya in the first century BCE, emphasizing the role of lineage and knowledge of the Vinaya over the role of synods. In the *Saddhammasangaha*, a work representing the Thai tradition, this council is seen as the fifth (Law 1952, 61–69).
8. Frasch (2000, 2013).
9. Frasch (1998b).

10. Frasch (2013).

11. For the various Southeast Asian traditions relating to this synod and its outreach see Frasch (2011, 387–389).

12. Nyanasamvara (1992). Thai tradition recognizes the three Indian councils detailed above and four Sri Lankan synods at Anuradhapura (third century BCE), Alokalena (first century BCE), Anuradhapura under Buddhaghosa (fifth century CE) and the attempt by King Parakkama Bahu I of Polonnaruwa to reunite the three Sinhalese *nikayas* in the middle of the twelfth century CE.

13. Blackburn (2001, 2010); Malalgoda (1976, 87–100, 161–172).

14. For the modernization of Burma after 1853, see U Myint Thant-U (2001, 104–129).

15. Dates follow U Than Tun (1977) and are based on the official history of Burma's last dynasty, the *Konbaungzet Mahayazawin-daw-gyi.*

16. U Than Tun (1977, 130).

17. U Than Tun (ed., 1988), July 10, 1870. The recitation of the texts was presided over by the Royal Preceptor or Thathanabaing.

18. U Maung Maung Tin (1968, 382–385). The account of the chronicle begins with a recapitulation of the previous four synods, listing the kings who sponsored them, the number of monks participating, the name of the leading monk and the subject of the synod, which was a recitation of the complete canon in every case. The account of the Mandalay synod is, for the most part, an eulogy of the king.

19. U Than Tun (ed., 1988), September 10, 1871.

20. Major works containing that mistake include Smith (1965, 26, 157); Bechert ([1966–1967]1988–2000, 2); Keyes (1977, 267); Devendra (1977, 524); U Tin Maung Maung Than (1993, 11); Bečka (1995, 84). But see Quigly (1956) and Bollée (1968), the latter being the first scholar to point out this mistake and actually assess the value of the stone library.

21. Malalgoda (1976, 161–172).

22. Bechert ([1966–1967]1988–2000, 22–23). For the factions within the *sangha* see also Ferguson (1978) and Charney (2006, 209–215).

23. Nyanasamvara (1992, 60); Saddhatissa (1974, 219). The ninth synod had been held in 1788 as part of the reorganization of the Siamese kingdom after the Burmese conquest of Ayutthya in 1767.

24. Chalmers (1898).

25. Chalmers (1898, 2–3).

26. Chalmers (1898, 8). For traditional forms of Thai Buddhist scholarship see Veidlinger (2006); for the adaption of Western scholarship see Jory (2002).

27. Grönbold (1984, 57).

28. Frasch (2013); Tinker (1957).

29. Tinker (1957, 174). The total expenses equated to c. £2 million. In addition to the financial contributions, numerous government officials were given paid leave to work as volunteers for the synod.

30. For the tasks given to the synod and its proceedings see Bechert ([1966–1967] 1988–2000, 104–106) and Tinker (1957, 172–175). A first assessment of the printed texts is Hamm (1962).

31. See Grönbold (1984) for further details.

32. The compilation of the *Encyclopaedia of Buddhism*, begun in 1955 and concluded in 2011, was the major state-sponsored project on the island. The impetus of the Buddhist revival there was quickly hijacked by the two major political parties and became a crucial factor in the Sinhalese-Tamil conflict that paralysed the country for the rest of the twentieth century.

33. For Ambedkar's conversion (and, more generally, a history of Buddhism from the perspective of the Navayana), see Omvedt (2003, 243–265). Nehru and the Government of India welcomed the Buddhist revival in India as part of India's own nation-building project. The Indian government sponsored a volume in felicitation of the anniversary of 2500 years (Bapat 1956).

34. For Nepal, see Levine and Gellner (2005); for Indonesia, see Bechert (1988).

REFERENCES

ALSDORF, L. 1959. Ashokas Schismenedikt und das Dritte Konzil. *Indo-Iranian Journal* 3: 161–74.

BAPAT, P. V., ed. 1956. *2500 Years of Buddhism*. Delhi: Ministry of Information and Broadcasting.

BAREAU, A. 1955. *Les premières conciles bouddhiques*. Paris: Musée Guimet.

BECHERT, H. 1961. Ashokas, 'Schismenedikt' und der Begriff des *samghabheda*. *Wiener Zeitschrift für die Kunde Süd- und Ostasiens* 5: 18–52.

BECHERT, H. [1966–1967]1988–2000. *Buddhismus, Staat und Gesellschaft in den Ländern des Theravada-Buddhismus*. Vols. 1–2. Göttingen: Originally Frankfurt: Metzner, and Wiesbaden: Harrassowitz Seminar für Indologie und Buddhismuskunde.

BECHERT, H. 1988. Buddhismus im heutigen Java und Bali. *Internationales Asienforum* 19: 17–33.

BECHERT, H. 1992. The Writing Down of the Tipitaka in Bali. *Wiener Zeitschrift für die Kunde Südasiens* 36: 45–53.

BEČKA, J. 1995. *Historical Dictionary of Myanmar*. Metuchen: Scarecrow Press.

BLACKBURN, A. 2001. *Buddhist Learning and Textual Practice in Eighteenth-Century Lankan Monastic Culture*. Princeton: Princeton University Press.

BLACKBURN, A. 2010. *Locations of Buddhism. Colonialism and Modernity in Sri Lanka*. Chicago: University of Chicago Press.

BOLLÉE, W. B. 1968. Some Lesser Known Burmese Pali Texts. In *Pratidanam. Indian, Iranian and Indo-European Studies Presented to Franciscus Bernardus Jacobus Kuiper on His 60th Birthday*, edited by J. C. Heesterman, and G. H. Schokker., 493–9. New York: de Gruyter.

CHALMERS, R. 1898. The King of Siam's Edition of the Pali Tipitaka. *Journal of the Royal Asiatic Society* : 1–10.

CHARNEY, M. W. 2006. *Powerful Learning. Buddhist Literati and the Throne in Burma's Last Dynasty, 1752–1885*. Ann Arbor: University of Michigan Press.

COLLINS, S. 1990. The Very Idea of the Pali Canon. *Journal of the Pali Text Society* 15: 89–126.

DEVENDRA, D. T. 1977. Burma. In *Encyclopaedia of Buddhism*, edited by A. W. P. Guruge, and D. W. Weeraratne. Vol. 3, fasc. 4. Colombo: Bauddha Mandalaya.

FERGUSON, J. P. 1978. The Quest for Legitimation by Burmese Monks and Kings: The Case of the Shwegyin Sect, Nineteenth-Twentieth Centuries. In *Religion and Legitimation of Power in Thailand, Laos and Burma*, edited by Bardwell L. Smith, 66–86. Chambersburg: Anima.

FRASCH, T. 1998a. Religious and Economic Development of Ancient Anuradhapura. In *Sri Lanka Past and Present. Archaeology, Geography, Economics*, edited by M. Domrös, and H. Roth, 61–81. Weikersheim: Margraf.

FRASCH, T. 1998b. A Buddhist Network in the Bay of Bengal: Relations between Bodhgaya, Burma and Sri Lanka, c. 300–1300. In *From the Mediterranean to the China Sea. Miscellaneous Notes*, edited by Claude Guillot et al., 69–93. Wiesbaden: Harrassowitz.

FRASCH, T. 2000. Der Buddhismus im Jahr 1000. *Periplus. Jahrbuch für Außereuropäische Geschichte* 10: 56–72 [The World of Buddhism in the Year 1000. In *Proceedings of the Myanmar Two Millennia Conference*, Vol. 3, 39–51. Yangon].

FRASCH, T. 2011. 1456: The Making of a Buddhist Ecumene in the Bay of Bengal. In *Pelagic Passageways: The Northern Bay of Bengal World before Colonialism*, edited by Rila Mukherjee, 383–405. Delhi: Primus.

FRASCH, T. 2013. Relics and the Rule of Righteousness: Reflections on U Nu's *dhammavijaya*. In *Buddhism and State Power in Asia: Cooperation, Cooptation, Confrontation*, edited by John Whalen-Bridge, and Pattana Kitiarsa. Basingstoke: Macmillan.

FRAUWALLNER, E. 1952. Die buddhistischen Konzile. *Zeitschrift der Deutschen Morgenländischen Gesellschaft* 102: 245–61.

GOMBRICH, R. F. 2006. *Theravada Buddhism. A Social History from Ancient Benares to Modern Colombo*. 2nd ed. London: Routledge.

GRÖNBOLD, G. 1984. *Der buddhistische Kanon. Eine Bibliographie*. Wiesbaden: Harrassowitz.

HALLISEY, C. S. 1991. Councils as Ideas and Events in the Theravada. In *The Buddhist Forum II*, edited by T. Skorupski, 133–48. London: SOAS.

HAMM, F.-R. 1962. Zu einigen neueren Ausgaben des Pali Tipitaka. *Zeitschrift der Deutschen Morgenländischen Gesellschaft* 112: 353–78.

JAYAWICKRAMA, N. A., trans. 1962. *The Inception of Discipline and the Vinaya-Nidana*. London: Luzac.

JORY, P. 2002. Thai and Western Buddhist Scholarship in the Age of Colonialism: King Chulalongkorn Redefines the Jatakas. *Journal of Asian Studies* 61 (3): 891–918.

KEYES, C. F. 1977. *The Golden Peninsula*. Honolulu: University of Hawai'i Press.

U MAUNG MAUNG TIN. 1968. *Konbaungzet Mahayazawin-daw-gyi* [Royal Chronicle of the Konbaung Dynasty]. Vol. 3. Rangoon: Ledi Mandaing Press.

LAW, B. C., trans. 1952. *Sasanavamsa. A History of the Buddha's Religion*. London: Luzac.

LEVINE, S., and GELLNER, D., eds. 2005. *Rebuilding Buddhism: The Theravada Movement in Twentieth Century Nepal*. Cambridge, MA: Harvard University Press.

MALALGODA, K. 1976. *Buddhism in Sinhalese Society, 1750–1900*. Berkeley: University of California Press.

U MYINT THANT-U. 2001. *The Making of Modern Burma*. Cambridge: Cambridge University Press.

NORMAN, K. R. 1983. *Pali Literature*. Wiesbaden: Harrassowitz.

NYANASAMVARA MAHATHERA. 1992. *Buddha Sasana Vamsa: A Buddhist Monastic Lineage*. Bangkok: Mahamakut Press.

OMVEDT, G. 2003. *Buddhism in India. Challenging Brahmanism and Caste*. New Delhi: Sage.

PREBISH, C. 1974. A Review of Scholarship on the Buddhist Councils. *Journal of Asian Studies* 33 (2): 239–54.

QUIGLY, E. P. 1956. *Libraries, Manuscripts and Books of Burma*. London: Probsthain.

SADDHATISSA, H. 1974. Pali Literature of Thailand. In *Buddhist Studies in Honour of I.B. Horner*, edited by L. Cousins et al., 211–20. Dordrecht and Boston: Reidel.

SMITH, D. E. 1965. *Religion and Politics in Burma*. Princeton: University Press.

U THAN TUN. 1977. Chronology of Mandalay. *Shiroku* 10: 127–55.

U THAN TUN, ed. and trans. 1988. *The Royal Orders of Burma, AD 1598–1885*. Vol. 9 (1853–1885). Kyoto: Center for Southeast Studies, Kyoto University.

U TIN MAUNG MAUNG THAN. 1993. Sangha Reforms and Renewal of Sasana in Myanmar: Historical Trends and Contemporary Practice. In *Buddhist Trends in Southeast Asia*, edited by Trevor Ling, 6–63. Singapore: ISEAS.

TINKER, H. 1957. *The Union of Burma. A Study of the First Year of Independence*. London: Oxford University Press.

VEIDLINGER, D. M. 2006. *Spreading the Dhamma. Writing, Orality, and Textual Transmission in Buddhist Northern Thailand*. Honolulu: University of Hawai'i Press.

THREE BOYS ON A GREAT VEHICLE: 'MAHAYANA BUDDHISM' AND A TRANS-NATIONAL NETWORK

Shin'ichi Yoshinaga

From 1915–1916 there was in Kyoto a trans-national group of Buddhists named the Mahayana Association, which published an English Buddhist periodical, Mahayanist. Two members of the Mahayana Association, William Montgomery McGovern and M. T. Kirby, were among the earliest cases of Westerners ordained in the tradition of Mahayana Buddhism in Japan. Kirby explored the temples of Jōdo Shinshū and the monastic life of Rinzai Zen and Theravada Buddhism in search of salvation. McGovern, on the other hand, had been searching for an alternative to Christianity, which he found unscientific and dissatisfying. He finally found Jōdo Shinshū, which he held to be the essence of Mahayana Buddhism. His understanding of Buddhism was influenced by D. T. Suzuki's version of Mahayana Buddhism. Utsuki Nishu, who helped McGovern and Kirby run the Association, joined the Theosophical Society (Adyar, India) while he was studying at Hollywood High School in Los Angeles and later helped Beatrice Suzuki run the Mahayana Lodge of the Theosophical Society. Drawing on forgotten documents discovered only recently in a Japanese temple, this paper offers a progress report on research into these documents and explores a significant but hitherto unknown side of the history of modern Japanese Buddhism.

Preface

In 1915, a Canadian and an American, Mortimer T. Kirby and William Montgomery McGovern, received Buddhist ordination. The former was ordained at the Rinzai sect's Engakuji in Kamakura and the latter at the Jōdo Shinshū (Pure Land, Nishi Honganji branch) Anryūji in Shiga. Both were among the earliest cases of Westerners ordained in the tradition of Mahayana Buddhism in Japan. While they had precursors such as William Sturgis Bigelow, who took 'lay ordination' in Japan in 1888 and gave a lecture on Buddhism after returning to Boston and Charles Pfoundes, who was ordained into Tendai, Shugendo and other traditions in the 1890s, these two men were different from their forerunners in several ways. First, they tried to enter a temple to lead the life of a priest as disciples, not as 'guests' or 'part-time' priests. Second, in the spring of 1915, in Kyoto, they organized a society for foreign sympathizers of Buddhism, the Mahayana Association (Daijō Kyōkai). Third, they published a monthly journal *Mahayanist* from July 1915 to around September 1916. Fourth, Japanese scholars and students helped them publish the periodical. So this was a truly international, or global, organization. A young student of Bukkyō University (now Ryūkoku University), Utsuki Nishū, helped them run the Association. McGovern, Kirby and Utsuki were on good terms and continued to communicate with each other until late in their lives.

However, in spite of their significance, the *Mahayanist* and Mahayana Association have not been mentioned in any recently published English articles on Buddhism (Peirce 2010): up until now, this was a completely forgotten episode. This is only natural, considering the lack of remaining copies of the journal. However, I was fortunate enough to uncover related historical materials such as the *Mahayanist*[1] itself and the association's members list at the Shōtokuji Documents Collection.

Shōtokuji is a Jōdo Shinshū (Pure Land, Nishi Honganji branch) temple in Takatsuki, Osaka. Utsuki Nishū was its twentieth chief priest. Colleagues and I started researching there in 2009 in order to know how and why a priest of the Jōdo Shin sect had written an article about the Cao Dai religion of Vietnam (then French Indo-China). When we started the research, all we knew about him was that he had been a professor of English at Ryūkoku University, had published some English books on Buddhism, had co-operated with Suzuki Daisetsu's wife, Beatrice Suzuki, in running a Theosophical lodge and had been sent to South East Asia in 1941 to investigate the religious situation there by Koa Bukkyō Kyōkai (Buddhist Society for the Promotion of Asia). Luckily, we found many of the documents preserved untouched in the storehouse of the temple right before they were going to be thrown away. There was more than we had expected: diaries from Utsuki's travels to America, Hawaii, and Southeast Asia and materials relating to the Mahayana Association and his activities as a Theosophist, including a certificate admitting him to the Theosophical Society (Adyar, India) signed by A. P. Warrington and Annie Besant. Through the Shōtokuji Documents Collection, the early years of trans-national communications between Japanese and foreign Buddhists in Kyoto and around the world have come to light. This paper is a progress report on research into the collection and an attempt to explore a forgotten side of the history of modern Japanese Buddhism.

William Montgomery McGovern (1897–1964)

William M. McGovern is a famous person, since he led an eventful and well-publicised life. He went on expeditions to Tibet and the Amazon, leading some to call him the "prototypic 'Indiana Jones'".[2] According to a short biography on Northwestern University's library website,[3] his life was as follows:

> William Montgomery McGovern was born in New York City on September 28, 1897. Much of his early life was spent in the Orient; he graduated with the degree of *soro*, or doctor of divinity, from the Buddhist monastery of Nishi Hongwanji in Kyoto, Japan, in 1917. After subsequent studies at the Sorbonne and the University of Berlin, he received his D.Phil. from Christ Church College, Oxford, in 1922.
>
> From 1919 to 1927, he held appointments as lecturer and/or examiner in Oriental Studies at the University of London. His service there was interrupted by two extended expeditions, one to Tibet in 1922–23, the second through the upper Amazon basin and Peru in 1925–26. On the former trip, after being refused entry into the country via normal channels, he disguised himself as a Tibetan coolie and succeeded in entering the capital city of Lhasa, one of the first Westerners to do so. This adventure was recounted in McGovern's most popular work, *To Lhasa in Disguise*. In 1927 McGovern returned to the United States as Assistant Curator of the Anthropology Department at Chicago's Field Museum of Natural History. In 1929 he was appointed Associate Professor of Political Science at Northwestern; he was promoted to full professor in 1936 and held that position until his death in 1964, developing a reputation as an exceptionally entertaining classroom lecturer.

Although this biography itself is correct, his early years before 1922 are difficult to trace and sometimes confusing.

McGovern's daughter describes his early years as follows.[4] William's father was a journalist, Chauncey (or Felix) McGovern, and his mother was Janet Stuart Blair Montgomery-McGovern. The young William was strongly connected to this unique woman. Janet graduated from Shorter College in Georgia and worked as a journalist in New York City. After William was born, his parents divorced and Janet often travelled with her little son to faraway places. In 1912, mother and son travelled to the Philippines where her ex-husband lived and they tried to re-start their marriage, in vain.

Janet played an important role in her son's life. She was an avid seeker of occult teachings before coming to Asia and her name appears in a historical study of Krotona Institute of Theosophy in Los Angeles (Ross 1989). She edited the journal published by a small intellectual occult group, the Oriental Esoteric Head Center, in Washington D.C., and while in USA also joined the American Section of the Theosophical Society (Adyar, India) led by A.P. Warrington. She appears to have been an independent person in spiritual matters, as is evidenced by her severing her relationship with the Society shortly before leaving the USA. It must have been Janet who connected her son's Mahayana Association with esotericists abroad.[5]

The exact year Janet and William came to Japan is not known. Janet began teaching English in some schools in Japan in 1914. William himself wrote that he studied Taoism in China before coming to Japan.[6] It is still unclear whether they came to Japan together or separately, and what route(s) they took after leaving the Philippines. In any case, William moved from Kagoshima to Kyoto in April 1915 and started teaching at the Heian Middle School of Nishi Honganji (Heian Gakuen 1986) in place of the aforementioned M. T. Kirby. Around this time Janet also came to live in Kyoto.

The McGoverns' stay in Kyoto did not last long. Janet decided to take up a teaching job at a Japanese women's school in Taiwan and left Kyoto in 1916. She carried out anthropological research on the traditional societies of Taiwan, which she would publish in 1922 (J. B. Mcgovern 1922). Whether William followed her to Taiwan in 1916 or stayed in Japan until 1917 is not known.

William McGovern underwent the 'kikyō-shiki' which is almost the same as 'lay ordination' on May 3, 1915 and was given the name of Shaku Shidō.[7] He was then ordained as a priest of the Jōdo Shin sect (Nishi Honganji) on December 16, 1915 as a 'shūto' (deacon) at Anryūji, of which Nogami Kakudō, an English teacher at Heian Middle School and the treasurer of the Mahayana Association, was deputy chief priest.

William appeared at a festival at Anryūji on January 5, 1916. According to an article describing this event, a thousand people gathered to see him make an English speech on Buddhism. This event became known when Nishi Honganji's official organ *Kyōkai Ichiran* reported the event (no. 598, February 1, 1916), featuring his photo on its front cover. In his speech McGovern talked about why he had converted to Buddhism. He stated that he became disappointed with Christianity after he came to know the natural sciences, and he could not find satisfaction in Vedanta philosophy, Islam or Theravada Buddhism. However, he had finally found Mahayana Buddhism, the essence of which he thought to be Jōdo Shinshū.

However, his version of Mahayana Buddhism was more philosophically sophisticated. We shall look at his rationalist explanation of Buddhism below.

Mortimer T. Kirby (1877–?)

Considerably less is known about M. T. Kirby's life, even though his travels covered England, Canada, America, Japan and Ceylon. He was born in Swaffham Prior, Cambridgeshire, UK in 1877.[8] Later, he emigrated to Canada and converted to Catholicism. After developing an interest in Buddhism, he travelled to Japan in 1913. First, on April 24, 1914, he joined a secular Zen group, the Sanmaji Kai (Society for Samadhi)[9] which was presided over by Hirai Kinza.[10] Soon after, in May 1914, he visited Engakuji with Suzuki Daisetsu and on July 11, 1915 he formally became a Zen monk at Engakuji under Shaku Sōen (1860–1919) and was given the Buddhist name Shaku Sōgaku. The *Mahayanist* reported that Shaku Sōen conducted a special Pali ritual for him.[11]

Kirby returned to Canada in February 1916 and started to propagate Buddhism there, by himself. From 1919–1926, he gave lectures on Buddhism at the temples of Nishi Honganji in San Francisco (1919–1921) and in Honolulu

(1921–1926). In 1919, he met and taught Zen to Samuel L. Lewis, who would become the Sufi Ahmed Murad Chisti.[12] From 1927–1929 he stayed in Japan again, visiting Nishi Honganji and temples of the Rinzai sect. Kirby then left Japan and travelled to Ceylon after staying for a while in Europe.

It seems that Kirby became more and more critical of Japanese Buddhism after his second visit to Japan. He wrote an article titled 'What of the Future?' for the *Young East* in 1927. In that article he criticized Japanese Buddhism for being a speculative system of metaphysics. He proposed a return to the Buddhism of the Buddha which, he said, was scientific and stressed the effort of the practitioners. He wrote, 'Truly it is the bonsan [priests] that first need salvation. Japan needs a purified priesthood, a possessionless priesthood, a priesthood on the Noble Path of Effort. Without this the future is not healthy; with this, the future is assured' (Kirby 1927, 129). After this, he seems to have turned to Theravada for salvation. He wrote a letter to Utsuki dated August 29, 1929, from the Island Hermitage in Ceylon.[13] In it he said he was satisfied with his simple life in the island, studying Pali and practising meditation.

Kirby was seeking not a metaphysical system but rather a psychological practice based on a rational system. In an earlier letter to Utsuki dated March 31, 1922, he had written 'Universe is LAW, and all mental, so we must find these LAWS and live in harmony with them'. It is natural that such a pursuit for a mental law led to a longing for the monastery life and disappointment with Japanese clerics (who were often married). However, one of his old colleagues from missionary work in Hawaii recalled that he was not satisfied even with Theravada and that in the end 'he abandoned Buddhism, which he had never really practiced, and he died ignominiously in a Salvation Army camp, cursing the Dharma as fit only for the "dirty Niggers" of Ceylon' (Hunter 1971).[14] Regardless of whether this account is true or not, we should pay proper attention to his life as an example of that of an early European practitioner of Buddhism.

The Mahayana Association

As mentioned above, the Mahayana Association was organized in the spring of 1915. The reason for starting such a society was the recognition by the founders that Mahayana Buddhism was still unknown to the Occident, and 'many of the few books written on Mahayana by foreigners are filled with gross mi[s]statements and misconceptions'.[15]

The aims of this association were: (1) to study Mahayana Buddhism; (2) to present it to the Western public; and (3) to make 'bonds of closer fellowship [among] those interested in the foregoing aims'.[16] Those who wanted to practise in a temple could get in touch with Japanese monks and scholars through this association.

The association had an impressive list of members. McGovern was the chancellor of the society, Kirby the vice-chancellor. After Kirby returned to Canada in 1916, Paul Carus took his place. The schoolteacher Nogami Kakudō helped them as a treasurer. Its executive council consisted of Hadani Ryōtai, a professor at Kyoto University and the sixth president of Ryūkoku University, Beatrice Suzuki, and

Nogami. Honorary presidents were Akamatsu Renjō, the first president of Bukkyō University and Sonoda Shūe, the second and fourth president of Bukkyō University (1905–1912, 1915–1921). Timothy Richard in China and Suzuki Daisetsu were also members of the honorary council ('The Mahayana Association: Notes and News' in *Mahayanist* 1 [2]). Other helpful members included Watanabe Ryūshō, principal of Heian middle school and Utsuki Nishū.

The member's list of this association, as of October 1916, contained over 100 names including Japanese university professors, priests, foreign researchers, and editors of journals such as *Theosophist, Quest* and *Buddhist Review.* Members included professors Sonoda Shūye, Morikawa Chitoku, Uno Enku, and Akamatsu Chijō of Bukkyō University, Yamaguchi Susumu and Izumi Hokei of Ōtani University, Nishi Hongwanji North American Missionaries Nakai Gendō, Mitsunaga Teiyū and Jisōji Tetsugai, A. J. Edmunds from the USA and Elizabeth A. Gordon from Japan.

Regardless of whether William was only 18 years old, as the biography quoted above says, or 23 years old as a contemporary Japanese person wrote, (Jisōji 1969, 312)[17] it would have been almost impossible for him to create such a network by himself. He might have been introduced to these people through Watanabe Ryusho, Janet McGovern, or Suzuki Daisetsu, whom he met at least once (Suzuki Daisetsu 2003, 397).[18]

The *Mahayanist*

The *Mahayanist* was published in the years between two important English periodicals, the *Light of Dharma* (San Francisco, 1901–1907) and the *Eastern Buddhist* (Kyoto, 1921–). It was smaller than the former, and not as academic as the latter. However, it had more higher-quality and scholarly articles than other previously published English Buddhist journals such as the *Bijou of Asia* (Kyoto, 1888–1889), *Hansei Zasshi* (Tokyo, 1897–1899) and the *Orient* (Tokyo, 1899–1900). Although most Japanese contributors were scholars and intellectuals, the overall atmosphere of the *Mahayanist* was not analytical but apologetic. Some articles were written by Zen priests, such as Shaku Sōen or Nukariya Kaiten, and some were by scholars of Jōdo Shinshū such as Tada Kanaye, Akamatsu Renjō, Izumi Hōkei, Tsumaki Jikiryō, Uno Enkū, Suzuki Daisetsu and so on. The most frequent contributors were William McGovern, M. T. Kirby, and Janet McGovern.

Obviously, there was no sect called 'Mahayana Buddhism' in Japan at the time. Mahayana Buddhism, as a trans-sectarian concept, originates from the middle of the Meiji Period (1868–1912). As Judith Snodgrass points out, it was used strategically against Western society to proclaim the superiority of Japanese Buddhism (Snodgrass 2003). In the case of the *Mahayanist*, Suzuki Daisetsu's version of a trans-sectarian 'Mahayana Buddhism' may have been the inspiration for the author of the title of the journal.

The editorial in *Mahayanist* 1 (6) (January 1916) is a good example of this strategic comparison. The writer sums up five points of similarity and difference between Christianity and Buddhism regarding God and Shinnyo (suchness), Christ and Gautama, and their laws of retribution. According to the article, the Absolute is a being possessed of boundless love, and uses various guises to realize its love. The guises can be grouped into three, so the Mahayana doctrine of the three bodies corresponds to the Christian Trinity. Yet the goal of salvation differs, so the editor writes.

> The only difference being that the Christian goal is Heaven, a place merely, while the Buddhist goal is Supreme and Perfect Enlightenment (Buddhahood), a condition of mind, which may either be gained here on earth or in the Sukhavati, of Amitabha the Universal Buddha or the Absolute.[19]

The approach characterizing Buddhism as a 'monotheistic' and 'pantheistic' (or 'panentheistic') system is commonly seen in the articles by Japanese contributors such as Shaku Sōen or Hadani Ryōtai.

Hadani's article, 'The Ideal Form of Monotheism' (*Mahayanist* 1 [1]) compares the 'Transcendental monotheism' of Christianity with the 'Pantheistic monotheism' of Buddhism, arguing for the superiority of the latter as follows:

> It is already quite clear without any illustration that there are two forms, Transcendental-monotheism and Pantheism, in all religions which stand upon the belief in only one Superhuman Being. The former declares that the Superhuman Being is the maker of the world and exists apart from it, as in Christianity and Islam: the latter, on the contrary, regards Him not as a Creator distinct from nature of the universe, but as Eternal Being existing inside it or identical with it; accordingly, in the view of Pantheism, there is nothing but the Supreme and everything is part of Him or a manifestation of Him. 'Tathagata' the object of faith in Mahayana Buddhism consists of the pantheistic idea, for He is an immanent infinite Being and the one All in All, like Spinoza's God.[20]

Pantheism is rational and can satisfy our reason, but it lacks in religious sentiment. Hadani wrote, 'Religion ought to be more closely connected with our heart than with our head,' continuing, 'We require heartily a religion holding together each excellent point of the two forms of Monotheism, in other words, being able to admit both the claims of head and heart'.[21]

The last statement of Hadani in this article is that this ideal religion is none other than the reformed Buddhism of Shinran. This strategy of using Western philosophy or comparative religion to argue for the superiority of Mahayana Buddhism, had often been used by intellectual Buddhists since Inoue Enryō and Nakanishi Ushirō (Hoshino 2009).

William McGovern's understanding of Buddhism was also influenced by this modernized and eclectic version of Japanese Buddhism. He contributed at least eight articles to the *Mahayanist* which would later become the basis of his *Introduction to Mahayana Buddhism* (1922). What characterizes his articles is a concern with the 'three bodies' in Buddhism and the Christian Trinity. Below is a passage about Dharmakaya (the Dharma body) from his article, 'The Nature of the Buddhist Trinity' (W. M. Mcgovern 1915).

> The Dharmakaya corresponds, as we have seen, in the Shodomon [the path of the sages], to the Christian God the Father, but though it is like the Christian conception of the Deity in as much as it is supposed to be the chief object of our worship, yet the Mahayana idea is apt to be more amplified, more universal, less restricted.... The Northern Buddhistic view of this Law-Body is not of a man made God-like, but rather of a principle self-manifested for the sake of aiding evolution. It is personal, I have said — yes, but care must be taken in understanding just what is meant by the word personal. If by personal we mean anthropopathic — man-like in feeling if not in actual shape, with a man's likes and dislikes, hates and partialities, the Dharmakaya is certainly not personal. Nevertheless it is not purely abstract and colourless — it is not merely Love, Reason, and Justice. It is a being endowed with those attributes and is, therefore, in that sense a person, but it far transcends the limits of a personality in the narrow sense in which the word is so often used. The Dharmakaya is not impersonal but rather than personal, we might call it super-personal.[22]

McGovern's discussion of the Dharmakāya and Trikāya shares similarities with Japanese modernized Buddhism, specifically that of Suzuki Daisetsu. Suzuki wrote *Outlines of Mahayana Buddhism* in America in 1907. Suzuki described the Dharmakāya as: (1) not transcendental but omnipresent; and (2) not an absolutely impersonal principle, both of which were characteristic of McGovern's interpretation of Buddhism. It is certain that McGovern borrowed Daisetsu's 'Dharmakāya'. Here is one passage from Suzuki's book.

> The Dharmakāya may be compared in one sense to the God of Christianity and in another sense to the Brahman or Paramatman of Vedantism. It is different, however, from the former in that it does not stand transcendentally above the universe, which, according to the Christian view, was created by God, but which is, according to Mahayanism, a manifestation of the Dharmakāya himself. It is also different from Brahman in that it is not absolutely impersonal, nor is it a mere being. The Dharmakāya, on the contrary, is capable of willing and reflecting, or, to use Buddhist phraseology, it is Karuna (love) and Bodhi (intelligence), and not the mere state of being. This pantheistic and at the same time entheistic Dharmakāya is working in every sentient being, for sentient beings are nothing but a self-manifestation of the Dharmakāya. Individuals are not isolated existences, as imagined by most people (D. T. Suzuki 1907, 46).

In other words, during the 1910s, the *Mahayanist* was the only periodical conveying Suzuki's modernist version of Buddhism to English-speaking people.

After the *Mahayanist*: Utsuki Nishū (1893–1951) and the Mahayana Lodge

There was a sequel to the Mahayana Association. Several years after it disappeared, another international group of Buddhists appeared in Kyoto, organized as a lodge of the Theosophical Society with the help of Utsuki Nishū. This was in 1924, the same year that Christmas Humphreys organized the Buddhist Lodge of the Theosophical Society in London.

In 1917, Utsuki had graduated from Bukkyō University and travelled to America with Sonoda Shūye, who was sent to Los Angeles by Nishi Hongwanji to settle some trouble there (Ama 2010). Utsuki attended the College Preparatory Course of Hollywood High School for a year and entered the University of Southern California in 1918, where he studied until 1920. He then left California and arrived in England in October 1920. There, he met McGovern again and taught Japanese at the School of Oriental Studies. In December 1921, he left London and after travelling through Europe arrived back in Japan in April 1922, where he became a lecturer in English at Ryūkoku University.

While in Hollywood, Utsuki became a member of the Theosophical Society, becoming part of the Krotona Institute of Theosophy and its community. The leader of Krotona was A. P. Warrington, who was also the general secretary of the American Section of the Theosophical Society (Adyar, India). Utsuki was introduced to Warrington by McGovern and was admitted to the Society on September 24, 1917. There is a letter dated October 2, 1917 from the Theosophical Society to Utsuki, whose address was the same as that of the Theosophical Society. It seems that he lived or worked in Krotona for a year while studying English at Hollywood High School.

Though it was a rare occurrence, Utsuki was not the first Japanese Buddhist priest to be involved with Krotona. Jisōji Tetsugai (1888–1980), a missionary of Nishi Honganji and one year senior to Utsuki, met A. P. Warrington for the first time on November 4, 1915 and visited Krotona several times while he stayed in Los Angeles (1915–1919). Jisōji would come back to Japan and become a lecturer at Ryūkoku University at an earlier time than Utsuki.

James Cousins, an Irish poet and a professor at Keiō University, formed an International Lodge connected to the Theosophical Society (Adyar, India) in Tokyo in 1920. Beatrice Suzuki, her mother (Emma Erskine Hahn), and Suzuki Daisetsu joined the lodge. They attended meetings six times between March and June. In 1921, Suzuki became a professor at Ōtani University, so the Suzukis left Tokyo and Suzuki's Theosophical activities ceased.

In 1924 a new lodge was formed in Kyoto at the Suzukis' house. Beatrice explained the birth of the new lodge as follows:

> On May 8, 1924 (White Lotus Day) a meeting was held at my home for the purpose of forming a lodge of the Theosophical Society. Five former members of the Society with three new members came together and decided to form a new lodge to be called the Mahāyāna Lodge of Kyoto. On June 14, another meeting took place at Ryukoku University, when six others joined. I am herewith enclosing the applications for fellowship in the Society of nine persons, who are joining for the first time. (Algeo 2005)

Beatrice took the initiative in forming the lodge and became secretary of the lodge. Utsuki helped her as the treasurer. Of the 14 members, 11 were professors of either Ryūkoku University or Ōtani University, and nine of them had been on the membership list of the Mahayana Association. In other words, the Mahayana Lodge was a successor of the Mahayana Association. This was brought about through the network around Utsuki Nishu.

On the other hand, Beatrice was also enthusiastic about the Order of the Star in the East (1911 – 1929), a kind of messianic movement with Jiddu Krishnamurti as its head. Suzuki Daisetsu took a critical attitude towards it,[23] as did other scholars. Jugaku Bunsho, who was himself a priest of the Shingon sect, described the meetings of the Order of the Star in the East as 'weird' (Hisamatsu, Yamaguchi and Furuta 1971, 209). Beatrice's association with the Order of the Star of the East was one of the reasons why this lodge had an 'esoteric' in addition to an 'exoteric' side.

From the perspective of its exoteric side, this lodge could be called the most excellent circle of scholars in Kyoto. Uno Enkū and Akamatsu Chijō were the founders of anthropological studies of religion in Japan. Izumi Hokei was a scholar of Sanskrit who translated the *Kama Sutra*. Yamabe Shugaku would become the president of Ōtani University, and Hadani Ryōtai and Morikawa Chitoku would become presidents of Ryūkoku University. Jugaku Bunshō would become a famous scholar of English. It seems the meeting was a kind of academic meeting, not a study group of middle class women as was usually the case for Theosophical Society groups around the world. Compared to the exoteric side, the esoteric side was more limited. The activities of the Order of the Star in the East were started as late as December 1927 and continued by Beatrice and Setti Line Hibino.[24]

The lodge members decreased in number for several reasons. Hadani later recalls that various inspiring themes were discussed at the monthly meeting of the lodge, but Japanese professors dropped out because reading a paper in English was a hard task (Hisamatsu, Yamaguchi and Furuta 1971, 470). To recruit new members, Beatrice used a Theosophy leaflet translated into Japanese, published by Suzuki Daisetsu in 1928. However, the number of lodge members did not exceed 15 people. Beatrice attributed this to the similarities between Japanese Buddhism and Theosophy. Her letter is interesting, so I have quoted it below.

> But with regard to Theosophy, Theosophy comes not as something new but as a variant of their own Buddhist teaching and for this reason they are slow to come to it. The appeal of Universal Brotherhood is the note that must be struck by theosophists for the Japanese. It is just the same too in regard to the Order of the Star. Their own great teachers like Kobo Daishi, Shinran Shonin, and others stand still too close to theirs in time and they feel that they have not yet fully absorbed the teachings of these great ones and therefore they do not feel the call to look elsewhere. In my opinion it is not because of their unspirituality that they fail to do so but on account of their strong religious feeling for their own religious leaders.[25]

While the Japanese may not have needed the universal spirituality of Theosophy, the reason might not only have been that there were 'great teachers' in the traditional sects, but also that, in the Taisho era (1912–1926), there appeared new religious movements with similar messages to that of Theosophy. One of the rapidly expanding religious movements was Ōmoto-kyo, which taught the doctrine of 'banshū dōkon' (all religions have the same root) and used the Swedenborgian concept of a spiritual world in their belief system, utilizing translations by Suzuki Daisetsu (Nishikawa 1977).

The Kyoto lodge stopped its activity in 1929, the same year that Krishnamurti dissolved the Order of the Star in the East. In the same year, Utsuki and other professors resigned from Ryūkoku University owing to the opposition between the conservative authorities of the sect and the liberal group, whose members were almost the same as the members of the Mahayana Association or the Mahayana Lodge. So even if it had not been for the dissolution of the Order, the Mahayana Lodge would have come to a halt.

As an aside, it is interesting that, in 1924, another Buddhist lodge of the Theosophical Society was organized in London by Christmas Humphreys. The lodge would become the Buddhist Society, and D. T. Suzuki's books on Mahayana Buddhism would be circulated around Britain and America thanks to Humphreys. Thus Buddhism became 'independent' of Theosophy.

Conclusion

Utsuki was later (from 1936–1941) appointed chairman of the publishing bureau of Nishi Honganji, where his job was to publish English texts on Buddhism. He was one of the best qualified persons to take the position, apart from Suzuki Daisetsu, as he knew well what Westerners sought for in Buddhism after his experiences in Theosophy. Furthermore, foreigners would come to visit Utsuki in order to be put in contact with Buddhist temples in Kyoto. He played the role of 'clerk at the window', in that he opened Buddhism in Kyoto to an international network of Buddhist sympathizers.

Remaining at Shōtoku-ji are some photos of an American family, taken at the top of Mt. Hiei in 1930. A husband, a wife, a daughter, a tutor, and Utsuki are in these photos. The name 'Everett' is written on the back of them. They are photos of Ruth Everett when she first visited Japan. Ruth was introduced to and enchanted with Zen on this trip. Needless to say, she would marry Sokei-an, Sasaki Shigetsu, and become one of the Zen pioneers in America. Her daughter, who climbed Mt. Hiei with Utsuki, would marry Alan Watts. The person who introduced Ruth to Utsuki and Suzuki Daisetsu was none other than William McGovern. Though the Mahayana Association was forgotten, its legacy still survives today.

ACKNOWLEDGEMENTS

The initial version of this paper was presented at the conference 'SE Asia as a Crossroads for Buddhist Exchange: Pioneer European Buddhists and Asian Buddhist Networks 1860–1960,' hosted by the Study of Religions Department,

University College Cork, Ireland, from September 13–15, 2012. The conference was funded by the Dhammakaya International Society of the United Kingdom as part of the 2012 postdoctoral fellowship, 'Continuities and Transitions in Early Modern Thai Buddhism'. The research in Shōtokuji temple has been done with the help of Ohsawa Koji, Nakagawa Mirai and Dylan Luers. It has been supported by two projects funded by the Japan Society for the Promotion of Science's Grants-in-Aid for Scientific Research (20320016 and 23320022). I am also grateful to the colleagues of the Shin Bukkyō Research Group (now Modern Religions Archive Research Group) and the 'translocative' exchanges with the Dhammaloka Research Group.

NOTES

1. The set of copies found at Shōtokuji Temple is incomplete, lacking at least Vol. 1, No. 11. Whether they continued to publish after Vol. 2, No. 1 is uncertain.
2. http://www.northwestern.edu/magazine/spring2010/feature/williammcgovern.html
3. http://files.library.northwestern.edu/findingaids/McGovern_William.pdf
4. Carol McGovern Cerf's e-mails to the author dated February 28, 2010 and March 2, 2010.
5. In his letter to Jisōji Tetsugai dated June 24, 1917, Utsuki Nishū wrote that McGovern introduced him to A. P. Warrington when he was in Taiwan.
6. *Mahayanist* 2 (1).
7. *Kyokai Ichiran* no. 585 (May 7, 1915). This article says McGovern was British and 23 years old.
8. From the 1891 England Census. I thank Professor Bocking for this information.
9. The name list of Sanmaji Kai (privately owned). Beatrice Suzuki also joined Sanmaji Kai on October 22, 1915.
10. Hirai Kinza (1859–1916) was a teacher of English at several schools and a secular practitioner of Zen Buddhism, though nominally he was ordained as a monk of Rinzai Zen. Reports on him which this author has edited are available. http://www.maizuru-ct.ac.jp/human/yosinaga/hirai_report.pdf
11. *Mahayanist* (August 1915), 1 (2), 1. But this is rather difficult to believe, as Beatrice Suzuki who was on the site did not mention it (B. Suzuki 1919).
12. Samuel L. Lewis (1978) *Incense from Roshis*, pp. 3, 4. http://murshidsam.org/Documents/Papers/Level1/Incense_From_Roshis.pdf. Lewis wrote about the hardship with which Kirby attained 'satori'. Lewis later studied Zen with Senzaki Nyogen and Sokei-an.
13. Professor Richard Jaffe (Duke University) has suggested that a famous priest-scholar of the Jōdo sect, Watanabe Kaigyoku (1872–1933) might have introduced Kirby to Nyanatiloka (1876–1957), founder of the Island Hermitage, because the latter stayed in Japan from 1921–1926, helped by Watanabe.

14. This part is based on the statement of Ernest Hunt to Louise Hunter, on November 4, 1965.
15. *Mahayanist* (July 1915), 1 (1), 2.
16. *Mahayanist*, (July, 1915), 1 (1), 5.
17. Jisōji Tetsugai wrote that McGovern was born in England, and was 23 years old as of May 5, 1915.
18. Suzuki wrote in a letter to Beatrice dated April 4, 1916 that he had met McGovern in Osaka.
19. *Mahayanist* (January 1916), 1 (6), 2.
20. *Mahayanist* (July 1915), 1 (1), 18–19.
21. *Mahayanist* (July 1915), 1 (1), 19.
22. *Mahayanist* (May 1915), 1 (4), 4.
23. See Daisetsu's letter to Beatrice dated August 4, 1930. Suzuki Daisetsu (2003, 547).
24. Setti Line Hibino was the wife of Hibino Shin'ichi (1888–1968), a botanist and a professor of Tohoku Imperial University.
25. Beatrice's letter to the president of the Theosophical Society dated November 28, 1928 (Algeo 2005, 12–13).

REFERENCES

ALGEO, ADELE S. 2005. Beatrice Lane Suzuki and Theosophy in Japan. *Theosophical History* 11 (3): 3–16.

AMA, MICHIHIRO. 2010. The Legal Dimensions of the Formation of Shin Buddhist Temples in Los Angeles. In *Issei Buddhism in America*, edited by Tomoe Moriya and Duncan Ryuken Williams, 65–86. Urbana: University of Illinois Press.

HEIAN, GAKUEN. 1986. *Heian Gakuen Hyakunen no Ayumi*. Kyoto: Heian Gakuen.

HISAMATSU, S., YAMAGUCHI, S., and FURUTA, S., eds. 1971. *Suzuki Daisetsu—Hito to Shiso*. Tokyo: Iwanami Shoten.

HOSHINO, SEIJI. 2009. Reconfiguring Buddhism as a Religion: Nakanishi Ushirō and his Shin Bukkyō'. *Japanese Religions* 34 (2), 133–154.

HUNTER, L. 1971. *Buddhism in Hawaii: Its Impact on a Yankee Community*. Honolulu: University of Hawaii Press.

JISŌJI, TETSUGAI. 1969. *Tenro Rekihen*. Yukuhashi, Fukuoka: Jisōji Tetsugai Sensei Choju Kinenkai.

KIRBY, M. T. 1927. What of the Future? *Young East* III (4): (September) 125–129.

MCGOVERN, JANET B. 1922. *Among the Headhunters of Formosa*. London: T. Fisher Unwin.

MCGOVERN, W. M. 1915. The Nature of the Buddhist Trinity. *Mahayanist* 1 (4): (May) 2–11.

MCGOVERN, W. M. 1922. *An Introduction to Mahayana Buddhism, with Especial Reference to Chinese and Japanese Phase*. London: K. Paul, Trench, Trubner.

NISHIKAWA, TAKESHI. 1977. *Kōdō Ōmoto-kyō Jiken Ni Kansuru Kenkyū,* reprint. Kyoto: Toyo Bunka Sha.

PEIRCE, LORI. 2010. Buddhist Modernism in English-Language Buddhist Periodicals. In *Issei Buddhism in America*, edited by Tomoe Moriya and Duncan Ryuken Williams, 87–109. Urbana: University of Illinois Press.

ROSS, JOSEPH E. 1989. *Krotona of Old Hollywood*. Vol. 1. Montecito: El Montecito Oaks Press.

SNODGRASS, J. 2003. *Presenting Japanese Buddhism to the West: Orientalism, Occidentalism, and the Columbian Exposition*. Chapel Hill: University of North Carolina Press.

SUZUKI, BEATRICE. 1919. The Zen Ordination Ceremony. *The Open Court* 1919 (4), article 6.

SUZUKI, D. T. 1907. *Outlines of Mahayana Buddhism*. London: Luzac.

SUZUKI, DAISETSU. 2003. *Suzuki Daisetsu Zenshu*. Vol. 36. Tokyo: Iwanami Shoten.

THE BIBLE, THE BOTTLE AND THE KNIFE: RELIGION AS A MODE OF RESISTING COLONIALISM FOR U DHAMMALOKA

Alicia Turner

While those who sought solidarity between Asians and Europeans in the colonial era often ended up replicating the colonial divisions they had hoped to overcome, the interstitial position of working class and beachcomber Buddhist monks allowed for more substantive modes of solidarity and critique. U Dhammaloka offered a sophisticated critique of British colonialism in its religious, cultural and material modes, but opted to focus his efforts on Buddhism as an avenue of resistance because it offered him a means of connection, like that which Leela Gandhi has identified as a 'politics of friendship.'

The colonial era saw many movements that brought Europeans to Asia and to the aid of Asians for various causes. However, all too often both the motivations and means underlying these movements served to reinforce European superiority instead of overcoming divisions between colonized and colonized. The turn of the century British feminist movements studied by Antoinette Burton offer a classic example of this. As Burton has shown, British feminists of this era highlighted the oppression of Indian women, not as a gesture of equality and solidarity, but to argue that European women should have a greater political voice and the vote so that they could intervene on behalf of what they portrayed as forever powerless and backward Indian women (Burton 1994). In this sense, British feminist interventions in Asia were meant not to break down power divisions between Asian and European women but instead to reinforce a fundamental difference between them, and in doing so prove British women's loyalty to the colonial project. While Burton's materials lay out this politics in particularly stark terms, many, if not most, attempts at cooperation between Asians and European movements in this period were plagued by the same problem of replicating white authority and privilege. In the history of the Buddhist revival in Theravadin South and Southeast Asia, Col. H. S. Olcott's career exemplified many of these issues—particularly the ways in which he was perceived as a white advocate for Sri Lankan Buddhists in their struggles against Christian missionaries, and yet came to promote, through his ubiquitous *Buddhist Catechism*, a particular interpretation of Buddhism shaped by his own American and Protestant background (Prothero 1995, 1996). Similarly, studies of other key Theosophists, particularly Madame Blavatsky and Annie Besant, have highlighted how each, while claiming a metaphysical connection to Asia and Asians, served to reinforce white colonial authority. As postcolonial theory has made clear, for the most part the movements of this era, anti-colonial nationalism included, served to reproduce, reinvent or invert the division but could never completely transcend colonial difference—the divisions between colonizer and colonized.

Postcolonial studies argues that, unlike the earlier nationalists who understood themselves and their values as completely antithetical to colonialism, nationalist discourse and the postcolonial state never escaped the grip of colonial power. Even after the end of empire, colonial power remained because colonialism's modes of thinking, its desires and its divisions remained deeply engrained in former colonized subjects, as well as former colonizers. Theorists, including Partha Chatterjee and Dipesh Chakrabarty, have argued that, even though nationalists had successfully reversed the priorities and power dynamics of the colonial state, elevating the Indian over the English and the spiritual traditions of the East over the material technologies of the West, all they had achieved was to invert the two sides of the power differential (Chakrabarty 2000; Chatterjee 1993). Their thinking still relied on the constructed division between colonizers and colonized that was the foundation of colonial power. So long as such a division survived in thinking, imperialism was alive and well. No matter how much a given European individual or movement claimed to side with the colonized, they were embedded in systems of thought and power that operated by defining 'European' and 'Asian' as radically different. Thus, when Europeans valorized Buddhism they relied on its difference from European religion for its attraction. And for most postcolonial theory, the prospects of overcoming this are bleak.

Leela Gandhi, starting from this postcolonial framework, sought to interrogate whether interactions in the colonial world *necessarily* replicated this power dynamic, arguing for the possibility of human interaction on a level that does not rehearse this fundamental division (Gandhi 2006). She found certain moments in branches of utopian socialism of the last decades in the nineteenth century which offered the potential to build direct connections between Asians and Europeans which stepped out of the dynamics of colonizer–colonized. These were sparks of insight and connections which Asians and Europeans fostered through a shared vision. Her most poignant example is the acceptance Mohandas Gandhi found, in his early days as a student in England, among a small group of English vegetarians—a connection he later referred to as an inspiration. Leela Gandhi argues that certain figures in these movements, all on the fringes of Victorian reform movements, were able to build real solidarity between Asians and Europeans and to offer a critique of colonialism that stepped outside the logic of colonial power. This was possible because the movements she highlights—particular strands of humanism embedded within Victorian vegetarian and homosexual activism—were able to imagine a mode of radical kinship and connection as part of a critique of colonialism. These movements' explicit critique of colonialism, posited as the root cause to be overcome in their various struggles, envisioned the end of imperialism as a utopia that also ended divisions between species and genders, as well as races. Leela Gandhi offers, in her text, a concept of a politics of friendship at the turn of the twentieth century that allowed a limited few activists genuinely to transcend colonial difference. I am not sure if I agree with Gandhi in all the aspects of her argument, particularly when she labels Theosophy as one of the movements with the potential to facilitate this radical connection. However, her focus on those on the margins, in particular, figures located at the intersections of Asian and European movements at the turn of the twentieth century, helps us to understand the implications of the connections built by European and Asian Buddhists.

The stories of marginalized working class Europeans in Asia, of the kind highlighted through our study of Dhammaloka, and marginalized Asians like those highlighted in this issue, have been left out of the history of British colonialism in Asia. Such figures operated at the margins of multiple divisions and cultures. Their presence alone belied the idea of a single and monolithic divide between colonizer and colonized, and forced consideration of the internal diversity of both 'sides' in terms of class, gender, culture, ethnicity and importantly, religion. As Gauri Viswanathan has argued, conversion to a minority religion served as a key marker of dissident identity and agency in this period (Viswanathan 1998). The mere existence of plebeian and working class men in Asia who not only declared an affinity and allegiance to Buddhism but publicly practised aspects of Buddhist culture, threatened the vision of Europeans as fundamentally distinct from Asian Buddhists. Moreover, the interstitial nature of these figures, existing on the margins and moving fluidly between multiple worlds —as the culture of sailors and beachcombers required—brought to light the heterogeneity of networks and connections that operated in late Victorian colonial Asia which allowed for connections, solidarities and friendships well outside the colonial frame.

Many of the figures discussed in this volume defied the expectations and transgressed the cultural boundaries of their time and context. All in their own ways challenged the larger frameworks and built unexpected connections across class, ethnic and cultural lines. In this they were rebels and reformers, whose actions made them implicit critics of the divisions that they crossed. Many of the people studied in this issue either rejected or removed themselves from the rules of their own societies and were able to breach the boundaries of their adopted locales under the guise of being 'out of place.' European Buddhist converts, and particularly working class and beachcomber monks, defied the categories and assumptions that defined Victorian colonial propriety. Their class and cultural backgrounds threatened the privileged status constructed for Europeans in colonial Asia and their chosen affinity for Buddhism and Asian Buddhists made them appear to be traitors to the colonial project. With little to lose, they occupied a unique position from which to critique colonialism and create real alliances between Europeans and Asians.

Dhammaloka as creative critic: Bible, the bottle and the knife

No critic was more outspoken or creative in his alliances than U Dhammaloka. The documented decade and a half of his life in Asia is littered with campaigns to rally Southeast Asians to the cause of Buddhism and opposition, always obliquely worded, to European colonial rule. U Dhammaloka was born in Dublin and spent much of his life as a sailor and hobo, travelling across North America and Asia, before finally arriving in Rangoon.[1] In Burma, he discovered an affinity and connection with Buddhism. He took up residence in a Buddhist monastery which, we now know, was a not infrequent occurrence for working class Europeans in Asia travelling without substantial means. Burmese monasteries offered free lodging and food to all comers, and this Irishman soon found that they offered quite a bit more in terms of identity, belonging and purpose. U Dhammaloka was ordained as a monk on July 8, 1900 at the Kyaikmantan Kyo monastery in Rangoon and lived near the Shwedagon pagoda in the Tavoy monastery, which became his headquarters.[2] In autumn 1900, he embarked on a vocal and provocative public career of promoting Buddhism and denouncing missionary Christianity, across Burma and Asia. He was welcomed by the Burmese in villages and towns across the colonial province during two major preaching tours in 1901 and 1907–1908. He founded schools and associations to promote Buddhism in Bangkok, Penang and Singapore and travelled as far as Sri Lanka, Japan and Australia to promote his cause. Dhammaloka thrived on confrontation; he was a natural rabble-rouser who was most in his element when questioning the status quo. His vitriolic critiques of missionary Christianity and, by implication, British colonialism, led to his eventual conviction for sedition in 1911.[3]

Witnesses sent to observe U Dhammaloka's speech to a crowd of 2000 people in Moulmein on November 1, 1910 allege that he represented Christian ministers as 'addicted to immorality and as going about each with a Bible, a bottle of whiskey and a knife' (Chaudhri 1911, 249). On November 5, the missionaries had sent a shorthand writer to record his sermon verbatim, but Dhammaloka did not offer a repeat of this particular phrase. The statement, however, was key to his conviction for sedition against the British colonial state, confirmed after appeal in January 1911.

Dhammaloka, in his defence at the trial, disputed the accuracy of some of the testimony about that sermon but did not dispute his use of this phrase. It would have been difficult to deny; at least twice before he had made the same accusation in print. In each instance, he deployed the combination of the Bible, the bottle and a weapon as evidence of the inherently corruptive nature of colonialism. In a 1907 newspaper article he had written, 'Christianity is the only drunken religion—at least Christians are the only drunken religionists... And yet, this, the least philosophical, the most vulgar and the meanest religion that ever civilization knew—a leprous mixture of India's royal line—goes to India to vanquish it! The missionary, fanatical fool or lazy knave, armed with the bible and the gin bottle' (Purser 1911, 271–318). That same year he published 'A Wicked Proclamation to His Fellow Beings, From the Sinner in Charge of the Buddhist Tract Society,' in which he argued, 'People who weep over the sufferings of the alleged "saviour" seldom weep much for the suffering man except he be nude and in Africa, without a bottle of "Guiding Star Brandy," a "Holy Bible" or a "Gatling Gun"' (Dhammaloka 1910, 60–61). For Dhammaloka, colonialism was a cold and heartless project, one that had no sympathy for the objects of its corruptive civilizing mission but only for its agents, who deployed these three evils in equal measure.

The refrain of the Bible, the bottle and the knife, presented in bombastic style, became a frequent theme in Dhammaloka's preaching and written work. It offered a pithy summary of the evils he perceived in British colonialism in Burma and across Asia. It could serve not just as a striking and sarcastic image, but as a piquant mnemonic device for both preacher and audience to dissect the problems of the day.

Like much else in Dhammaloka's writings and sermons, the phrase was lifted from the broader literature of the era. The juxtaposition of the Bible and the bottle was a fairly frequent metaphor deployed by the Christian temperance movement against Christian ministers and missionaries who did not meet the ideal of total abstinence. These temperance advocates, like U Dhammaloka, denounced British colonialism for bringing the evils of alcohol to the colonies and profiting from the trade.

One Christian temperance advocate cited a missionary to the Maori who had accused Europeans of offering a contradictory message:

> Captain J. C. Johnstone, in his volume *Maoria*, a sketch of the manners and customs of the aboriginal inhabitants of New Zealand, bears his testimony, 'to the truth, honour, generosity, hospitality and virtue which distinguished the inhabitants of Maoria before the advent of pakeha (white man). With the Bible in one hand and the rum-bottle in the other, we flattered ourselves,' he continues, 'that we had in a few years Christianized and civilized the owner for broad lands we had appropriated. But our presumption has been heavily rebuked, for the race has morally and physically deteriorated in the attempt and promises to become extinct in the process'. (Grindrod 1884, 184 citing Johnstone 1874, viii)

The author concluded that, 'To preach the Gospel of peace with the Bible in one hand and the whiskey-bottle in the other, however it may be the practice of modern Christians is not the practice of Christ' (Grindrod 1884, 184).

Temperance advocates, seeking to imply a contradiction in any colonial or missionary endeavour that did not promote total abstinence, often attributed the criticism of alcohol to the colonial subjects. This approach even found its way into parliamentary debate in English where it was reported that an 'important Indian newspaper asked—Was it not a ridiculous spectacle which the Christian presented in India, having a copy of the Bible in one hand and a bottle of rum in the other?'

(*Hansard* 1881, 335). Those opposed to the bottle saw allies around the colonial world. Similar comments were attributed to Native American Christian converts.

> The Rev. George Copway, who is also a North American chief, affirmed that his tribe had been nearly all burnt up by this 'great Evil Spirit;' and in speaking of our early missionary efforts, he said: 'You, English, are a very strange people. You send out to my country the Bible—that is very good—and a good man to explain it to us—that is also very good. He builds a chapel for us on one side of the road, and teaches us, there, the road to heaven. Then his brother comes, and he builds a rum shop on the other side of the road, to show us the way to the devil—that is very bad . . . You send out, as it were, to the poor savage a man with a Bible in one hand, and a bottle of rum in the other!' (Cruikshank 1853, 25)

For the Christian temperance advocates, the Bible and the bottle were antithetical to each other. Such an accusation was meant to show the futility and hypocrisy of any Christian missionary work that was not intimately connected with temperance advocacy.

For Dhammaloka, in contrast, the Bible and the bottle were not contradictory influences but all of a piece—separate incarnations of the same general threat. His accusation against the missionaries—that they used the Bible and the bottle together—was meant not to point out their hypocrisy, but to reveal the consistency of the threat they posed. Some of this sentiment was shared by satirical literature in the West. One parody, written in the voice of a fictitious colonial Muslim writing his observations of England, indicted the Bible and the bottle as tools of capitalism.

> Missionarism has always been a special feature of this country. I remember that long years ago, when I was a boy, I had among my coloured prints one which represented Mdme. Britannia dressed in a debardeur costume, and about to start on a voyage round the world, with a Bible in one hand, and a bottle of rum in the other. By- and-by, when I grew older, I perceived that the Bible and the bottle were merely accessories, and that the real meaning of missionarism was to civilize the world, chiefly with a view to throw open as large a market for your industry as you could possibly get. (Thieblin 1870, 120)

The tripartate combination of the Bible, the bottle and the knife (or at times the gun), had appeared elsewhere in late Victorian publications as well, cited by European critics who quoted unnamed natives of Africa, the Middle East or North America, as an oblique criticism of the violence of colonialism.[4] The knife or the gun in this context pointed to the violent means used to enforce acceptance of the Bible and the bottle. The Europeans referencing the phrase were able to shield themselves from the repercussions of such a critical stance by attributing it to an unnamed colonial subject: curiously the wording was the same whether that person was African, Asian or North American. However, Dhammaloka, in keeping with his bombastic style, sought none of this cover. He owned the accusation against the missionaries, to the point of a conviction for sedition, and his criticism of the Bible, the bottle and the knife became a signature line of his public persona.

A sophisticated critique of colonialism

Despite the fact that the accusation was explicitly levelled at Christian ministers, no one in 1910 Burma interpreted Dhammaloka's accusation as an attack on religion *per se*. Instead both those who supported and those who denounced Dhammaloka agreed that his was an attack on the entirety of the colonial project and the colonial state. The India Acts provided an entire section of laws against statements that defamed religion, but the Crown chose to prosecute U Dhammaloka on charges of sedition instead; namely that he intended 'to provoke feelings of enmity or hatred between different classes of His Majesty's subjects' (Chaudhri 1911). This seems to have been the common interpretation because as far as we know neither the complaining witnesses—themselves likely missionaries—nor U Dhammaloka's attorneys raised the objection that the harms of his action adhered to religion and not to the state. It had seemed patently obvious to everyone at the time, if not to scholars today, that the object of U Dhammaloka's criticisms was colonialism writ large and not simply Christianity.

If we accept his comments to be seditious, as they were found to be, and therefore a criticism not merely of missionary Christianity but of colonialism as a whole, U Dhammaloka emerges as a sophisticated, if never subtle, critic. He offered in his refrain a tripartite critique of colonial power and the threat it posed to the Burmese, one that was consistent with his broader efforts. His accusation divides colonial power into three interrelated assaults: religious, cultural and material. First, is the religious threat—the Bible's power in the hands of Christian missionaries to destabilize Buddhist worldviews and threaten the Buddha's teachings. Second, with the bottle, he references colonial interventions into local cultures and the changes in desires, orientations and values that colonial regimes sought to create. Finally, the knife referred to the rarely distant threat of violence and material domination—ever present in the military troops stationed at the Shwedagon Pagoda, as well as the police and prisons that detained a higher percentage of the population in Burma than anywhere else in the British empire (Brown 2007). The knife was also a symbol that would not have been far from Burmese thinking, many having witnessed the bloody 'pacification' campaigns that followed the arrival of British power two decades earlier. If this is the critique that U Dhammaloka intended to encode, there is little doubt his intention was seditious. He was standing on the side of the Burmese and looking to strike a blow to the organizational heart of British colonialism.

Seen from this angle, it was a remarkably sophisticated analysis. The theme of the Bible, the bottle and the knife resonated in Dhammaloka's sermons and written work because it was an easy and concrete means of encapsulating the whole problem of colonialism. While there were many movements concerned with the state of Buddhism, and with religious and cultural changes in Burma at the time, few among the activists in 1907 would have explicitly identified British colonialism as the source of the threat on the religious or cultural fronts in such stark terms (Turner 2009). These were the earliest days of anti-colonial nationalist thinking in Burma and not many would have identified religion and culture as specific modes of colonial power in the ways that Dhammaloka quite clearly implied. Although the critique of cultural modes of power has become central to our historical understanding of colonialism after the birth of postcolonial studies, few at the time could have offered such an analysis and certainly not in such stark terms.

Encapsulating his career

In many ways, the refrain of the Bible, the bottle and the knife encapsulated not just Dhammaloka's critique but his career and his activist programme. Dhammaloka's public mission was defined by three clear passions: a vitriolic hatred of Christian missionaries, a commitment to warning the Burmese of the dangers of drink, and criticism of British colonialism informed by his experiences of Ireland. Put more simply, he was committed to a brand of freethinker atheism, temperance and anti-colonialism.

Dhammaloka's first appearance in print was in a small advertisement, published not long after his monastic ordination, warning Christian missionaries to desist from proselytizing on the pagoda grounds. From then on, the denunciation of Christian missionaries, whom he called 'sky pilots', a term lifted from the sailors' vernacular, was central to all of his public preaching. He warned Buddhists that Christian missionaries sought to turn them away from their 'blessed religion' through the violence and lies he saw perpetrated in Christian theology. This was a message he carried to the small towns across Burma and which gained him popularity with audiences of thousands of Burmese Buddhists. When asked to preach on Buddhism he often demurred, deferring to other monks as better able explain Buddhist philosophy or ethical practice. Instead, what he felt he could best offer his new Burmese friends and admirers was an analysis and warning of the harms of Christianity.

Similarly the denunciation of drink, the second major thread in Dhammaloka's public career, fostered a strong personal connection with Burmese Buddhists. Like many at the time, Dhammaloka was an unfailing advocate of temperance and became an officer in the 'Pride of Rangoon' branch of the International Order of Good Templars (IOGT), one of the most prominent temperance organizations of the day.[5] Dhammaloka carried this affiliation with him to Singapore, Bangkok and Australia in his later work. For European temperance advocates in Asia at the turn of the century, temperance organizations were part of a transformative mission that sought to civilize and thus, to this extent, reinforced a division between colonizer and colonized.[6] However, for Dhammaloka, temperance and the knowledge of the dangers of drink were not truths bestowed by Christianity or European scientific enlightenment but instead values, learned from his own experience, that he found mirrored in Buddhism. Temperance was among a set of shared ideals that could be deployed together against the threats of colonial Christianity. While he did not renounce his membership in the European IOGT, he frequently denounced other branches and the policies of the larger organization when these restricted the full participation of non-Christian Asians. Moreover, some of his most vitriolic language was reserved for temperance advocates who denied self-determination to Asians, for example accusing them of holding a Japanese woman against her will to further their religious ideals (An International Degree Good Templar 1909).

Likely to be acutely aware of the dangers of preaching outright sedition or revolution, the critique of the knife did not play a public role in Dhammaloka's career. As far as we know, despite examples in Irish, labour and anarchist movements of the time, Dhammaloka never suggested addressing the material or coercive modes of colonial power. Instead, the problem of the 'knife' in his rhetoric was left as an open question. Local defeats including the fall of the Burmese monarchy in 1885 and the bloody 'pacification' campaigns that followed, as well as those from farther afield including the failures of Fenian efforts, rendered the knife an ineffective option for an activist programme. This was a period when, unlike later nationalist movements in both Ireland and Asian, physical and material force was not considered a viable option to pursue anti-colonial ends. Dhammaloka did not particularly emphasize socialist or other critiques of colonial capitalism, although some of those whose writings he published in his Buddhist Tract Society series encouraged such analysis.

And yet, if Dhammaloka gave voice to a feeling of threat from imperialism in three modes—religious, cultural and material—his own response demonstrates a clear priority among the three. The bulk of U Dhammaloka's words and of his work between 1900–1913 was focused on religion—both in his vociferous denunciations of missionary Christianity and his efforts to promote Buddhism among Asians and plebeian Europeans alike. The majority of his time was spent founding and promoting Buddhist institutions—schools, associations, networks—or practicing and preaching Buddhism. Early on, he set out to reconvert those Burmese who had become Christians and bring them back to Buddhism. He spoke of their own religion, Buddhism, as a way forward and a clear antidote to the threats that British colonialism posed.

Why did he feel so fervently that colonialism could be best critiqued and redressed by religion? Why, of the three modes of colonial power he knew so intimately, both in Ireland and Burma, did he think the battle was best fought through religion—through promoting Buddhism?

In many ways, Dhammaloka's emphasis on religion is the most Irish aspect of his campaigns. Religion as a potential field of solidarity and confrontation reflected his Irish background. In this period, Irish nationalism and anti-colonialism were organized through religion and religious difference. So despite his rejection of Catholicism, the idea of religion as a site of resistance would have been familiar to Dhammaloka from his Irish roots. However, he seems to have taken this much further than other Irish anti-colonial dissidents in Asia.

Buddhism offered Dhammaloka a medium both to critique colonialism as the root cause of other injustices and to build connections outside of colonial divisions. Buddhism, and, in particular, the pragmatic and lived Buddhism which Dhammaloka engaged in, served as a medium for a direct and personal solidarity.

It not only defied the colonizer-colonized, Asian-European, and class divisions that defined so much of his world, but provided a means of connection that set such divisions aside. His approach to being Buddhist and promoting Buddhism managed not to invert or reproduce the power differentials but offered a means of relationship and connection defined in very different terms.

Dhammaloka found in his Buddhism something that superseded the otherwise unbreachable divisions between Asians and Europeans that undergirded colonial power. Rather than replicating the operations of power of the romanticized or scientific European interpretations of Buddhism, Dhammaloka's approach had offered him direct and visceral connections with others in Burma. It is this connection that allowed Dhammaloka to prescribe Buddhism not just as an answer to the problems of alcohol or the threats of missionary Christianity but as an antidote to the whole of colonialism, because it released him from the tyranny of the colonial framework.

Buddhism offered a connection across the colonial divide and a mode of solidarity and belonging for a person who was very much out of place. It offered a type of utopianism, like that observed by Leela Gandhi in other movements of this era, which could label colonialism as the root cause of other social wrongs and provide a bridge between otherwise fragmented groups. It offered Dhammaloka a politics of friendship. Like the radical connection in Leela Gandhi's work on turn of the century utopianism, Dhammaloka's Buddhism offered a vision that transcended colonial thinking and colonial power. Dhammaloka did not make claims to greater knowledge of Buddhism than the Burmese—he was not replicating Orientalist knowledge—nor did he romanticize the mystic East in ways that reinforced its difference from Europe. Dhammaloka's Buddhism was performative, and it was this performance —from the margin and embedded in multiple networks — that he perceived as offering liberation from the power relations of colonialism; a life away from the Bible, the bottle and the knife. His critique of colonialism, like that of the advocates for vegetarianism and homosexuals that Leela Gandhi highlights, identified colonialism as a threat to Europeans and Asians alike. And he found in Buddhism a viable way forward that was, if not utopian, certainly a bridge of friendship.

ACKNOWLEDGEMENTS

This paper was originally presented at the conference Southeast Asia as a Crossroads for Buddhist Exchange: *Pioneer European Buddhists and Asian Buddhist Networks 1860–1960* hosted by the Study of Religions Department of University College Cork, Ireland, September 13–15, 2012 and funded by the Dhammakaya International Society of the United Kingdom as part of the 2012 postdoctoral fellowship 'Continuities and Transitions in Early Modern Thai Buddhism'. I would like to thank Brian Bocking and Laurence Cox, my collaborators on the Dhammaloka project, for their ongoing support and suggestions on this article and Kate Crosby for her wise editorial eye.

NOTES

1. U Dhammaloka's biography is the subject on an ongoing collaborative research project between Laurence Cox, Brian Bocking and myself. For a preliminary outline of his life see Bocking (2010), Cox (2010), Turner (2010), Turner, Cox, and Bocking (2010).
2. 'The Ordination of an Englishman as a Monk with the Name of Dhammaloka' (in Burmese) (1900) *The Hanthawaddy Weekly Review*, July 14.
3. European Buddhist's Case (1911) *Times of India*, February 1.
4. Dhammaloka's substitution of the Gatling gun was particularly apt in the context because it referenced the unequal military encounters between European and Asian forces.
5. International Order of Good Templars (1907) *Burma Echo*, September 21.
6. See, for example, in Burma (Swift 2003). On broader issues of the International Order of Good Templars and racial divisions see Fahey (1996).

REFERENCES

BOCKING, BRIAN. 2010. A Man of Work and Few Words'? Dhammaloka Beyond Burma. *Contemporary Buddhism* 11 (2): 125–47.

BROWN, IAN. 2007. A Commissioner Calls: Alexander Paterson and Colonial Burma's Prisons. *Journal of Southeast Asian Studies* 38 (2): 293–308.

BURTON, ANTOINETTE M. 1994. *Burdens of History: British Feminists, Indian Women, and Imperial Culture, 1865–1915*. Chapel Hill: University of North Carolina.

CHAKRABARTY, DIPESH. 2000. *Provincializing Europe: Postcolonial Thought and Historical Difference, Princeton Studies in Culture/Power/History*. Princeton, NJ: Princeton University Press.

CHATTERJEE, PARTHA. 1993. *The Nation and its Fragments: Colonial and Postcolonial Histories, Princeton Studies in Culture/Power/History*. Princeton, NJ: Princeton University Press.

CHAUDHRI, S. D. 1911. Lower Burma Chief Court Criminal Revision No. 378B of 1910, January 31. *The Criminal Law Journal of India: Containing Full Reports of All Reported Criminal Cases of the High Courts and Chief Courts, &c. in India* 12: 248–50.

COX, LAURENCE. 2010. The Politics of Buddhist Revival: U Dhammaloka as Social Movement Organizer. *Contemporary Buddhism* 11 (2): 173–227.

CRUIKSHANK, GEORGE. 1853. *The Glass and the New Crystal Palace*. London: J. Cassell.

DHAMMALOKA, U. 1910. A Wicked Proclamation to His Fellow Beings, from the Sinner in Charge of the Buddhist Tract Society. In *The Teachings of Jesus Not Adapted to Modern Civilization*, 60–3. Rangoon: Buddhist Tract Society, at the Burma Echo Press.

FAHEY, DAVID M. 1996. *Temperance and Racism: John Bull, Johnny Reb, and the Good Templars*. Lexington: University Press of Kentucky.

GANDHI, LEELA. 2006. *Affective Communities: Anticolonial Thought, Fin-De-Siècle Radicalism, and the Politics of Friendship*. Durham, NC: Duke University Press.

GRINDROD, RALPH BARNES. 1884. *The Nation's Vice: The Claims of Temperance on the Christian Church*. London: Hodder & Stoughton.

HANSARD'S PARLIMENTARY DEBATES. 1881. 3rd series, vol. CCLXV. London: Cornelius Buck.

AN INTERNATIONAL DEGREE GOOD TEMPLAR [*PSEUD.* U DHAMMALOKA]. 1909. Good Templary in Rangoon. In *Buddhism: The Highest Religion*, edited by U Dhammaloka, 27–9. Rangoon: Burma Echo Press.

JOHNSTONE, J. C. 1874. *Maoria: A Sketch of the Manners and Customs of the Aboriginal Inhabitants of New Zealand*. London: Chapman and Hall.

PROTHERO, STEPHEN. 1995. Henry Steel Olcott and 'Protestant Buddhism'. *Journal of the American Academy of Religion* 63 (2): 281–302.

PROTHERO, STEPHEN. 1996. *The White Buddhist: The Asian Odyssey of Henry Steel Olcott*. Bloomington: Indiana University Press.

PURSER, WILLIAM CHARLES BERTRAND. 1911. *Christian Missions in Burma*. Westminster: Society for the Propagation of the Gospel in Foreign Parts.

SWIFT, JOAN W. 2003. *Hattie: A Woman's Mission to Burma*. San Geronimo, CA: Half Meadow Press.

THIEBLIN, NICOLAS LEON. 1870. *A Little Book about Great Britain by Azamat-Batuk*. London: Badbury, Evans & Co.

TURNER, ALICIA. 2009. *Buddhism, Colonialism and The Boundaries of Religion: Theravada Buddhism in Burma 1885–1920*, Ph.D. diss., Divinity School, The University of Chicago, Chicago.

TURNER, ALICIA. 2010. The Irish Pongyi in Colonial Burma: The Confrontations and Challenges of U Dhammaloka. *Contemporary Buddhism* 11 (2): 149–171.

TURNER, ALICIA, LAURENCE COX, and BRIAN BOCKING. 2010. Beachcombing, Going Native and Freethinking: Rewriting the History of Early Western Buddhist Monastics. *Contemporary Buddhism* 11 (2): 125–147.

VISWANATHAN, GAURI. 1998. *Outside The Fold: Conversion, Modernity, and Belief*. Princeton, NJ: Princeton University Press.

ANANDA METTEYYA: CONTROVERSIAL NETWORKER, PASSIONATE CRITIC

Elizabeth J. Harris

Ananda Metteyya (Charles Henry Allan Bennett 1872–1923), according to some representations of Buddhism's transmission to the West, was a respectable member of an elite group of converts to Buddhism at the beginning of the twentieth century, who, in effect, stole recognition from a non-elite group. Whilst not contesting this basic premise, I first suggest in this paper that Ananda Metteyya was neither elite nor always, at least in the eyes of the Buddhist Society of Great Britain and Ireland, 'respectable'. In fact, he came to pose a threat to the identity that the Society sought to create for itself. I then turn to three contexts within which Ananda Metteyya placed himself: international networks for the spread of Buddhism; anti-missionary networks within Sri Lanka and Burma; antiimperialist networks. His main vehicle within the first was the Buddhasāsana Samāgama, *the international Buddhist organisation he founded in 1902 and the journal that accompanied it, which was sent to between 500 and 600 libraries throughout the world. Also significant was Ananda Metteyya's call for five men from four countries to come to Burma to be trained for higher ordination. Ananda Metteyya's anti-missionary agenda was realized through the promotion of Buddhist education in Burma and through a ruthless written critique of Christianity and Christian proselytisation. An anti-imperialist agenda was implicit within this and is extended in his writing. This paper argues, therefore, that Ananda Metteyya was a central figure in the global networking of a substantial number of those interested in Buddhism in the early years of the twentieth century. He was also an early Engaged Buddhist, a critic of the West and a robust promoter of the East.*

Charles Henry Allan Bennett or Venerable Ananda Metteyya, a British person who received higher ordination (*upasaṃpadā*) in Burma in 1902, has been represented in two main ways. The cover of my first study of Bennett was graced with a romanticized crayon drawing of him by Alexander Fisher, held by The Buddhist Society, London.[1] Bennett's shoulders are covered with the robes of a *bhikkhu*, beautifully draped. His back is straight. His eyes are downcast, and his features are sharp and aristocratic. Lines of illness, particularly the dark circles under his eyes characteristic of some photos we have of him, are erased. John Crow, on the

FIGURE 1
Crayon Drawing of Ven. Ananda Metteyya by Alexander Fisher, courtesy of The Buddhist Society, London. Used on the cover of Harris (1998)

other hand, chose a different kind of image for the cover of his published Research Master's dissertation on Bennett. Here, Bennett is pictured as a lay person. He wears a tight-fitting, dark suit with waistcoat. His eyebrows are thick. His hair is black, uncombed and bushy. There is a stoop to his back and pallor to his skin. Dark rings lie below his eyes and there is slight upward twist to his lips. It is the picture of an intense, rather sinister young man with chronic asthma.[2]

Fisher's drawing is the image that the Buddhist Society of Great Britain and Ireland wanted to project of the *bhikkhu* whose mission to Britain from Burma in 1908, the first formal Buddhist mission to the West, occasioned the founding of the Society.[3] The second is the one that the esoteric counter-culture of late nineteenth century England wanted to project and, indeed, that those interested in this world continue to project, of the person who, according to Alistair Crowley, was known all over London in the 1890s as, 'the one Magician who could really do big-time stuff'.[4]

It was the first representation of Bennett that attracted me when I first read his poetic and animated writings on Buddhism in the late 1980s.[5] It was the second that, at first, brought John Crow to Bennett in the first decade of this century. The influence of Allan Bennett or Ananda Metteyya, however, cannot be understood unless both images are taken into account. Although Buddhism was the driving force in his life after his *upasaṃpadā*, he did not lose his contacts within the world of esotericism but engaged with them in the light of his new commitments.[6]

It was this fusion that made him such a controversial figure, especially to The Buddhist Society of Great Britain and Ireland. He was by no means its respectable face, although his mission to Britain and his work in Burma was lauded. In fact, he highlighted faultlines in the Society that could not be owned publicly. From its inception, the Society struggled for academic and religious respectability, and for funds, at a time when the popular mind cast Buddhism as nihilistic, exotically romantic or esoteric.[7] One of the ways the Society did this was to distance itself from theosophy and nineteenth century esoteric movements, even though some of its members might have had sympathy for the former. In this, it acted in synergy with the Buddhist modernism emerging in the two Asian countries that donated money to the new Society, Burma and Ceylon. One particularly influential Buddhist modernist and donor to the Society was the brother of the Anagarika Dharmapala, Dr Hewavitarana, who, according to Cassius Perera, came to London to sort the Society out.[8] In January 1914, he is recorded as giving the Society £111.13.8 for its Housing Fund.[9] All this meant that the Society became suspicious if any hint of theosophy or the esoteric re-appeared in Bennett's involvements.

There is a telling entry in the Minute Book of the Society for March 31, 1910, when the Society accepted Ananda Metteyya's offer of 1500 copies of his 'handbook to Buddhism' with the following caveat, 'It was agreed to accept the offer on condition that the book was not identified with Theosophy in any way.'[10] It is possible that members knew that an article by Ananda Metteyya had been published in *The Theosophist* the year before or that parts of the book he was offering might soon be published in the same journal.[11]

Even in the 1990s, when the General Secretary of the Society, Ron Maddox, suggested that a gravestone should be placed on Bennett's unmarked grave in Morden, Bennett was so controversial that Maddox could not take the Society with him.[12] It meant that those who researched Bennett were wary of keeping documents about the non-Buddhist part of his life. Maddox, for instance, suggested I contact Jean Pemberton, a woman who, he told me, was hoping to write a biography of Bennett. When I did, I received a letter from her husband saying that Jean had died. He added:

> My wife wished that her papers concerning Alan Bennett should be destroyed... One of the reasons Jean wished her papers to be destroyed was that they contained photocopies of Golden Dawn rituals written by A.B. These Jean copied from the originals in Gerald Yorke's possession.[13]

Mr Pemberton added, however, that Jean would never have destroyed the originals and 'had strong views on Christmas Humphrey's destruction of material referring to A. B which he thought better suppressed'.[14]

Allan Bennett, therefore, was a controversial figure before and after his death. Towards the end of his life, he took a more active part in The Buddhist Society. At Vesak 1918, for instance, he gave to the Society what Christmas Humphrey called 'a "fighting speech" which aroused the listening members to fresh enthusiasm'.[15] Two years later, he was editing their journal. However, he remained someone who was never quite 'respectable'. Valued for his contribution to Buddhism in the West, his capacity for networking and his fluent writing, pitied and feared because of his illness and poverty,[16] he was both a liability and a strength for a fledgling organization seeking public recognition. For contemporary Buddhist Studies, however, I would suggest that he can be seen as emblematic of a significant moment in the reception of Buddhism by the West, a moment when the definition of Buddhism was uncertain and contested, caught in a nexus of interpretations that included the esoteric, the romantic, the nihilistic and the modernist.

This paper will first survey Bennett's life, before examining his role in initiating and developing an important global and pan-Asian Buddhist network at the beginning of the twentieth century. I will use colonial period names for Sri Lanka and Myanmar, namely Ceylon and Burma, and will refer to Allan Bennett as Bennett when examining his time as a lay person and Ananda Metteyya when discussing his time as a *bhikkhu*.

Allan Bennett's life

Bennett was born in 1872 to Roman Catholic parents. His father, a civil and electrical engineer, died when he was young. His mother struggled to bring him and his sister up. He was educated in Bath and developed a strong interest in science, particularly chemistry. Chronic asthma, however, a condition that remained with him throughout his life, prevented him from gaining the qualifications he hoped for or holding down a permanent job. Crow convincingly argues, contesting my own earlier conclusion, that Bennett did not actually qualify as an analytical chemist, but nevertheless developed 'a broad set of skills' in this area and within scientific knowledge generally, to the extent that he patented at least two mechanical devices during his life that he hoped might allay his financial difficulties.[17] Crow also points out, agreeing with Brunton,[18] that, in the early 1890s, for a short time, he attended the Colonial College at Hollesey Bay, which was set up to teach men of lower socioeconomic status the skills to serve the Empire.[19]

It was scientific discovery plus, I would suggest, the suffering he saw in the world and in his own poverty-stricken and illness-filled life that turned him away from the Roman Catholicism of his childhood. With this, Bennett moved from simply being an intelligent, aspiring scientist thwarted by poverty and his own body to becoming a mirror on late Victorian religious 'seekership'. Science, for Bennett, was 'far more ... than technical knowledge'.[20] It was an integral part of his search for truth and, as such, was linked to his religious quest. At the age of 18 years old, he read Edwin Arnold's lyrical presentation of the Buddha in *The Light of Asia*. However, I agree with Crow that Buddhism did not feature greatly in his initial religious quest. Yogic forms of breath control, esoteric practice and the study of alchemy and astrology were more important. In the early 1890s, this led him to join two religious new movements that dealt in spiritualism and the esoteric. The first was the Theosophical Society, which he joined through the Brixton Lodge in 1893. The second was the Hermetic Order of the Golden Dawn, which he joined in 1894, having probably met the founders through theosophy.[21]

Within the latter, he took the magical name *Iehi Aour*, Hebrew for 'let there be light'.

In 1998, I explained this as follows:

> By the year 1899, therefore, Bennett was deeply interested in the religious heritage of the East ... He was widely read and had practised some forms of meditation, probably using yogic methods of breath control and trance-inducement ... He was interested in Western esoteric practice and magic and had discovered that he possessed certain psychic powers.[22]

In the light of Crow's research, I would now add that esoteric practice played such an important part in his life that it is possible, although be no means certain, that he was a member of the Esoteric Section or School of the Theosophical Society.[23]

His membership of the Theosophical Society ended in 1895 due to an internal conflict within the Society, although his contact with theosophists continued. His membership of the Order of the Golden Dawn, however, persisted. He became known not only for personal magical and psychic powers, his skilful use of a wand for instance,[24] but also for his ability to write occult rituals. A significant development came in 1898, when he became the teacher of a new member of the Order, Aleister Crowley, who later declared, 'I was instantly aware that this man could teach me more in a month than anyone else in five years'.[25]

According to Crowley, however, by the end of 1899, Bennett had lost interest in magic and 'cared only for Yoga'.[26] In 1900, Crowley facilitated a passage to Asia for him to save his health. An intriguing statement in a speech by J. F. McKechnie on Bennett's tenth death anniversary suggests that Bennett was destined for Japan and only stopped off at Colombo.[27] If this was true, and Crow doubts it, Bennett did not continue his journey. He remained in Ceylon for between 1–2 years, decided to become a *bhikkhu* and travelled to Burma, probably because he had been given to believe that Buddhism was purer there than in Ceylon.[28] He also changed his identity, claiming that he had been adopted by a Mr McGregor and took his name.[29] From Burma, he planned a Buddhist mission to Britain, which took place in 1908.[30] Returning to Burma in the same year, he remained there until 1914, disrobing before this date. He then sailed to England, hoping for an onward passage to California with his sister but this was refused because of his health. Bennett was cared for by a doctor who was a member of the Liverpool Branch of The Buddhist Society, but the pressure on his family of having a prematurely old and sick person with them became too great. Jean Pemberton visited a member of this family, who had been a young girl when Bennett had stayed. She 'had only a vague memory of an ill old man whose arrival had meant the children of the family sharing a bedroom and a growing atmosphere of concern and worry surrounding his presence'.[31] In 1916, the Buddhist Society referred to his case as 'sad' and appealed for funds so that he was not placed, 'in some institution supported by public charity'.[32]

Help did come to him in the last decade of his life from friends in Britain and Sri Lanka, particularly Cassius Perera, a long-term friend with whom he had an almost telepathic form of communication,[33] and Dr Hewavitarana. As previously mentioned, he returned to active work for The Buddhist Society in London, eventually taking over the editorship of *The Buddhist Review*. Paul Brunton, who first met him at this point and helped his editing work, gives an engaging picture of Bennett, at this time, in the years before his death:

> He lived in the same humble room which he had occupied during his youth. There he would sit amid heavy Victorian furniture, his table covered with books and palm-leaf classics, the floor around his chair littered with a miscellaneous assortment of manuscripts, letters and scientific instruments. Some statuettes of Gautama would rest on the mantelshelf, gazing benignly down at the disorderly scene. The white yogi would lean back in the large and battered arm-chair, in which I invariably found him, throw his head up and to one side, gaze reflectively through the window into the little garden and answer my questions in lengthy sentences .... He taught me the lofty ethic and stern ascetic philosophy of his faith .... He helped me towards two precious possessions: a rational balanced outlook and a desire to bring some light from archaic Asia to help the adolescent West.[34]

Bennett died in 1923 and was buried in an unmarked grave in Morden Cemetery, the money for this coming not from the Buddhist Society but from Dr Hewavitarana in Ceylon.

Buddhist networks and Allan Bennett

The paper turns now to the global network of Buddhists and those interested in Buddhism that Bennett helped to create from Burma when he was Ven. Ananda Metteyya. He centred the network around three main topics: the spread of Buddhist teaching and humanitarian ethic; opposition to Christian missionary activity; anti-imperialism.

Ananda Metteyya's primary tools for creating this network was the *Buddhasāsana Samāgama*, the international Buddhist organization that Ananda Metteyya founded from Burma in July 1902,[35] and its journal, *Buddhism: An Illustrated Review*, edited by Metteyya. In the first issue, he expanded on the formal constitution of the Society and the aims of the journal in this way:

> [I]t may not be out of place to present here in greater detail the programme of BUDDHISM as well as the objects of the Society in producing it. *Firstly*, to set before the world the true principles of our Religion, believing, as we do, that these need only to be better known to meet with a wide-spread acceptance among the people of the West .... *Secondly*, to promote, as far as lies in our power, those humanitarian activities referred to in the latter portion of THE FAITH OF THE FUTURE: and *Thirdly*, to unite by our Journal, as by a common bond of mutual interest and brotherhood, the many Associations with Buddhist aims that now exist.[36]

The humanitarian activities included in Ananda Metteyya's introductory editorial article that he named 'The Faith of the Future' (Metteyya 1903b), were centred on the practical application of the five precepts: substituting 'rational arbitration' for warfare and thus reducing armaments; abolishing capital punishment; desisting from eating animal flesh and drinking alcohol; creating gender equality; developing educational systems that taught mind culture. Internationalism and an early form of modernist engaged Buddhism is present here.

There was an aspect of Buddhist networking, however, that Ananda Metteyya did not prioritize: networks with Buddhists in Tibet and, more widely, with Mahāyāna Buddhists, although he made an exception for China and Japan. His attitude to Tibet was similar to that of the orientalist, T. W. Rhys-Davids[37] and the Buddhist modernism that was developing in Sri Lanka, which doubtlessly influenced him. In the third issue of *Buddhism*, he could, therefore, declare:

> We may state incidentally, in view of the wild rumours to the contrary, that the Buddhists of Burma, and we presume all Buddhists in the British Empire, view with absolute indifference the affairs of the Dalai Lama of Tibet, generally, with which they have nothing in common; and that the fiction that Buddhists regard the former in the same light as they do Roman Catholics the Pope is too absurd for serious discussion.[38]

In a similar vein, he could express concern that European scholars first met 'northern' Buddhism and likened this to scholars of Christianity first encountering, 'the later, garbled and miracle-teeming writings of medieval monks'.[39] His interpretative model was that of revival/decline. Buddhism was pure at the outset. As the centuries passed and it spread north from India, it declined through the entry of the superstitious.[40] Metteyya's networking, therefore, differed that of the later western Buddhist figure, Christmas Humphreys, who ardently believed that the different Buddhist schools could be united.

The journal, *Buddhism* was eventually sent to between 500–600 libraries throughout the world for free, on the condition that the copy should be left on the table in the reading room until the next was received. Burmese donations funded this. The journal itself reflected the internationalism of its distribution. It contained articles on Buddhism by Metteyya, columns for news from other countries and sections entitled 'How Others See Us', 'Correspondence' and 'News and Notes'. Representatives in different countries were appointed. The first edition named representatives in Austria (Karl Neumann), Upper Burma (Maung Thaw), Ceylon (W. A. de Silva & R. L. Perera), China (Kong Yu Wei), Germany (Arthur Pfungst) and Italy (Guiseppe de Lorenzo), and Honorary Members from England, USA, Denmark, Burma and Sri Lanka, including Edwin Arnold, Paul Carus, Caroline Rhys Davids, Viggo Fausböll and Ven Hikkaḍuwē Sumaṃgala.[41] Metteyya also claimed that he was arranging for representatives in England, Russia and the USA, and that he was seeking them for Japan, Siam and India.[42] Not unsurprisingly, given Metteyya's friendships, news from Ceylon was particularly visible in the journal. However, correspondence from the other countries networked also appeared.

I suggest that the journal, *Buddhism*, was the first Buddhist publication in English, distributed from an Asian country with the specific aim of creating an international network of Buddhists and scholars of Buddhism. Yet there was at least one precedent. One influence on Ananda Metteyya could have been a journal published in Sri Lanka from 1889, entitled, *The Buddhist*. The first editor was Charles William Leadbeater, an Anglican priest who became a theosophist and, later, a leading figure in modern esotericism.[43] *The Buddhist* also had an international focus but its international contributors tended to be theosophists such as A. P. Sinnett, whose writings were serialized extensively in the first volume (1888–1889). Moreover, its focus was more explicitly linked than that of *Buddhism* to the local, anti-missionary struggle, through, for instance, setting itself up as foil to Christian missionary publications such as the Methodist Wesleyan journal, *The Ceylon Friend*.[44]

There is no doubt that *Buddhism* was internationally influential. Many of the articles in it by Metteyya were later published in Europe.[45] Nevertheless, its existence was short-lived. The last issue was in 1908 shortly before Ananda Metteyya left for England. The nascent network lost its main driver.

The presence in Burma of ordained Buddhists from the West, however, was another significant part of Ananda Metteyya's vision of an internationalized and networked Buddhism. In the first issue of *Buddhism*, Metteyya called for five men from four countries, USA, England, France and Germany, to come to Burma to be trained for higher ordination as *bhikkhus*.[46] He was careful to list conditions such as not eating after noon and asked for detailed personal particulars. Not as many people as he hoped responded. We know that some reached Burma with little or no influence from Metteyya, U Dhammaloka for instance. I know of only two who came to Burma because of Metteyya but the first could not have been influenced by this appeal. Anton Walter Florus Gueth decided that he would become a *bhikkhu* before the date of Metteyya's ordination and travelled first to Egypt, Bombay and Ceylon.[47] He left Ceylon for Burma because, by that time, there was a 'Scotsman' (Ananda Metteyya) there who had become a Buddhist monk.[48] Gueth was accepted as a novice in September 1903 and lived for a month in a single room with Metteyya before moving to Kyandaw Monastery, where, in January or February 1904, he received the higher ordination (*upasampadā*) as Nyāṇatiloka. Metteyya was not his teacher. Nyāṇatiloka's autobiography records only one piece of advice from Ananda Metteyya—that he should concentrate on learning Burmese rather than Pali—and he ignored it.[49] J. F. McKechnie, the second person, travelled to Burma after reading the first issue of *Buddhism*. He was particularly influenced by Metteyya's aricle on *nibbāna* and offered himself initially as a business advisor. Nevertheless, he was eventually ordained as Ven. Sīlācāra in 1906.

Both Sīlācāra and Nyāṇatiloka became influential monks, although the former disrobed in 1925. Nyāṇatiloka eventually became the father of western renunciants in Ceylon. I have a copy of a wonderful letter dated February 10, 1905, written by Ananda Metteyya to Cassius Perera, commending Nyāṇatiloka and asking if Cassius's father could give assistance. It contains these words: 'He does not smoke, not eat meat, not have asthma (I wish I didn't); he is an easily-contented mortal, with a very gentle and considerate nature'. Nyaṇatusita and Hecker list 42 monk disciples of Nyāṇatiloka, including Sīlācāra, 35 of whom were from outside Asia.[50]

Ananda Metteyya did not have a pivotal role in creating a Buddhist monastic Sangha in the West, in spite of his 1908 mission. His example and his compassionate pastoral care, however, contributed to creating a western monastic Sangha in the East. Nyāṇatiloka eventually overshadowed him as preceptor of western *bhikkhus* but it would be an injustice to Metteyya if his role in this was ignored.

The anti-missionary agenda

When Ananda Metteyya returned to Burma in 1908 after his six month mission to Britain, he did not edit further issues of *Buddhism*. One reason was his failing health. Perera records that his health began to fail rapidly after his return to Burma with gallstone problems superimposed on his asthma.[51] But I would argue that there was also another reason. Crow points out that the interests of the *Buddhasāsana Samāgama*, after 1908, 'focussed mostly on promoting Buddhist education'.[52] The *Buddhasāsana Samāgama* had been committed to furthering Buddhist education from its inception but I would suggest that the threat from Christian missionary work in Burma had so increased by this time that its members believed they had no option but to address it more directly, leaving less time for international networking. Britain gained complete control over Burma in 1885, although western missionaries had been active before then, including Roman Catholic orders. American Baptists arrived in 1813 and the British-based Society for the Propagation of the Gospel established a Diocese of Rangoon in 1877.[53] Wesleyan Methodists arrived in Upper Burma in 1887. Reports from missionary sources claim that opposition from Buddhists towards Christian missionary work was intensifying by the beginning of the twentieth century. Opposition had, in fact, begun earlier but in a more subtle way, through education. Metteyya's patron, Mrs Hla Oung (Daw Mya Me), for instance, had founded two Buddhist schools in the 1890s. At the beginning of the twentieth century, however, an apparent tolerance of the missionaries by Buddhists changed to defensive confrontation.[54] The influence of Sri Lanka's anti-Christian Buddhist revival cannot be discounted here, given the high level of communication between the two countries in the colonial period. I would suggest, however, that Ananda Metteyya and monks such as U Dhammaloka were also important drivers of this, networking with Ceylonese revivalists and possibly the theosophists who continued to work in Ceylon alongside Buddhists.

The strategy of Ananda Metteyya and the *Buddhasāsana Samāgama* was to create opportunities for Buddhist education to equip Buddhist children to withstand the arguments of the Christian missionaries. I disagree with Crow that these aims were 'less ambitious' than their previous, more international ones.[55] They were simply different in a context where the need to address an increasingly threatening missionary presence was becoming urgent, and there was some success. For instance, The Buddhist Society of Great Britain and Ireland noted on December 3, 1909 that the Government of India had granted permission for the teaching of Buddhism in schools in Burma and congratulated Ananda Metteyya and his colleagues for this victory.

Their other defensive strategies were the pen and the symbolic message that western *bhikkhus* could embody. As Crow notes, after 1908, more lectures by Ananda Metteyya and Sīlācāra were published and re-published in Burma. Within these, not only was Buddhism promoted but Christianity was undermined. Ananda Metteyya's indictment of Christianity and Christian proselytization had always been ruthless. Christianity with its belief in god and a soul was locked in childhood and delusion. It was utterly bankrupt and was losing its grip on the western mind.[56] His early serialized article on the Shwe Dagon Pagoda confirmed this message, by comparing the richness and beauty of lived religion in Burma with a memory of Easter Monday at Battersea Park, which he described in this way:

> Beneath the hideous glare of flaming of oil, men, women and children were running to and fro; girls and men bandying coarse jests, their speech incardine with senseless oaths. Hard by, a monstrous engine, grinding raucous vulgar airs upon an organ, spun dizzy couples round on circling wooden horses... And I remembered how I had felt ashamed, how I had slunk home by the least frequented paths, and marvelled what evil I had done in former lives, that I should take birth as countryman of such as these.'[57]

The implicit question behind his words was, of course: 'And how can missionaries have the arrogance to believe that they can convert a people with such a deep spirituality?'

In the second volume of *Buddhism*, Ananda Metteyya published a comment from the newly founded German Buddhist monthly, *Der Buddhist*, on the quality of converts to Buddhism, and the quality of converts to Christianity, namely that adherents of Buddhism in the West were from the intelligent thinking classes and converts to Christianity in India and Ceylon were from the lower ranks.[58] It was a comment that bolstered Metteyya's view that Christianity was for the non-intellectual child and Buddhism for the thinking adult who sought knowledge.[59]

Ananda Metteyya's strategy, in the face of Christian mission, therefore, was to strengthen Buddhists in their own faith, through education and the disseminating of articles about Buddhism, and to demonstrate that Buddhism was attractive to the West. For if the Burmese could see that white people could become Buddhists, then their confidence might be strengthened enough to resist the missionary. In this, he drew strength from and networked with Buddhists and theosophists with a similar agenda.

Imperialism

The relationship between British missionaries and the colonial administration in Burma and Ceylon was antagonistic at times.[60] However, to Ananda Metteyya, the two appeared united. Ananda Metteyya's indictment of imperialism, therefore, was implicit in his critique of Christianity, and his opposition to Christian mission was also opposition to British imperialism. His strategy, however, was not to urge open opposition to the British. The British could be praised where praise was due, for example when they re-instated the position of the Head of Burmese Buddhism, the *thathanabaing*.[61] As I have shown, they could also be negotiated with when it came to Buddhist education. However, the fallacy of believing the West, and Britain in particular, was more advanced than Burma, had to be pointed out and Ananda Metteyya did this with vigour, overturning the accepted rhetoric of Empire, networking himself with other contesters of Empire and all who read his journal. Therefore, in the first issue of *Buddhism*, he declared of Britain:

> Apart from the misery that that civilization has spread in lands beyond its pale, can it be claimed that that in its internal polity, that for its own people, it has brought a diminution of the world's suffering, any diminution of its degradation, its misery, its crime, above all, has it brought about any general increase of its native contentment, the extension of any such knowledge as promotes the spirit of mutual helpfulness rather than the curse of competition?[62]

I can do no better, at this point, than to quote from my earlier study of Ananda Metteyya:

> 'No' was his answer. Next, he criticized the West's war machine, tearing ten million men away from useful service, "waiting but a word to let Hell loose on earth"; then he turned to alcohol, 'crowded taverns', 'overflowing gaols,' and 'sad asylums' to prove that there had been no increase in happiness in the West because it had concentrated too much on, 'the multiplication of material possessions,' ignoring 'the culture of the highest faculties of the mind.'[63] In the fourth issue of *Buddhism*, the condemnation was even more pointed. He went through recent centuries in the West to highlight the barbarism present; that children could be hanged for stealing anything over the value of a shilling; that a man killed by lightening could be denied a Christian burial because it was thought to be a punishment from God; that Simpson of Edinburgh could be condemned for discovering that chloroform could be used as an anaesthetic; that Darwin could be the subject of bitter invective. He linked such things to 'primeval savageries'[64] flowing from the Christian heritage and the ferocity of its persecution of knowledge.[65]

Therefore, when Japan, which Ananda Metteyya saw as a Buddhist country, found itself at war with Russia, Metteyya vigorously supported Japan. For him, the war was an example of a country oppressed by western imperialism, rising up in opposition, repudiating subservience, fighting for civilisation against, 'the most despotic, the most reactionary and the most ruthless of the Christian powers'.[66] He hoped that it would teach the West that it had underrated the intelligence and ability of the Japanese. In effect, Metteyya justified defensive war in Buddhism, in a way that prefigured arguments used by Asian Buddhists later in the twentieth century.

Concluding remarks

This paper has argued that Ananda Metteyya was central to the global networking of educated Buddhists and those interested in Buddhism in the early years of the twentieth century and that he deserves recognition for this. He was an early 'engaged' Buddhist, a strong critic of the West and of Christianity, and a robust promoter of the East to the extent that he could endorse defensive war by an eastern power. On the other hand, he was orientated towards the West, retained contact with free-thinkers and Buddhists there even when in Burma, and sought its transformation through Buddhism. In the narrative of the West's reception of Buddhism, he lies between more 'respectable' monks such as Nyāṇatiloka and more 'disreputable' monks such as U Dhammaloka, for he fell into neither category. He was both inspiration and a problem for The Buddhist Society for Great Britain and Ireland, and an enigma for his theosophist and occultist friends. He was a seeker and a missionary, a poet and a pastor. He embodied and lived out the tensions within the West's reception of Buddhism. Brunton wrote, 'His sombre yet tranquil face was so unusual that it still haunts my fancies'.[67] May Allan Bennett continue to grip the imagination of those who seek an accurate history of Buddhism in the West.

ACKNOWLEDGEMENTS

The initial version of this paper was presented at the conference *SE Asia as a Crossroads for Buddhist Exchange: Pioneer European Buddhists and Asian Buddhist Networks 1860–1960* hosted by the Study of Religions Department, University College Cork, Ireland, September 13–15, 2012 and funded by the Dhammakaya International Society of the United Kingdom as part of the 2012 postdoctoral fellowship, 'Continuities and Transitions in early Modern Thai Buddhism'.

NOTES

1. Harris (1998). See Figure 1.
2. See Crow (2009).
3. The Sri Lankan revivalist, the Anagarika Dharmapala, predated him informally in 1893, when he visited London on his way to the Parliament of the World's Religions in Chicago, with a form of mission in mind. See Guruge (1991, xxxvii).
4. Grant (1972, 85), quoted in Harris (1998, 6).

5. Most particularly Bennett (1923, 1929).
6. For his ongoing engagement with theosophy see Crow (2009, 55–62), Harris (2008).
7. See Harris (2006).
8. Perera (1923, 6). See also Minutes of the Council Meetings of the Society for 1911 and 1912, when Dr Hewavitarana's signature often appears (held at the Headquarters of The Buddhist Society, London)
9. Minutes of the Council Meeting of The Buddhist Society of Great Britain and Ireland, January 9, 1914.
10. Minutes of the Council Meeting, March 31, 1910.
11. Ananda Metteyya (1909) and Ananda Metteyya (1911), as mentioned in Crow (2009, 166).
12. Personal conversation with Ron Maddox.
13. Letter to Elizabeth Harris from Mr T. Pemberton dated October 26, 1994.
14. Letter to Elizabeth Harris from Mr T. Pemberton dated October 26, 1994.
15. Humphreys (1968, 14).
16. In the late nineteenth century, the remedies prescribed for asthma included cocaine, opium and morphine. Bennett was heavily dependent on these in Britain and this may, periodically, have affected his lucidity and personality. See Harris (1998, 7n).
17. Crow (2009, 21–22). See also Harris (1998, 4).
18. Brunton (1941, 1st page of article).
19. Crow (2009, 20).
20. Harris (1998, 4).
21. Crow (2009, 25).
22. Harris (1998, 7).
23. Crow (2009, 26).
24. See Harris (1998, 6).
25. Symonds and Grant (1989, 181); quoted in Harris (1998, 6).
26. Crow (2009, 43).
27. Crow (2009, 44).
28. Symonds and Grant (1989, 180), cited in Harris (1998, 9).
29. Bennett in Britain had become very close to Samuel Liddell MacGregor Mathers, one of the founders of the Order of the Golden Dawn and it is probable that he wished to claim him as a father figure. See Crow (2009, 50–52). Evidence of this came to me in a conversation with Ven Balangoda Ananda Maitreya Thera (1896–1998), a person with first-hand memories of Bennett, who insisted that Bennett had kept the name McGregor until he died.
30. For accounts of his mission see Harris (1998, 11–13); Crow (2009: 71–77).
31. Personal letter from Mr T. Pemberton to Elizabeth Harris, October 26, 1994.
32. *The Buddhist Review* (1916) 8, 217–219; quoted in Harris (1998, 15).
33. Personal conversation with Alec Robertson, an associate of Cassius Perera, in the early 1990s.
34. Brunton (1941, 3rd page of article).

35. Crow contested the date that I had originally discovered.
36. Ananda Metteyya (1903d, 163–167).
37. See, for instance, Rhys-Davids (1894, 199–211), where Rhys-Davids accuses Tibetan Buddhism of being antagonistic to early Buddhism.
38. Ananda Metteyya (1904b, 497–520).
39. Bennett (1929, 5).
40. See particularly Ananda Metteyya (1908).
41. *Buddhism* (1903) I (I), iii.
42. Ananda Metteyya (1903d, 165).
43. See Tillett (1982).
44. See Harris (2012, 299–302).
45. See Crow (2009, 168–170).
46. *Buddhism* (1903) I (I), 161–163.
47. Bhikkhu Nyanatusita and Hecker (2008, 22–24). This part of the book is a translation from German of the autobiography of Nyanatiloka, published in 1948.
48. Bhikkhu Nyanatusita and Hecker (2008, 24). That Nyanatiloka refers to Metteyya as a Scotsman confirms that Metteyya's re-making of himself in Sri Lanka had been successful.
49. Bhikkhu Nyanatusita and Hecker (2008, 25).
50. Bhikkhu Nyanatusita and Hecker (2008, 192–195).
51. Perera (1923, 6), quoted in Harris (1998, 14).
52. Crow (2009, 77).
53. Leigh (2011, 10).
54. Leigh (2011, 78–84).
55. Crow (2009, 77).
56. See for example Ananda Metteyya (1903b).
57. Ananda Metteyya (1903a, 111–112).
58. *Buddhism* 2 (1), 115.
59. Ananda Metteyya rejected the theosophist view of the evolution of the soul but, nevertheless, thought in evolutionary terms. There was an evolution in the realm of compassion and one in the realm of wisdom. 'In the area of wisdom, childhood was the realm of blind faith ... Adolescence was the age of investigation and questioning, and adulthood the age of understanding' (Harris, 1998, 48–49, drawing on Ananda Metteyya, 1908, 182–187).
60. See Leigh (2011, 40–60); Harris (2012, 294–295).
61. 'And we would venture to express to Sir Hugh Barnes, as the Representative of the Imperial Government, the heart-felt thanks and gratitude of the Burmese people for the boon that the Government has granted them' (Ananda Metteyya, 1903c, 208).
62. Ananda Metteyya (1903b, 12).
63. Ananda Metteyya (1903b, 13).
64. Ananda Metteyya (1904a, 535–536).
65. Harris (1998, 45).
66. Ananda Metteyya (1904c, 649).
67. Brunton (1941, 3).

REFERENCES

BENNETT, ALLAN. 1923. *The Wisdom of the Aryas*. London: Kegan Paul, Trench, Trubner.

BENNETT, ALLAN. 1929. *The Religion of Burma and Other Papers*. Adyar: Theosophical Publishing House.

BRUNTON, PAUL. 1941. A Pioneer Western Buddhist. *Ceylon Daily News Vesak Number May 1941*, unnumbered pages.

CROW, JOHN L. 2009. *The White Knight in the Yellow Robe: Allan Bennett's Search for Truth*, Privately printed by the author.

GRANT, KENNETH. 1972. *The Magical Revival*. London: Frederick Muller Ltd.

GURUGE, ANANDA. 1991. *Return to Righteousness: A Collection of Speeches, Essays and Letters of the Anagarika Dharmapala*. Colombo: Ministry of Cultural Affairs and Information.

HARRIS, ELIZABETH. 1998. *Ananda Metteyya: The First British Emissary of Buddhism*. Kandy: Buddhist Publication Society.

HARRIS, ELIZABETH. 2006. *Theravāda Buddhism and the British Encounter*. London: Routledge.

HARRIS, ELIZABETH. 2008. Ananda Metteyya: Contester of Misinterpretations of Buddhism. In *Dharma to the UK: A Centennial Celebration of Buddhist Legacy*, edited by Mahinda Deegalle., 37–52. London: World Buddhist Foundation.

HARRIS, ELIZABETH. 2012. Memory, Experience and the Clash of Cosmologies: The Encounter between British Protestant Missionaries and Buddhism in Nineteenth Century Sri Lanka. *Social Sciences and Mission* 25 (3): 265–303.

HUMPHREYS, CHRISTMAS. 1968. *Sixty Years of Buddhism in England (1907–1967)*. London: The Buddhist Society.

LEIGH, MICHAEL D. 2011. *Conflict, Politics and Proselytisation: Methodist Missionaries in Colonial and Postcolonial Upper Burma 1887–1966*. Manchester: Manchester University Press.

METTEYYA, ANANDA. 1903a. In the Shadow of Shwe Dagon. *Buddhism* 1 (1): 101–12.

METTEYYA, ANANDA. 1903b. The Faith of the Future. *Buddhism* 1 (1): 6–38.

METTEYYA, ANANDA. 1903c. The Thathanabaing. *Buddhism* 1 (2): 177–208.

METTEYYA, ANANDA. 1903d. Ourselves. *The Buddhist* 1 (1): 163–167.

METTEYYA, ANANDA. 1904a. The New Civilization. *Buddhism* 1 (4): 529–60.

METTEYYA, ANANDA. 1904b. News and Notes. *Buddhism* 1 (3): 497–520.

METTEYYA, ANANDA. 1904c. News and Notes. *Buddhism* 1 (4): 649–656.

METTEYYA, ANANDA. 1908. Propaganda. *Buddhism* 1 (2): 169–92.

METTEYYA, ANANDA. 1909. The Extension of the Empire of Righteousness in Western Lands. *The Theosophist* 30 (9): 302–9.

METTEYYA, ANANDA. 1911. The Religion of Burma. Parts I & 2. *The Theosophist* 32 (7): 51–77, 32 (8): 215–241.

NYANATUSITA, BHIKKHU, and HELLMUTH HECKER. 2008. *The Life of Nyanatiloka: The Biography of a Western Buddhist Pioneer*. Kandy: Buddhist Publication Society.

PERERA, CASSIUS. 1923. The Late Mr Allan Bennett. *The Buddhist*, April 28, 2466-1923: 6.

RHYS-DAVIDS, T. W. 1894. *Buddhism: Being A Sketch of the Life and Teaching of Gautama, The Buddha*. rev. ed. London: SPCK.

SYMONDS, JOHN, and GRANT, KENNETH, eds. 1989. *The Confessions of Aleister Crowley: An Autohagiography*. Harmondsworth: Penguin.

TILLETT, GEOFFREY. 1982. *The Elder Brother A Biography of Charles Webster Leadbeater*. London: Routledge and Kegan Paul.

TAI-BURMESE-LAO BUDDHISMS IN THE 'MODERNIZING' OF BAN THAWAI (BANGKOK): THE DYNAMIC INTERACTION BETWEEN ETHNIC MINORITY RELIGION AND BRITISH–SIAMESE CENTRALIZATION IN THE LATE NINETEENTH/EARLY TWENTIETH CENTURIES

Phibul Choompolpaisal

Drawing on extensive Thai literary and oral history sources this article sets out to explain the complex social, political, ethnic and religious framework within which the opening by 'the Irish Buddhist' U Dhammaloka of a free, bilingual and multi-ethnic Buddhist school at Wat Ban Thawai, Bangkok in May 1903 acquires a broader and deeper significance. The article documents the mutual relationships between the local Buddhisms of Tai, Burmese and Lao ethnic minorities and the politics of British-Siamese alliance in the period before and during the First World War. It examines the British-Siamese support of these Buddhist communities in Bangkok and explores the British-Siamese use of their diplomatic relationship with the Tai, Burmese and Lao ethnic minorities in Ban Thawai and elsewhere (i.e. across the borders between Siam and Burma) in order to centralize power. It also discusses the anomalous effect of British and French influence in Ban Thawai which allowed local resistance to Siamese centralization and saṅgha reform.

Introduction

U. DHAMMALOKA, the Irish Buddhist now in Bangkok, has started a school at Wat Ban-ta-wai for the instruction of Siamese and Chinese boys in English. Already a large number of pupils have begun to take advantage of the opportunity afforded them of learning English, some 50 scholars attending daily.

> The class is held in a new building which was specially erected for the purpose of a schoolroom. No charge is made for attendance at the class. (*Bangkok Times Weekly Mail*, May 2, 1903, 6)

In the only account published so far of U Dhammaloka's period of residence in Bangkok so far, an account based almost entirely on reports in English-language newspapers of the time, Bocking (2010) noted that prior to Dhammaloka's arrival in 1903 he resided in the Tavoy monastery in Rangoon; that he travelled from Singapore to Bangkok with the Saophawa of Kengtung and was suspected by some of being a British agent; that on arrival in Bangkok he found a welcome at a temple called 'Wat Bantawai' where he founded a bilingual Buddhist school and that he associated with an Anglican, Canon Greenstock, in the cause of temperance. However, Bocking could offer little to explain any of these events. Drawing on new archival and fieldwork research in Bangkok, the present article helps to explain how these seemingly disparate elements are in fact connected and locates Dhammaloka's activities during February–August 1903 within the larger socio-political and religious context of the modernization and centralization of the emerging Siamese nation-state.

The geographical focus of this article is a strip of land running alongside the Chao Phraya river in the city of Bangkok. Now integrated into the urban sprawl of the city, the area known in the 1900s as Ban Thawai was, for a time, a linear outgrowth of the expanding city, providing a home for new commerce, ethnic minority settlement, foreign diplomatic missions, new forms of education and religious diversity.

From the nineteenth to early twentieth centuries, when the British and French were competing to colonize Southeast Asia, ethnic minorities from Tai, Burmese and Lao regions including the Thawai (aka Tavoy/Davoy), Shan, Mon and Lao, migrated into Ban Thawai (present name, 'Yannawa').[1] The Buddhist temples—Wat Don Thawai, Wat Thung Kula, Wat Lao and Wat Yannawa—located in this area became the most important temples and communal centres for these migrants in Bangkok.

At the time, Siam was struggling both to fend off the interests of the two colonizing powers that lay to the East and West (the French in Indochina and the British in Burma) and to forge a national identity out of smaller, former tributary kingdoms with distinctive cultural and religious traditions.

In modernizing Ban Thawai, the British and Siamese governments together lent support to religious, socio-political and educational diversity of Buddhist and Christian practices, such that the first Buddhist and Christian bilingual schools and the most important Western-supported Christian churches in Siam became established in the area. The advantage for the British-Siamese alliance was in establishing diplomatic relationships with Tai, Burmese and Lao ethnic migrants and using these relationships to centralize power at local, national and international levels. The advantage for the ethnic minority communities in this area was that, for a while, they enjoyed some degree of autonomy, particularly freedom from full implementation of the 1902 Saṅgha Act which sought to homogenize Buddhist practice. In these and other respects the Ban Thawai area in the early 1900s can aptly be described as a 'Buddhist crossroads'.

British colonization and British-Siamese centralization mid-nineteenth to early twentieth centuries

To contextualize the rapid development in nineteenth to early twentieth century Bangkok of global networks involving different ethnic groups, religions and European powers in educational and religious affairs that took place in the Ban Thawai area, one must first examine the dynamics of political and economic competition that developed during the colonial period between these groups and the Siamese state.

From the seventeenth to eighteenth centuries, prior to European colonization, the Siamese and Burmese were the two major players competing to take control of the many different ethnic groups that resided in Burma, the Shan states, Siam, Lanna and the borders between the upper parts of the Shan states and the southern part of China (hereafter referred to as 'the Tai-Burmese area'). The main ethnic minorities relevant to this article that migrated into 'modernized' Bangkok are the Thawai ('Tavoy'/ 'Dawei'), the Shan, the Mon, the Lanna and the Lao. The Thawai, the Shan and the Mon are Tai-Burmese ethnic minorities who live in Burmese or Siamese territories. The Thawai refers to the ethnic people who originally resided in the Tanaosri area in southeastern Burma near the border with Siam.[2] In Siam, other terms were used to refer to the Thawai, including Aracanese, Ayakhiang and Yakhai (Sathienkoset 2003, 96).[3] The Mon originally lived in the southern part of Burma—some in the same area as the Thawai, many along the southern part of the Burma-Siam border. The Shan ('Tai' or 'Tai Yai') are the ethnic group whose homeland is in the Shan State, in the southern part of China, the north of Thailand, east of Burma and west of Laos. The) Lanna lived in Chiangmai, Chiangrai, Lamphun, Lamprang, Phayao and Phrae before their integration into Siam (Charoenmuang 1999, 4–5). The Lao are the ethnic group that lives in Laos, on the eastern side of Thailand.

By the late nineteenth century, to the west and northwest of Siam, the British had colonized Burma and taken complete control of the Burmese, Shan, Thawai and Mon areas, while, on the eastern side of Siam, the French had colonized the Lao, Cambodia and the Vietnamese. Siam thus became a buffer state between the British and the French, ultimately responding with its own expansionist policies. The Siamese government helped preserve its own independence and sovereignty by conceding to some of the trading, settlement, territorial and military demands of the British and French. In turn, these European powers helped with the process of modernization, so that Bangkok was rapidly transformed socially, politically and economically, though Siam continued to be ruled by an absolute monarchy until the reign of King Rama VII in 1932.[4]

From the nineteenth to early twentieth centuries, the Siamese government developed a stronger relationship with the British than with the French. The British in turn played a more dominant role than the French in supporting modernization (Choompolpaisal 2011, 212; Keyes 1977, 291–301, 1989, 128–129; Thompson 1941, 30–48, 184–186). British intervention in the Tai-Burmese area changed the shape of Siamese-Burmese politics. The British success in defeating the Burmese had, in part, been due to the substantial support the British received from the Siamese government and many of the ethnic groups within the Tai–Burmese region (Chao Kong Tai, Saowapha of Kengtung for example) who did not want to be under Burmese control. In return, these ethnic groups received political support from the British and the Siamese and greater freedom than before to govern their own affairs (Sawangsri 2009, 19–21, 30–33, 40). With the support of these ethnic groups, the British–Siamese political alliance allowed Britain to maximize its political and economic power in the Tai–Burmese region and enabled Siam to centralize its power with British support and without having to confront the Burmese directly. Thus a pact evolved among the British, the Siamese and various ethnic groups within what had been Burmese territory, which led initially to the downfall of the Burmese and subsequently to the mutual empowerment of the British, Siamese and minority ethnic groups in the region (Sawangsri 2009).

Siam had, nevertheless, by the early twentieth century conceded a substantial amount of its newly centralized territory to Britain and France (Choompolpaisal 2011, 263, n.27; Thompson 1941, 163–165).[5] Special trading treaties gave the British and French (and to a lesser extent other Western powers) considerable economic benefits within Siamese territory. French encroachment from the east and British expansion from the west stimulated King Chulalongkorn (r. 1868–1910) to tighten Siam's control over all peripheral areas, including through the introduction of a new system of political administration from the 1870s. By the early 1890s, high-ranking commissioners had been sent into many rural areas, particularly the remote northeastern parts of Siam and neighbouring Laos. These commissioners occupied a new position intermediate between the Siamese Court and the local hereditary elites. In the 1890s, Chulalongkorn further centralized the political administration, dividing the whole country into provinces and downgrading the status of many local gentry. Local governors, who used to exercise relative autonomy, were subordinated to the Court (Keyes 1977, 291–301, 1989, 128–129; Choompolpaisal 2011, 212).

The palace also centralized ecclesiastical power structures in this period, tightening control over Buddhist monks nationwide. This was highly significant as many urban and rural monks were influential in society, acting as community leaders as well as religious teachers and advisors. They could even become leading figures in violent uprisings against government centralization policies, especially in the north and northeast of Siam from the 1890s to 1910s. In its attempt to centralize power in the religious sphere, from the 1850s to 1930s, the palace privileged royalist Thammayut (Dhammayutika) monks, using them to control all monks nationwide. The Thammayut sect, established by Prince Mongkut in 1837, was a relatively small group of monks who supported the centralizing policies of consecutive kings, namely Mongkut (r. 1851–1868), Chulalongkorn (r. 1868–1910) and Rama VI (r. 1910–1925). Thammayut control extended over the Mahanikay sect. From the 1880s to the 1920s, Thammayut monks assisted in the nationalizing of 'Bangkok-centralised', that is 'Thai', Buddhist identity. This 'Siamese Sangha' discriminated against rural, local Buddhist practices and vernaculars, instead promoting Pali textual studies and practices approved by Thammayut monks (Choompolpaisal 2011, 134–135, 159–161, 231–257). The 1902 Sangha Act established a centralized hierarchy for the political administration of all Sangha affairs and a national system of clerical education. Scholars such as Charles Keyes see this Act as bringing about 'the incorporation of all monks into a national structure' (Keyes 1971, 555–556). Krajaang Nanthapho and other Thai scholars see it as creating a new system prejudiced in favour of the Thammayut, with their close ties to the crown (Choompolpaisal 2011, 258–281).

Key events: treaties, transformation of the urban landscape and migration

Three related key events took place between the 1850s and 1910s as part of the colonial process of centralizing power: (1) the signing of the Bowring and other special Treaties from the mid-1850 to 1870s; (2) the transformation of the urban landscape in Bangkok from the 1860s to 1890s; and (3) the rapid migration of Tai, Burmese and Lao migrants into Bangkok from the 1880s to the early 1900s. These events were interlinked. The process of modernizing Bangkok elevated the Ban Thawai (Yannawa) area into a newly modernized centre for commercialism, religious diversity, education, dynamic interactions between the Europeans and the Tai, Burmese and Lao Buddhist migrants, and the politics of geographical centralization which linked Bangkok to the Tai-Burmese region.

The Bowring and other treaties and their consequences

In 1855, the British and Siamese governments signed the Bowring Treaty. Articles I–III and V created a new political identity, that of 'British subject(s)' resident in Siam but under British control. 'British subjects' included not only British people but also ethnic migrants such as the Thawai, the Mon and the Burmese who had migrated into Siam under British control (Ministry of Foreign Affairs 1968, 27–30; Khumsupha 2010, 78–84, 91–92).[6] These had to be 'registered' with the British consulates in Bangkok, Chiangmai or Kengtung. The Siamese government could not then interfere with the authority of the British consular representatives over these subjects; among them several monks (ibid.; Charoenmuang 1999, 9; Jumsai 1970a, 140, 1970b, 55–56).

Articles IV and VIII of the Treaty allowed British subjects and Westerners to settle, do business, employ local people and buy and rent land in central Bangkok.

This led to a rapid increase in Western settlers and Christian missionaries and the expansion of trade and business between the West and Siam. The major ports of Bangkok became increasingly busy and prosperous. The European consulates servicing these activities were located in the Ban Thawai/Yannawa area, the location of one of the most important docks in Bangkok and, as business expanded, many Burmese, Mon, Shan, Thawai and Singaporean Chinese migrated into this area to work for Western companies (Ministry of Foreign Affairs 1968, 29, 30–31; Khumsupha 2010, 65–96).

In contrast to the Siamese government's increasingly centralized control of the religion of Siamese subjects through the Thammayut hierarchy, Article VI in the Bowring Treaty specified that all British subjects and Westerners in Siamese territories had freedom of religion. The British supported Christianity but also Buddhism, the religion of the majority of their ethnic subjects (Ministry of Foreign Affairs 1968, 30; Loos 2006, 41–42, n39). British support for Christianity led to the establishment of Christian churches during the period from the 1860s until the early 1900s. Christ Church (in Thai, 'Krittajak Angklit', literally translates as 'the Christian Kingdom of the British') was the first British Protestant church in Bangkok, established in 1861 after King Mongkut gave land in the Ban Thawai area to American and British missionaries (Mcfarland 1999, 55–63).[7] From then until the early 1900s—the era George Bradley McFarland calls 'the period of expansion' in Bangkok—other Protestant and Catholic missionaries from France, Italy, America and elsewhere came to promote their religion in Ban Thawai and other parts of Bangkok (Mcfarland 1999, 51–70; Sathienkoset 2003, 316–354). The presence of Christian missionaries had a significant impact in terms of bilingual education, the introduction of Western medical methods and the Press, which at the earliest stage belonged to American and British missionaries (Sukhum 2005, 3–16, 77–80). The Treaty's promotion of freedom of religion also contributed indirectly to the establishment of Western societies and clubs that promoted religious values. For example, a small group of British women founded the Women's Christian Temperance Union ('Temperance Club') in 1869 in Sathon, close to Ban Thawai. This club and two other British institutions, the Ladies' Bazaar Association and the Neilson Hays Library, became important for British social networking during subsequent decades (Mcfarland 1999, 68–70, 82).

A year after the Bowring Treaty, in May 1856, the British and Siamese signed the Harris Park Treaty. It was similar to the Bowring Treaty but legislated in greater detail. In August of the same year, the Diplomatic Treaty between France and Siam was signed. This, with its major revision in 1872, was similar to Bowring, especially regarding the rights of French subjects under French control in Siamese territories, that is the rights to settle, do business, buy and rent lands in central Bangkok, have freedom of religion, and so forth. 'French subjects' included not only French people, but also ethnic migrants such as the Lao, the Cambodian and the Vietnamese who migrated into Siam under French control (Khumsupha 2010, 78–79; Fabre 2007, 4–5, n.3–5).[8]

The transformation of the urban landscape in Bangkok

From the 1860s to 1890s, the rapid colonial modernization of Bangkok transformed the urban landscape and provided an improved modern infrastructure. This speeded up domestic and international travel, improved transportation for trade and provided far more residential and commercial space for British and French subjects, other Westerners and the Chinese. A new network of roads replaced canals throughout central Bangkok. As early as 1861 Jaroen Krung Road (literally, 'modern/new city road' aka 'New Road'), was constructed (Sathienkoset 2003, 18; Wongthes 2005, 186–192), replacing the canal that had cut through the heart of the Ban Thawai area. It enabled commuters to travel easily from central Bangkok to the port in Ban Thawai where ships from Kwangtung (China) and Singapore docked (The Ministry of Police Officer 1905; Wongthes 2005, 139–141; Phraphromvachirayan 2006, 59). In subsequent decades, the modernization of Jaroen Krung Road and its extension to join the new Sathon Road (aka Poh Yom Road), created a new modern centre for commercial buildings and banks, Western hospitals, European clubs, Christian churches and bi- and multi-lingual schools. Sathon Road has remained the prime area for commercial buildings and banks (Khumsupha 2010, 65–96; Sathienkoset 2003, 102–104).

In the late nineteenth century, the river side of Jaroen Krung Road was the location for dynamic interactions between Westerners, the Siamese and several ethnic minorities. Located there were Western consulates (British, French, German, Danish, Portuguese for example), a major Bangkok port serving trade and international travel, the British-supported and influential Christ Church, the royal Thai temple Wat Yannawa, the Lao temple Wat Lao, the bilingual school Assumption College, residential accommodation for Westerners and ethnic migrants and the famous European graveyard, the Bangkok Protestant Cemetery. On this side of the road, the Chinese and Thawai provided the most dense population, while other main settlers included Westerners, Indians, Lao, Chinese and others. On the city side the Thawai were the most densely settled, with other major ethnic groups including Mon, Burmese, Chinese and European settlers (Sathienkoset 2003, 106–107). On this side of the road were two important temples: the long established Thawai temple, Wat Don Thawai and the Burmese temple, Wat Thung Kula. They were surrounded by fields, the Western-supported St Louis Hospital, the new buildings of Assumption College, a shopping centre and the Chinese graveyard.

Jaroen Krung ('New') Road was one of the most significant in Bangkok for three major reasons. Firstly, it became the locale with the highest population of multi-ethnic migrants and travellers living together and was thus the major point of contact between Westerners, the Siamese and Tai-Burmese-Lao and Chinese migrants. Most British subjects migrated into Ban Thawai in the 1880s, especially after Burma lost independence to Britain in 1886. According to official statistics, in 1894, the total population of Bangkok was approximately 169,000, comprising

93,000 Thai; 23,000 Chinese (Singaporean and mainland Chinese); 10,000 British subjects (British, Indian, Thawai, Shan, Burmese, etc.); 6,000 French subjects; and 300 other Westerners (Khumsupha 2010, 79). The Thawai population was around 1000–2000 people.[9]

Secondly, the transformation of the urban landscape started on both sides of Jaroen Krung Road in the early 1860s and continued until the early twentieth century, when most of central Bangkok was reached by the new roads throughout. Thirdly, the area became the centre for the British and French governors to exert political, educational and economic control over their immigrant subjects. The consulates in Ban Thawai became the most significant political centres of both the British and the French. As the Treaties allowed the British and French governors to exercise ultimate control over their subjects, we can observe in Ban Thawai a high level of complex relationship and competition between the British, the French and the Siamese. Wat Don Thawai and Wat Thung Kula, serving the Tai and Burmese Buddhist communities, came under British and to a lesser extent Thawai-Siamese alliance support and control. Wat Lao, serving the Lao community, was under French control, its activities supported by the French and Siamese. The royal Siamese temple Wat Yannawa, serving Siamese, Chinese and some Thawai, was under Siamese control and support. In the educational sphere, this area became the modern centre for bilingual English–Thai—and sometimes multilingual, including French or Spanish (or even more)—education. Modern bilingual education was provided by Christian missionaries, European travellers and settlers at Assumption College, at Western supported churches and at Buddhist temples including Wat Don Thawai, Wat Yannawa and Wat Lao. New medical technologies were available at the St. Louis and other Western hospitals in the area and a new generation of Siamese doctors learned about Western methods of treatment that became increasingly popularized.[10]

Migration, mid-1880s to early 1900s

In the mid- to late-nineteenth century, the migration of Tai, Lao and Chinese people into the Ban Thawai area occurred mainly for economic reasons. The Anglo-Thai Company (previous names: Mitsakalak Saw Mills, Siam Forest Company) founded in the mid-nineteenth century by Max R. West (alternative name: Fred S. Clark), employed local Thawai, Chinese and other ethnic immigrants. In the late nineteenth century, under G. M. B. Cohen, the company's name was changed to Bombay Burmah Trading as the company rapidly expanded into teak, sawmills and other related enterprises in Ban Thawai, Chiangmai, Kengtung and Burma (Sathienkoset 2003, 19–21, 102).[11] Due to rapid expansion, in the 1880s Bombay Burmah Trading was short of workers and so brought many Shan, Karen, Burmese and Lanna people to work in Bangkok. In addition to Bombay Burmah Trading, three other British companies were involved in the teak business employing Thawai, Shan, Karen, Burmese and Lanna people; namely British Borneo, Siam Forest and Louis T. Leonowens (Huabjareun 2008, 118–120).

Ranking second behind teak in importance was the export of rice. Markwald, the once-famous German company located in Ban Thawai also employed Chinese and Tai migrants (Sathienkoset 2003, 20–21). When the Briton David Williams was Assistant Director of the Siamese government's Department of Customs in Ban Thawai, the Department also employed British, Siamese, Thawai and Mon staff (Sathienkoset 2003, 93, 121–124).

The peak time for migration of Tai, Burmese and Lao people into and out of Ban Thawai was the mid-1880s to early 1900s. The first factor to speed up such migration was the British-supported construction of railways in the mid- to late-1880s from north and northeast Siam to Bangkok. The British company Panchard MacTaggart Lother helped plan the network of railways and the first line from Chiangmai and Chiangrai in the north to Rama IV Road (Bangkok) was constructed in 1887. In 1890, the line from Nakon Ratchasima to Rama IV Road was constructed.[12] Since there were now trains linking the north and northeast to Rama IV Road, which was connected to Sathon Road and only two kilometres from Jaroen Krung Road, the whole trip from Kengtung, Chiangmai and Lao to Sathon Road and Jaroen Krung Road became easy and convenient. The journey became even easier after 1902 with new British-constructed road and rail links from Kengtung and other Shan states to Chiangmai (Sawangsri 2009, 48–50). By the early 1900s it took a day to travel from Kengtung to Bangkok, a journey which in the 1870s had taken up to three months by boat or elephant.[13]

The construction of railways brought a political advantage to the British, French and Siamese authorities who could easily check the identity of travellers intending to cross borders. From the mid-1880s onwards, identity checks took place at international train stations before departure and after arrival (Sathienkoset 2003, 101).[14] As Britain attempted to tighten control over its subjects, it sought to prevent them crossing borders without permission. Most Tai-Burmese migrants needed, as British subjects, to register at either the Kengtung or Chiangmai consulates before coming to Bangkok, as well as registering after arriving in Bangkok.[15]

Royal marriages

Another important factor that contributed to migration as well as to strengthening relations between Siam and Mon, Lanna and Kengtung, was the marriage relationship between the royal courts of Siam and elsewhere. In the 1850s, the Mon Princess Jaojom Son Klin (1835–1925) migrated to Bangkok and became a wife to King Mongkut. In the late nineteenth century, five other Mon migrants; On, Eam, Erb, Arb and Eun, became wives of King Chulalongkorn and thus part of the Siamese royal family. From the 1850s to early 1900s, these Mon wives of Mongkut and Chulalongkorn played an important role in promoting Mon culture and supporting Mon communities in both Bangkok and Samutprakarn, the two largest places of Mon settlement (Kasetsiri and Banjun 2008, 32–87).

From the 1880s to early 1900s, the Siamese palace also made strategic royal marriages to tighten its control over the Lanna region, a vassal state to Siam, and to strengthen its relations with Kengtung with the help of Lanna governors (Charoenmuang 1999, 2–13). In 1883, the 10 year old Princess Dararatsamee, a daughter of Inthavichayanon, the last governor of Lanna/Chiangmai, was engaged to King Chulalongkorn. In 1886, Chulalongkorn asked Inthavichayanon to send Princess Dararatsamee to settle in Bangkok and serve the Siamese court. From then until 1908 Dararatsamee was not allowed to visit Chiangmai and in the late 1880s she became a wife to Chulalongkorn. In 1897, when Inthavichayanon passed away, Lanna became integrated into Siam (Charoenmuang 1999, 9–11). Having Dararatsamee as a wife enabled Chulalongkorn to easily centralize economic, political and religious power in Lanna.

Due to the significant political role of Inthavichayanon and Princess Dararatsamee in both Chiangmai and the Tai-Burmese regions, the British Queen Victoria had made attempts to establish a direct relationship with them, thus competing with the influence of the Siamese court. Although Chulalongkorn managed to have Dararatsamee as one of his wives, he had to challenge British power to do so. Queen Victoria had written directly to Dararatsamee requesting that she become her daughter-in-law under her direct patronage, instead of being engaged to Chulalongkorn (Huabjareun 2008, 120–122).

Lanna's integration into Siam meant that many ex-Lanna people became legally Siamese and could readily travel to Bangkok for work without concern about identity checks. In the religious sphere, after the promulgation of the 1902 Sangha Act, senior Thammayut monks were sent to Chiangmai, Chiangrai and Lamphun in order to work towards the nationalizing—spreading—of the centralized/Bangkok identity. At the same time, many ex-Lanna Siamese monks were recruited into the national Sangha for administrative and educational work. Some remained in the north of Siam, others migrated to central Siam and Bangkok and a few switched affiliation to the Thammayut order. So, as part of Siamese centralization during the early 1900s we can see the increasingly rapid speed of monastic migration from the north to Bangkok and vice versa (Charoenmuang 1999, 10–13).

Family relations between the Siamese courts and Kengtung courts were established indirectly through intermarriages between members of the Lanna and Kengtung royalty from the 1880s to 1930s. In the 1910s, Princess Thada of Lanna was married to Prince Suwansongkhram of Kengtung. In 1932 Princess Sukhantha, a daughter of Inthalang (ruler of Kengtung), was married to Prince Inthanon of Chiangmai.[16] In the early 1930s, Princess Thipawan of Lanna was married to Prince Sirisuwan of Kengtung (Sakda 2005, 43–52). Princess Dararatsamee and other Lanna royalty played an important role in maintaining the strong relationship between Siam and Kengtung, and intermarriages between the courts of Kengtung and Lawksawk helped Siam maintain good relations with Lawksawk. In 1921 Hkun Has, Prince of Lawksawk, was married to Ven Kio, Princess of Kengtung (Sawangsri 2009, 95). With British support and through their good relationship, the Kengtung ruler and the Siamese government agreed to allow many Shan people, subject to the approval of the British authorities in Kengtung, to settle in Bangkok to work for British companies. In the religious sphere, the diplomatic relationship between Siam and Shan and their joint support for Buddhist monks gave privileged status to Tai monks to cross borders and travel to Bangkok. While identity checks at train stations were strict for lay travellers, this was not the case for monks.

The events documented above illustrate the British and Siamese political alliance and a degree of competition between them to exert influence and gain advantage within Siamese territories and beyond Siam's borders. Both were attempting to consolidate their power in the region.

Tai-Burmese-Lao Buddhist communities at four important temples in Ban Thawai under British-Siamese support and control

Political control of temples

In Ban Thawai, the British governors had in principle ultimate control over the monastic communities at Wat Don Thawai and Wat Don Kula while the French governors controlled Wat Lao and the Siamese government Wat Yannawa. In practice, the British and French governors would consult and co-operate with the Sangharat (the Supreme Patriach) or a high-ranking Siamese monk from the area. In most cases, the abbot of Wat Yannawa headed the monastic hierarchy in Ban Thawai District. For example, in 1911, Jan Janthasaro, the Thawai abbot of Wat Don Thawai, was in conflict with Min Ong, the Burmese abbot of Wat Thung Kula. To resolve the problem a committee headed by British governor Morris and the Sangharat Prince Vachirayan took responsibility for considering the case (Phraphrommoli 2009, 91–105).

Under the authority exercised by the local British governor in Bangkok, the British authorities had the power to control British subjects with the help of the Siamese authorities. In the case of Tai and Burmese migrants, authorities based in the Tai-Burmese home region would usually send local leaders to be stationed in the Ban Thawai area to ensure local control of their own ethnic community. In turn, these local leaders in Ban Thawai would appoint the abbot of the temple. Where communities did not have their own temples, the Shan and Burmese, for example, monks of those ethnicities had to stay at Wat Ban Thawai, as indeed Dhammaloka did. Local community leaders would appoint a senior monk from their own community as the head monk of its own local monastic community in the area (Sawangsri 2009, 35–36).

At Wat Don Thawai (present name: Wat Barom Sathon; previous names: Wat Don and Wat Ban Thawai), the Thawai monk 'Jan Janthasaro' was abbot of the temple from the 1880s until 1919. The temple was established under the royal patronage of King Rama I (r. 1782–1809) by the first Thawai migrants into the Ban Thawai area during his reign.[17] From then, until the late 1920s, the abbot was always Thawai, appointed by the 'Jangvang', the local leader of the Thawai (Sathienkoset

2003, 14). Due to the Siamese government's support of the Jangvang, in the early twentieth century the Siamese palace supported the Jangvang and gave honorific titles to each Jangvang.[18] From the late eighteenth to early twentieth centuries, there were regular contacts between the Thawai community in Ban Thawai and the Thawai people residing in their homeland on the Burma – Siam border in the West of Siam. Most Thawai migrants in Ban Thawai either came to Bangkok in the late eighteenth century under Siamese control or, from the 1880s onwards, under British control. Ultimate authority over Wat Don Thawai hence shifted from the Siamese to the British in the late nineteenth century. Monks from other ethnic origins who took either lifelong or short-term residence at Wat Don Thawai included Burmese, Mon and Shan monks, mostly after Burma lost its independence in 1886 and before the 1910s when the Siamese Sangha attempted to centralize Bangkok identity and so limited the migration of Tai-Burmese monks into Siam. The abbots of Wat Don Thawai were Thawai monks from the late eighteenth century until 1919. In 1919, the Sangharat Pae Tissatheva appointed the Siamese monk Kuen (Phrakhru Kanlaya) to become abbot (Sathienkoset 2003, 122).[19]

Another important temple in the area, Wat Yannawa (previous names: Wat Khok Kwai and Wat Khok Krabue) is located on Jaroen Krung Road, next to the Bangkok Dock, and a short walk from Wat Don Thawai and Wat Don Kula. Wat Yannawa was a Siamese temple under royal patronage and throughout its history the abbots were always royalist monks of Siamese ethnic origin.[20] Wat Yannawa played a leading role in maintaining Bangkok/centralized Siamese Buddhist identity, that is teaching in central Thai language, organizing centralized forms of Buddhist ritual and promoting Pali study for monks (Sathienkoset 2003, 42 – 44).[21] Its abbots had authority over all monks in the Ban Thawai area who were not British and French subjects. The abbots of Wat Yannawa also acted as consultants for British and French officers in relation to monastic disputes and other matters amongst the Tai, Burmese and Lao communities in Ban Thawai. As indicated above, in serious disputes the abbots of the royal Wat Yannawa and/or higher ranked monks in Bangkok (in some cases, the Supreme Patriarch) acted on the committee with the British governor.

Finally, Wat Lao (present name: Wat Sutthivararam) was another important temple. Located less than a kilometre further down from Wat Yannawa along Jaroen Krung Road, it was near the French consulate in the Ban Thawai area and under French control. Many Western consulates were located between Wat Yannawa and Wat Lao. Wat Lao provided Buddhist activities for the local Lao and Siamese. The abbots of Wat Lao were Lao monks until the 1910s and, thereafter, Siamese monks became the abbots.

Unexpected fruits of this control

Under British, French and Siamese support the Thawai, Burmese, Mon, Shan and Lao ethnic minorities had their own Buddhist activities organized at each temple. Until the 1920s, each of these temples could to a large extent preserve the cultural identity of each ethnic minority since they had Tai, Burmese and Lao abbots and monks. At Wat Don Thawai, the Thawai monks taught their Thawai supporters in Thawai language. On Songkran, New Year's Day, the temple organized traditional Thawai Buddhist activities including the morning offering of 1000 *khao-pan-khata-phan* rice, building up a small model of a sand-made stupa, *mahājāti* (ritual preaching), etc. On important days, the Thawai would perform the practice of worshiping Yay Wat (literally, 'grandmas of the temple'), the female divine ancestors of the Thawai ethnic migrants. Thawai food such as *yam thawai* ('Thawai spicy salad') was available on some festival days. After the Lent period, there was a traditional *mahājāti* teaching.[22] The Burmese, Mon, Shan and Lao monks also taught their supporters in their own languages. This differed from the teaching of monks in most other temples in Bangkok, which was delivered in the central Thai language. From the 1930s onwards, each of these temples acquired Thai abbots and the teachings in other languages in public were replaced by central Thai language, apart from personal communication on an individual level.

The sacred objects that still remain in these temples indicate how the Buddhist identity of ethnic minorities contrasts with that of the Bangkok/centralized Siamese. For example, Wat Don Thawai to this day has Buddha statues and other sacred objects in its main *Ubosot* (prayer room), whose characteristics are different from central Thai, and at the gate of Wat Don Thawai there is still a sacred statue of the Thawai leader. The Thawai community had a traditional ceremony of worshipping their own ancestors, especially those whom they believed to be their national or local heroes.[23] The Thawai ceremony for worshipping their ancestors was similar to Chinese practice but differed from central Thai practice.

In its socio-political aspect, the combination of British, French and Siamese support allowed the lay leaders and abbots of ethnic minorities to enjoy some freedom to control their communities. The Thawai, Burmese and Lao abbots had the power to administer Wat Don Thawai, Wat Thung Kula and Wat Lao. As a consequence of British or French support of these temples, the Siamese Sangha could not directly intervene in religious affairs at these temples without the permission of the British or French governors. Unlike most other temples in Bangkok, including Wat Yannawa, that were strictly under the control of the Siamese Sangha, the abbots of these ethnic minority temples did not have to follow the centralized 1902 Sangha Act and the Siamese Sangha's policies.

The presence of European missionaries and settlers in Ban Thawai brought substantial educational benefits to local Tai, Burmese, Lao and Chinese migrants. According to Sathienkoset, whose writing was based on personal observation of his childhood during the early 1900s, the majority of English teachers in the area of Ban Thawai were French, Spanish or Irish rather than British, and most of them either were Christian missionaries or helped Christian missionaries to teach local people in the area (Sathienkoset 2003, 337–341). The only important group of British teachers in the area comprised the Christian missionaries at Christ Church, under the leadership of Rev. Canon William Greenstock, from 1894 to the early 1900s.[24] U Dhammaloka and Greenstock were worlds apart religiously but they were close neighbours in Ban Thawai and in respect of education and temperance it seems they held very similar ideals. The work of Christian missionaries in teaching local people, especially in multi-ethnic communities, was seen not only in Ban Thawai but also in many other places in Burma.[25]

On 2 May 1903, Wat Don Thawai school (present name: Wat Don Bilingual School or Wat Don School) became the first Buddhist bilingual English–Thai free school in Siam on record. The pioneer Irish monk U Dhammaloka, ordained in Burma in 1900, played a leading role in establishing the school (Bocking 2010, 248). Recent research by Brian Bocking, Alicia Turner and Laurence Cox suggests that from at least 1900–1902, Dhammaloka was residing as a monk in a Thawai monastery in Rangoon (the Tavoy monastery in Godwin Road) and that he came to stay at Wat Ban Thawai in Bangkok from February to September 1903. During this period, Dhammaloka established a bilingual school and taught local residents in the area (Bocking 2010, 246–254.). In his account of the school, Bocking said 'it seems unlikely that the school survived for long without Dhammaloka', but in fact it still exists today, with only a few years interruption in its work between the early 1920s and 1932.[26] The establishment of this bilingual school is highly significant at a national level in its educational aspect because it was the first time that English was taught at a Buddhist temple in Siam and at that time only a very few of the Siamese elite would have a chance to learn English (Choompolpaisal 2011, 134–135). The Wat Don Thawai School was only the fourth or fifth such bilingual school in the country. Wattana School (Presbyterian) was the first in 1874, the Assumption School (Catholic) the second in 1887; Bangkok Christian High School (present name: Krungthep Christian) the third in 1888; and a possible fourth in the late1890s/early 1900s was the School of Christ Church (Sukhum 2005, 77–80; Suriya and Buasri 2005, 53).

Despite the significance of the establishment of Buddhist bilingual education at Wat Don Thawai, there is limited reporting of such education in Thai sources. This may be because the Siamese government's nationalization of Thai identity has for many decades had an impact on Siamese authors' representation of the Thawai people's history and presence in Ban Thawai.[27] The fact that Dhammaloka's time in Siam has yet to be mentioned in any Thai material may be due to his role being connected to, and actually supportive of, the Thawai in both Burma and Bangkok.[28]

Wat Don School (Figure 1) is nowadays a two-storeyed building. It was part of, and located within, the boundary of Wat Don Thawai until the 1940s. In the 1950s a new boundary wall was constructed to set the school apart from the temple. In 1932, the duty of looking after the school shifted from the abbot of Wat Don Thawai to a lay Director (Wat Don School 2007, 23).

In 1904, one year after Dhammaloka opened his bilingual Buddhist school at Wat Don Thawai, the royal temple of Wat Yannawa became the second institution to offer a bilingual Buddhist education. Christian missionaries and Western volunteers taught English there to Chinese, Thawai and others.[29] In 1911, Wat Lao School (present name: Suttivararam School) provided trilingual education—French, English

FIGURE 1

Sign outside the Wat Don (formerly Wat Ban Thawai) bilingual school founded by the Irish Buddhist U Dhammaloka in 1903. The design incorporates (top right) the letters A and Z and (top left) the corresponding first and last Thai letters ก ko and ฮ ho. The letters are supported by a chalice (of knowledge) held by cupped hands. Photo: Phibul Choompolpaisal, 2012.

and Thai—for Lao residents in the area. Sometime after the First World War it discontinued French provision, but retained English and Thai.[30]

We can see that the setting up of bilingual or trilingual Buddhist education schools, adopting the model of bilingual education taught in Christian Churches from the 1880s to 1900s, became popularized in the Ban Thawai area and benefited local citizens from 1903 to the 1910s. In the 1930s, Satree Sri Suriyothai School was built in the area to provide bilingual education for female students and much later, when in 1968 the Mon established their own temple Wat Prok near Wat Don Thawai, bilingual education was also taught there.[31]

Conclusion

In this account we have seen the playing out of mutual influences between regional and colonizing nations and the unexpected effects on local ethnic Buddhist communities in the Ban Thawai area. The dynamic interaction of three interests, Siam, Britain and 'the Thawai', is demonstrated through the physical development of the Ban Thawai locale. This area became the crucible for the modernization and commercialization of Bangkok, in large part through provision of space for 'British subjects' from colonized ethnic communities in Burma and elsewhere. Migration to Ban Thawai resulted in larger and diversified Buddhist communities of multi-ethnic groups flourishing under joint British, Siamese and local Thawai control. At the same time, both Siam and Britain were able to exercise political control in the region and Tai, Burmese and Lao communities were successfully established within the modernized Thai context.

While Britain did not colonize Siam, it nevertheless was able, through the co-operative arrangements described here, to extend its control of 'British subjects' into Siamese sovereign territory, to maximize the commercial advantage it had gained from its control of Upper Burma through improved infrastructure links through Siamese territory and to obtain a competitive advantage over the French. These arrangements also allowed better control of Britain's own colonial subjects both at home (in Burma) and abroad (in Siam), simultaneously undermining autonomous Siamese political control within Bangkok. At a Southeast Asian regional level, the alliance between the British, the Siamese and the Tai-Burmese-Lao migrants allowed the British to maximize their power over both their Burmese subjects and their European political and business rivals, especially the French and to a lesser extent the Germans, throughout most of Siam and Burma.

Siam itself strove for a balance of colonial presence that would preserve its own existence, free from major colonial interference. Both France and Britain sought and obtained concessions within Siamese territorial and commercial interests, but within the same framework Siam was able also to work to centralize and strengthen its country by the imposition of centralized administration, education and religion. Control of ethnic minority groups was from the Siamese point of view advantageously shared with Britain, albeit at the price of the loss of some internal control, while threats from the French presence in Indochina were successfully kept at bay. At a national level, the Siamese government's tolerance of the locally ethnic forms of Buddhism enabled it to maintain good relationships with Tai-Burmese ethnic migrants into Siam while allowing the British to exert ultimate control over them. The British–Siamese alliance that had developed by the time Dhammaloka arrived in Bangkok in 1903 was able to establish diplomatic relationships with Tai, Burmese and Lao ethnic migrants and use these relationships to centralize power at local, national and international levels.

Within Ban Thawai, the religious and educational activities of the local communities fostered cultural, religious and political links between the 'British subjects' Tai-Burmese in Ban Thawai and their homeland. Ethnic identities were thus preserved and a degree of local autonomy achieved within Ban Thawai itself; particularly freedom from full implementation of the 1902 Saṅgha Act. Eventually, this autonomy was lost with the imposition of Thai abbots in Ban Thawai temples. The Buddhist activities in Ban Thawai—led by important monastic travellers, including the Irish monk Dhammaloka and the lay leaders of Thawai, Shan and Mon states—played an important role, contributing to the strengthening of the links of each ethnic group across borders. Local ethnic Buddhist identities could be protected against the most extreme effects of the 'nationalised' Siamese Buddhist identity promoted by the emerging centralized Siamese state.

ACKNOWLEDGEMENTS

The initial version of this paper was presented at the Conference *SE Asia as a Crossroads for Buddhist Exchange: Pioneer European Buddhists and Asian Buddhist Networks 1860 – 1960* hosted by the Study of Religions Department, University College Cork, Ireland, 13–15 September 2012 and funded by the Dhammakaya International Society of the United Kingdom as part of the 2012 postdoctoral fellowship 'Continuities and Transitions in early Modern Thai Buddhism'.

NOTES

1. Until the early twentieth century, the area was also called Khok Kwai and Otiachia, the latter used by Chinese ethnic migrants and referring to 'Ban Phung Dam', meaning 'the accommodation of those who have black stomachs'. For more see Sathienkoset (2003, 13). The influential, prolific Thai author Sathienkoset (Phrayaanumanratchthon) (1888–1969) grew up in Ban Thawai and lived there from 1888 until the mid-1950s. Sathienkoset (2003) is the fourth edition of Sathienkoset's writing, first published in 1957. The oral history component of his writing reflects his own experience and observation of the area.
2. For consistency of transliteration, this article mainly employs the 'Royal Thai General System of Transcription'. So, while most academics would write 'Tavoy', I transcribe it as 'Thawai' here and hereafter.

3. See Note 2.
4. This article covers mainly the period 1850–1920 and the country's name was officially changed from 'Siam' to 'Thailand' only in 1939, so I use the name 'Siam' throughout.
5. After World War II and the withdrawal of the French and British, these territories would become parts of the newly independent neighbouring countries, Cambodia, Laos and the Union of Burma. Siam lost several territories to France in 1893, 1904, 1906 and 1907, and to Britain in 1892 and 1908. These pieces of land later belonged to Lao, Burma and Malaysia.
6. For the detail of the Treaty see Bowring (1857). I wish to give special thanks to Ms. Boonyarat Deadson for her help during August 2012 in reading Thai material on all the British and French Treaties from the mid-1850s to 1890s.
7. See also http://www.anglicanthai.org/historythai.htm (accessed February 9, 2013).
8. For the detail of Harris Park Treaty and the Diplomatic Treaty between France and Siam, see Ministry of Foreign Affairs (1968, 35–46, 57–70).
9. This figure of 1000–2000 Thawai people is based on my calculation, confirmed by an interview—the total number of British subjects was 10,000 (of which Malays 1,800, Indians 700, several thousand Singaporean Chinese and several hundred British). This leaves us with the number of other British subjects as 3000–4000 including Thawai, Mon, Burmese and others. Since amongst these ethnic minorities the Thawai had the highest population, I speculate that the number of Thawai people is at least 1000 but not more than 3000. Somphong Wongsangam, an 82 year old ex-monk lay supporter of Wat Don Thawai in an interview on 29 December 2011 informed me that the population of Thawai surrounding Wat Don Thawai was around 300–500 in the early 1900s and, in total, in Ban Thawai there would be over 1000 Thawai people in the area at that time. Somphong has lived his entire life in the area and is a competent witness to the community here. His knowledge is based on oral tradition and personal experience.
10. In part I am drawing on public and tourist information signage for information. On the increasing uptake of Western medicine in the nineteenth century, see Sukhum (2005, 10–11).
11. For details of Bombay Burmah Trading's business in Chiangmai, see also Ian Bushell's (2012) Merchants and Missionaries—Western Incursions into Lanna between 1829 and 1921, presentation paper (May 22, 2012). Some of these ethnic migrants migrated into Siam as early as the Ayutthaya period; the majority arrived in Siam during the reign of King Chulalongkorn.
12. www.railway.co.th/home/srt/about/history.asp (accessed February 9, 2013)
13. Bushell (2012) Merchants and Missionaries – Western Incursions into Lanna between 1829 and 1921, presentation paper (May 22, 2012).
14. See also www.railway.co.th/home/srt/about/history.asp (accessed February 9, 2013)

15. It is specified in Article 5 that each British subject needs to report to the British officers at the nearest consulate both before leaving and after arriving at their destination (see above).
16. http://www.lannaworld.com/cgi/lannaboard/reply_topic.php?id = 15149 (accessed February 9, 2013).
17. Learning Resources Relating to the Construction and Refurbishment of Wat Don, Yannawa, Bangkok-Thonburi City. [บรรณสารการสร้าง และปฏิสังขรณ์ วัดดอน ยานนาวา นครหลวงกรุงเทพธนบุรี]. No publisher's detail. Wat Don publication (n.d. 1–10).
18. Wat Don publication (n.d. 1–10). The second Jangvang in the early twentieth century, ruling the Thawai from the 1910s to 1920s, was a close friend of Sathienkoset, whose writings I use here.
19. See also Wat Don Publication (n.d. 7–10).
20. Wat Yannawa publication (n.d. 7–8, 26–30).
21. Wat Yannawa publication (n.d. 22–25).
22. Interview with Somphong (29 December 2011) and Sathienkoset (2003, 106–107).
23. Interview with Somphong (29 December 2011) and Sathienkoset (2003, 106–107).
24. http://www.anglicanthai.org/historythai.htm. For Greenstock's life, see McFarland (1999, 207–208).
25. For example, in 1928 there were 40 churches in the Thawai-Mergui area in Burma. Most of these churches offered English language classes. This information is taken from *Sixty-third Annual Report. Burma Baptist Missionary Convention*, page 44 (no detail of author). It records the meeting held in Tavoy in October 26–28, 1928.
26. Wat Don School publication (2007, 18–23) and interview with Somphong (December 29, 2011).
27. For the issue of the impact of the Siamese politics of centralization on the authors' under-representation of non-centralized and non-Thai identity and view, see Choompolpaisal (2011, 134–153).
28. During fieldwork from March to May 2012, I reviewed Thai books which discuss Western Buddhist monks. Not a single Thai source mentions Dhammaloka. For a further detailed analysis of Dhammaloka's role in relation to the Thawai ethnic minorities, see Choompolpaisal (in preparation).
29. Wat Yannawa publication (n.d. 28–29); and interview with Somphong (29 December 2011).
30. Interview with Somphong (December 29, 2011). In part I am drawing on public and tourist information signage for information.
31. Interview with Somphong (December 29, 2011) and interview with anonymous Mon monk residing at Wat Prok (April 25, 2012).

REFERENCES

Material in Thai

CHAROENMUANG, TANET [ธเนศวร์ เจริญเมือง]. 1999 [2542BE]. *100 Years of Siamese-Lanna Relations 1899–1999 [100 ปี สายสัมพันธ์สยาม-ล้านนา พศ 2442–2542]*. Chiangmai [เชียงใหม่]: Local Government Studies Project, Faculty of Social Sciences, Chiangmai University [โครงการศึกษาการปกครองท้องถิ่น คณะสังคมศาสตร์ มหาวิทยาลัยเชียงใหม่].

FABRE, SUNANTA [สุนันท าฟาเบรอ]. 2007. Siam in the Press of France During the Reign of King Rama IV ["สยามในสิ่งพิมพ์ของฝรั่งเศสสมัยรัชกาลที่ 4"/ Le Siam du règne de Rama IV dans la Presse française]., Paper presented at Mae Fah Luang University (no date).

HUABJAREUN, LAMJUL [ลำจุล ฮวบเจริญ]. 2008 [2551BE]. *When the Shadow of Imperialism Casts Over Siam and Lanna According to Our Memory [เมื่อเงาจักรวรรดินิยมปกคลุมสยาม และล้านนา ในความทรงจำ]*. Bangkok [กรุงเทพ]: The Knowledge Centre [เดอะโนเลดจ์เซ็นเตอร์].

KASETSIRI, CHARNVIT, and BANJUN [ชาญวิทย์ เกษตรศิริ และองค์ บรรจุน], ONG, eds. 2008 [2551 BE]. *The Mons in Siam (Thailand): Race, Role and Lessons [มอญในสยาม ประเทศ (ไทย): ชนชาติ บทบาท และบทเรียน]*. Bangkok [กรุงเทพ]: Foundation for the Promotion of Social Sciences and Humanities Textbooks Project [มูลนิธิโครงการตำราสังคมศาสตร์ และ มนุษยศาสตร์].

MINISTRY OF FOREIGN AFFAIRS [กระทรวงการต่างประเทศ]. 1968 [2511 BE]. *Bilateral Treaties and Agreements between Thailand and Foreign Countries and International Organizations (Vol.1 1817–1869) [สนธิสัญญา และความตกลงทวิภาคี ระหว่างประเทศไทยกับต่างประเทศ และองค์กรระหว่างประเทศ (เล่ม 1 พ.ศ. 2360–2412)]*.

THE MINISTRY OF POLICE OFFICER [กระทรวงนครบาล]. 1905 [2448 BE]. *The 1903 Thai Maritime Act [พระราชบัญญัติเดินเรือน่านน้ำสยาม ร.ศ. 124]*. Phranakorn [พระนคร]: Bamrungnukit Press [โรงพิมพ์บำรุงนุกูลกิจ].

PHRAPHROMMOLI, (VILASYANAVARO) [พระพรหมโมลี (วิลาศญาณวโร)]. 2009 [2552 BE]. *Revealing the Legend of Wat Don [เปิดตำนานวัดดอน]*. Bangkok [กรุงเทพ]: Animate Print and Design [อะนิเมทพรินท์แอนด์ดีไซน์].

Phraphromvachirayan [พระพรหมวชิรญาณ]. 2006 [2549 BE]. *Phraphromvachirayan and His Religious Activities in the Year 2006 CE [พระพรหมวชิรญาณกับศาสนกิจ ปี 2549]*, Special publication on the special occasion of the 70th year birthday of Phraphromvachirayan, the abbot of Wat Yannawa, Bangkok.

SAKDA, PHARADON [ภราดร ศักดา]. 2005 [2548BE]. *Letters from the Shan States, the Kingdom of 19 Princes [จดหมายจากรัฐฉาน แผ่นดิน 19 เจ้าฟ้า]*. Bangkok [กรุงเทพ]: Roso 229 Press [สำนักพิมพ์ รศ 229].

SATHIENKOSET, (PHRAYAANUMANRATCHATHON) [เสฐียรโกเศศ (พระยาอนุมานราชธน)]. 2003 [2546BE]. *Reviving the Past Events, Book No.1 [ฟื้นความหลัง เล่ม 1]*. Bangkok [กรุงเทพ]: Sayam Press [สำนักพิมพ์ศยาม], 4th ed. First edition published in 1967 [2510 BE].

SAWANGSRI, KANOK-ORN [กนกอรสว่างศรี]. 2009 [2552 BE]. *Socio-Economic and Cultural Changes under the British Rule 1886–1948 [รัฐฉานกับการเปลี่ยนแปลงทางเศรษฐกิจ*

สังคม และ วัฒนธรรม ภายใต้การปกครองของอังกฤษ คศ 1886–1948], Master diss., Faculty of History, Silapakorn University, Thailand.

SUKHUM, PRASONG [ประสงค์ สุขุม] 2005 [2548BE]. 150 Years: From the Chinese Commual Area to the Groups of Missionaries and Education in Thailand. [150 ปี จากกุฎีจีนถึงประมวล มิชชันนารี กับการศึกษาไทย] Bangkok [กรุงเทพ]: Chulalongkorn University Press [สำนักพิมพ์แห่งจุฬาลงกรณ์มหาวิทยาลัย].

SURIYA, SRINAT, and SIRI BUASRI, SIRI [ศรีนาถ สุริยะ และ ศิริ บัวศรี]. 2005 [2548BE]. "Madam Cole Who Did Pioneering Work on the Reform of Female Education in Thailand" ["แหม่มโคล ผู้ริเริ่มการปฏิรูปการศึกษาสตรีไทย] Recollecting the Virtue of Ms Edna S. Cole; The 150 Years of the Establishment of Wattana Vitthayalay [รำลึกพระคุณ มิสเอ็ดน่า เอส. โคล ๑๕๐ ปี การก่อตั้งวัฒนาวิทยาลัย]. Bangkok [กรุงเทพ]: The Students of Wanglang-Wattana Association [สมาคมศิษย์วังหลัง-วัฒนา].

WAT DON PUBLICATION [เอกสารตีพิมพ์วัดดอน]. no detail of published year. Learning Resources Relating to the Construction and Refurbishment of Wat Don, Yannawa, Bangkok-Thonburi City. [บรรณสารการสร้าง และปฏิสังขรณ์ วัดดอน ยานนาวา นครหลวงกรุงเทพธนบุรี]. No publisher's detail.

WAT DON SCHOOL [โรงเรียนวัดดอน] 2007 [2550 BE]. Book in the Commemoration of the 75 Years of Wat Don School. [หนังสือที่ระลึก 75 ปี โรงเรียนวัดดอน]. No publication detail.

WAT YANNAWA PUBLICATION [เอกสารตีพิมพ์วัดยานนาวา]. no detail of published year. A History of Wat Yannawa [ประวัติวัดยานนาวา]. No publication detail.

WONGTHES, SUJIT [สุจิตต์ วงษ์เทศ] 2005. *Bangkok: A Historical Background*. [กรุงเทพ มาจากไหน] Bangkok ["กรุงเทพ]: Ruen Kaew Kan Phim [เรือนแก้วการพิมพ์].

Material in English

BOCKING, BRIAN. 2010. 'A Man of Work and Few Words'? Dhammaloka Beyond Burma. *Contemporary Buddhism* 11 (2): 229–80.

BOWRING, JOHN. 1857. *The Kingdom and People of Siam: with a Narrative of the Mission to that Country in 1855*. London: John W. Parker.

BURMA BAPTIST MISSIONARY CONVENTION. 1929. *Sixty-third Annual Report. Burma Baptist Missionary Convention*. Report of the meeting held in Tavoy, October 26–28, 1928. Rangoon: American Baptist Mission Press.

BUSHELL, IAN. 2012. Merchants and Missionaries—Western Incursions into Lanna between 1829 and 1921. Paper presented May 22. Notes of this talk received from rels-tlc@groups.sas.upenn.edu

CHOOMPOLPAISAL, PHIBUL. 2011. *Reassessing Modern Thai Political Buddhism: A Critical Study of Sociological Literature from Weber to Keyes*, Ph.D. thesis, School of Oriental and African Studies, University of London.

CHOOMPOLPAISAL, PHIBUL. in preparation. Buddhisms of Tai-Burmese Ethnic Minorities in Ban Thawai (Bangkok) in the Mid 20th Century: Local Buddhisms and the International Politics of Tai, Burmese and Siam.

JUMSAI, MANICH. 1970a. *King Mongkut and Sir John Bowring*. Bangkok: Chalermnit.

JUMSAI, MANICH. 1970b. *History of Anglo-Thai Relations*. Bangkok: Chalermnit.

JUMSAI, MANICH. 1989. Buddhist Politics and Their Revolutionary Origins in Thailand. *International Political Science Review* 10 (2): 121–42.

KEYES, CHARLES. 1971. Buddhism and National Integration in Thailand. *Journal of Asian Studies* 30 (3): 551–67.

KEYES, CHARLES. 1977. Millennialism, Theravada Buddhism and Thai Society. *Journal of Asian Studies* 36 (2): 283–302.

KEYES, CHARLES. 1989. Buddhist Politics and Their Revolutionary Origins in Thailand. *International Political Science Review* 10 (2): 121–142.

KHUMSUPHA, MALINEE. 2010. Changing Bangkok 1855–1909: The Effects of European Settlers and Their Subjects. *Rian Thai: International Journal of Thai Studies* 3: 65–96.

LOOS, TAMARA. 2006. *Subject Siam: Family, Law, and Colonial Modernity in Thailand.* Ithaca, NY: Cornell University Press.

MCFARLAND, GEORGE BRADLEY, ed. 1999. *Historial Sketch of Protestant Missions in Siam 1828–1928.* Bangkok: Bangkok. [Originally published in October 1928 *by the Bangkok Time Press*].

THOMPSON, VIRGINIA. 1941. *Thailand: The New Siam*. New York: Macmillian.

RETHINKING EARLY WESTERN BUDDHISTS: BEACHCOMBERS, 'GOING NATIVE' AND DISSIDENT ORIENTALISM

Laurence Cox

Recent research on the life of U Dhammaloka and other early western Buddhists in Asia has interesting implications in relation to class, ethnicity and politics. 'Beachcomber Buddhists' highlight the wider situation of 'poor whites' in Asia—needed by empire but prone to defect from elite standards of behaviour designed to maintain imperial and racial power. 'Going native', exemplified by the European bhikkhu, highlights the difficulties faced by empire in policing these racial boundaries and the role of Asian agency in early 'western' Buddhism. Finally, such 'dissident Orientalism' has political implications, as with specifically Irish forms of solidarity with Asian anti-colonial movements. Within the limits imposed by the data, this article rethinks 'early western Buddhism' in Asia as a creative response to colonialism, shaped by Asian actors, marked by cross-racial solidarity and oriented to alternative possible futures beyond empire.

Introduction

Phr'a Kow-Tow and Marco Polo

We will almost certainly never know who the first western Buddhist monks were. One of the first *attested* cases is an Austrian jokingly known as 'Phr'a Kow-Tow', ordained in Bangkok on 8 July 1878.[1] This ordination was said to be partly for the requirements of work in the Siamese state[2] (Khantipalo 1979, 167–168) and partly to learn Pali (thus the *Straits Times*).

'Phr'a Kow-Tow' was hardly the first European to find himself in this situation: Colley (2000, 181) estimates that in the early *seventeenth* century as many as 5000 Europeans had been in the service of native rulers in South Asia alone—soldiers, technicians and the like. Obviously, many South and Southeast Asian rulers were not Buddhist and 'Kow-Tow's' situation was probably unusual (Alicia Turner, pers. comm.), but these numbers alone make it very likely that the first such ordination will not now be recoverable.

Conversion, of course, is not identical to ordination; and Europeans had long been present in Asia, not only as state employees:

> Economic disaster, poverty, religious bigotry, intolerance, oppression and lack of opportunity at home drove ambitious or disgruntled Europeans not only to Asia but to flee from their mother countries to neighbouring states... But no call was stronger or more insistent than that of the Orient. (Scammell 1992, 645)

Indeed, when Marco Polo arrived at the court of the Great Khan in 1275, he found Europeans from many countries already present (Hudson 1954, 300). No doubt such people, changing culture and starting families, sometimes transferred their religious loyalties in one form or another, while their children or grandchildren must sometimes have been brought up in local religions. As Sutin (2006) notes, from one perspective the first western Buddhists were Bactrian Greeks; at which point perhaps the concept appears as an artificial separation which rules out many everyday conversions or transitions of this kind.

If it is nonetheless worth paying attention to late nineteenth and early twentieth century *ordinations* in particular—and if we can follow them to some extent through newspaper reports—this is for two reasons. Firstly, European colonial presence in Buddhist Asia was increasingly extensive, and in the aftermath of the 1857 Revolt increasingly direct; in the imperial areas, racial boundaries (including those of intermarriage and religious affiliation) were increasingly tightly policed; and the colonizing mission was increasingly justified in religious terms (not least to secure popular support at home). Secondly, European Buddhist monks were increasingly visible, and perhaps increasingly problematic, within reforming and more centralized sanghas (Choompolpaisal 2013). The figures discussed here, then, are significant not so much for chronological reasons, but because as Buddhist monks in a time of increasing *boundaries* between Europeans and Asians they posed particular challenges to political and cultural power relations.

U Dhammaloka: a window into wider worlds

In most cases such figures are recorded only in the moment of their transition. U Dhammaloka's career is particularly well-attested because his Buddhist activism continued to thematize the challenge. In this sense, he is a window into wider worlds: unusual by definition, but indicating broader power relations which remain less visible in other western Buddhist experiences.

If the invisible and unrecoverable Europeans who settled down and perhaps converted to Buddhism in parts of early modern Asia were part of the 'flow that followed western penetration of the maritime economy of the East' (Scammell 1992, 641), the far more visible western Buddhists of this later period can be seen in a world-systems perspective (Hall 2000) as being thrown into sharp relief (and the historical record) by the construction of a new kind of global capitalism which brought them to Asia, tightened the boundaries which they nevertheless crossed and perhaps also provoked them to resist, in one way or another, this same process (Cox 2013). This article discusses three dimensions of this later experience.

Firstly, it looks at social *class*, and 'beachcomber Buddhists' (Turner, Cox and Bocking 2010) such as Dhammaloka. It proposes that we should see such conversions as the result of personal encounters and situations in plebeian Asia rather than, as has often been assumed, textually-grounded convictions or purely individual religious crisis.

Secondly, it explores *racial* boundaries, and the process of 'going native'. As against the relationships of western power/knowledge often thematized (Almond 1988) in interpretations of early western Buddhism, it argues that Asian agency has to be understood as central in enabling Europeans to become monks in the first place, and—for those who left significant historical traces—in creating the contexts within which they could make a public impact.

Thirdly, it discusses the politics of empire and the particular role of *Irish* Buddhists' cultural or political resistance. Following Clarke (1997), it argues that such figures should be seen as embodying *dissident* Orientalisms, deploying Buddhism against empire, whether as insider critique in western circuits of communication or as outsider challenge.

These were significant challenges to the late nineteenth century colonial order in which, following the Indian Revolt, it was a matter of official policy that British settlers should be only civil servants, officers, capitalists, professionals, missionaries and philanthropists (Mizutani 2006, 3). Furthermore, from a social movements perspective (Diani and Della Porta 1999), we can ask after the position of early western Buddhists within the movements of *Asian* Buddhist revival which were to prove central in the construction of successful nationalisms from Japan to Ceylon.

As members of plebeian classes who were needed for the construction of empires and discarded when the job was done, who crossed the racial barriers which separated 'white' from 'native' and 'Christian' from 'heathen', and who challenged the imperial logic of *western* (scholarly, upper-class) power/knowledge, their public visibility was no accident and enabled them to play creative and, at times, significant roles in the Buddhist revival.

'Pauper lunatics and beachcombers'

> The colonies... are always having to repatriate pauper lunatics and beachcombers, the white men who have got into distress in Singapore and Colombo. (House of Commons 1910, 1)

When Buddhist Studies was establishing itself as a discipline in the 1960s and 1970s, it sought academic respectability by dissociating itself from widespread representations of Buddhism as hippie (eg Jack Kerouac's *The Dharma Bums*) or what would later be called New Age (eg T. Lobsang Rampa's *The Third Eye*) (Turner, Cox and Bocking 2010; Lopez 1998; Tonkinson 1995). However, as the example of

Dhammaloka suggests, Gary Snyder (fictionalized in *The Dharma Bums;* see also Snyder 2000) is not that far off the 'main sequence' of western Buddhists; migrant workers, with experience of sailing and other trades like logging (Snyder) or fruit picking (Dhammaloka), with backgrounds in the anarchist Industrial Workers of the World (Snyder) or other forms of radical politics (Dhammaloka). Many Buddhist organizations in the west pursued a similar path from marginality to would-be mainstream (Cox 2013).

In this, contemporary scholars and western Buddhists repeat the gesture of respectability which was strategically central in our period. If a figure like Dhammaloka attracted the hostility of Christian missionaries, colonial authorities and white journalists, their number one charge against him was that he was no gentleman—in his birth, education, clothing or behaviour. Although, as we now know, he was able to ordain between 13 and 15 western monks[3]—a figure considerably higher than Ananda Metteyya and comparable with Nyanatiloka in this period—one of the factors in Dhammaloka's later disappearance from histories of western Buddhism was not simply that his lineage apparently died out, but equally importantly that he made no attempt to claim the scholarly and gentlemanly credentials which the other two sought.

Nor was this solely a western concern: as Bocking (2010) has shown, part of his failure in Japan (compared to Singapore or Burma) was due to his inability to compete on the terms then becoming common in the more sophisticated environment there; while his later erasure from Burmese nationalist histories is no doubt conditioned by his not being Burmese and thus not suiting the narratives of later nationalist historiography (Turner 2011a).

It is for precisely these same reasons, of course, that Dhammaloka is interesting to research, as someone whose (unusually well-attested) existence fills in much of what is left blank by the more powerful accounts of Asian and western Buddhist organizational and scholarly genealogies. To rephrase E. P. Thompson (1963), the pauper lunatics and beachcombers may have more to say than the vantage point of respectability allows.

The Dhammaloka project has found that hobos (migrant workers), beachcombers or loafers (white members of the Asian lumpenproletariat) and drifters were well-represented among the first early European Buddhist *monastics* (and not simply converts as might be thought). Given the disparity in access to the 'intellectual means of production' of such figures, and the persistent attempts by those who did have access to present even such popular and visible figures as Dhammaloka as being barely worth a mention (while nonetheless having to mention them), it would be foolhardy to assume that there were not more such beachcomber Buddhists who have not had the dubious good fortune to be recorded by travel writers, criticized in the colonial and missionary press or (in Dhammaloka's case) tried for sedition.

In fact, beachcombers as such (let alone the Buddhists among them) are an under-studied group in Buddhist Asia, unlike the situation in the South Pacific where the key intermediary role they played between island societies and traders, colonizers and missionaries is better studied (Elleray 2005). For mainland Asia as a whole, more seems to have been written on the moral panics and legislation that accompanied the rise of European poverty in the later nineteenth century (see Ganachari 2002) than on the beachcombers themselves. The responses of a concerned middle-class public or a modernizing colonial administration are apparently of greater interest than the victims of this disciplinary activity (Foucault 1991), despite the large volume of data generated by the workhouses which were its practical expression (see Fischer-Tiné 2005).

The many-headed hydra

> [The white loafer] is generally of the lower middle or labouring class; sometimes a ci-devant soldier, sailor, or man-servant; occasionally a skilled artisan, or a whilom subordinate Government official; and rarer still, a *sahib* or gentleman, born and bred. (Hervey 1913, 95)

The major sources of the later nineteenth century European poor in India (where some research has been done) were according to Fischer-Tiné (2005) ex-sailors and ex-soldiers—together with ex-railway employees and ex-telegraph workers those who made imperial power and colonial trade and migration possible—Australian horse grooms (!) along with 'domiciled Europeans' and 'Eurasians' (Mizutani 2006) and women, who were a particular target of anxiety. If poor whites in general might transgress racial hierarchies by taking on menial work or indeed adopting Asian dress, the prospect that poor white women might marry Asians or turn to prostitution was on a par with European conversion to 'native' religion in its threat to the colonial moral order. Finally, Ghosh (2011, 498) mentions India as a traditional destination of escaped Australian convicts.

These and similar groups—increasingly large as the century wore on, ultimately representing nearly half of all whites in a country like India (Mizutani 2006, 6) were created by the normal processes of colonialism, including, in particular, the creation of groups of people who had not been able (or not wanted) to return 'home' once retired or demobbed, who did not have the resources to send their children 'back' to ensure their continued position at the top of the racial ladder, or who failed to make marriages that would keep them within polite society. In turn they represented what Siddiqi rightly calls 'an imperial lumpenproletariat' (2008, 75). A problem when it was surplus to requirements, as in the period following the Indian Revolt (Fischer-Tiné 2005, 304ff), while at other times of economic boom this class could be drawn on as a 'reserve army of labour' willing to work at cheap rates.

One migrant worker's trajectory

> It often, very often, happens, that men who declare themselves [enter workhouses] do not give a correct history of themselves, and we have no means

> of testing the truth of their stories. (Madras workhouse governor, 1876, cited in Fischer-Tiné 2005, 319)

In the nature both of record-keeping then and research now, such lives are hard to recover in anything like a qualitative or continuous way. Dhammaloka's reported biography is valuable in this sense. If correctly identified, he was the youngest son of lower-middle class parents from Booterstown, then a village in South County Dublin; leaving school by 14 to work in his father's provisions shop, he subsequently sought and failed to find work in Liverpool and worked his way across the Atlantic at 16 in a ship's pantry (see Tweed 2010).

In the US he claimed to have been a sailor, kitchen porter, hobo, shepherd, fruit-picker, truckman [transporting goods], docker and, finally, the watch officer on a trans-Pacific ship. In Asia he is variously said to have been a sailor, tally-clerk, soldier, beachcomber, pearl-diver or member of the Salvation Army. He is also said to have been a Catholic priest; together with the equally implausible lay name William Colvin, this seems to have been part of the later Dhammaloka's 'cover identity' used in particular when dealing with the authorities.

Research on all this is currently underway. At present it seems likely that he did indeed travel via Liverpool and New York on the dates given (although he may have been born three years earlier in Dublin's working-class inner city), and that the basic outline of his time as a hobo in the States stands up. He may have remained in the US for longer than he suggests, particularly if it was here that he acquired the reasons for later changing identities, faking his death and so on. In Asia, arriving at an uncertain date between c. 1874–1900, a role as beachcomber in Ceylon seems among the more probable pasts on the information available to date.

Alternatively, he may have remained a sailor for longer than he suggests and shared in the experience of a later contributor to the MahaBodhi Society's *British Buddhist:*

> I got a ship that was bound for the East, and at last we reached Colombo, Ceylon, as nice a little harbour as you could wish to see. I went ashore one morning early before the heat of the day began, and there I saw passing along in between the green trees a procession of yellow-dressed men. A strange sort of thrill of pleasure passed through as I watched them pass along the road . . . I thought them and their yellow robes the most beautiful thing I had ever seen . . .
>
> I have had many a talk since my first one, with Buddhist monks, and have always enjoyed learning more about their religion from their own lips; it somehow comes more freshly to me that way, than by reading about it in books . . . And when I am away in the west again, I feel as if I am away from home; and begin to feel bright and cheered again, as soon as I have passed Aden, and know I am getting nearer again to the home of Buddhism, Ceylon, where I now have among the Buddhists of this Island all the best, most real friends, I have in this world. ('A Sailor' 1928, 7–8)

Whatever Dhammaloka's personal history, it is clear from 'A sailor' and other accounts and encounters that this kind of plebeian life, for those who came to call Asia home and in some cases came to identify with local culture and religion, was far from unusual. In a period so obsessed by respectability it is unclear why Dhammaloka should tell his beachcomber tales unless they were moderately plausible or, in other words, representative of other people's experience.

Loafers and bhikkhus

> There's a bunch of one-time beachcombers scattered among the Burmese monasteries. (Dublin-born beachcomber John Askins, 1905 [Franck 1910, 272–3])

'A sailor' is unusual not only as a firsthand account by a plebeian Buddhist, but also as an account of a beachcomber Buddhist who did *not* become a monk; in the nature of things yellow-robed European monastics were more likely to attract attention and to have opportunities to speak, write or publish.

In previous work (Turner, Cox and Bocking 2010) we have given some illustrative examples of beachcomber Buddhists. As part of that same project we began to encounter other, previously unknown early western Buddhists.[4] Much as Deslippe notes (2013), once we start looking we bump into them everywhere. Here I want to make some general comments on what can now be said about the class background of early western Buddhists.

Some, of course, *do* fit the existing 'gentleman scholar' model—although Harris (2013) argues that this is not as true of Ananda Metteyya as later scholarship (and perhaps the man himself) claimed. For others we have no details whatsoever. Given how gossipy the colonial press of the day was, there may well be class implications to this silence—that these were figures unknown to the club-frequenting writers who acted as journalists in such contexts. In my own attempts to find early *Irish* Buddhists (Cox 2013), I found a similar picture. Many are simply noted as 'Irish', with no further information, on the basis of once-off encounters with a colonial author; only a handful were writers and so able to speak for themselves in any detail. A few were in the middle ground, having less control of the intellectual means of production themselves but nevertheless chronicled in something more than their 'bare life'.

Other monks are more definitely plebeian, at various levels. Thus, for example, we find an unnamed ex-sailor at the Tavoy monastery in Rangoon, the disgraced Alois Fuehrer (who had faked the discovery of relics of the Buddha) seeking ordination in Ceylon, an Englishman M. T. de la Courneuve (ordained by Dhammaloka in Singapore) who gave a false background but was fleeing debts, and two American beachcomber bhikkhus recorded on a Burmese train. Dhammaloka was not alone.

In newspaper accounts, respectability appears as constantly problematic for western Buddhist monks. While there was no doubt an element of the class prejudice mentioned above, the details are often telling. Disrobings are relatively frequently recorded, particularly in relation to issues around alcohol and money. Colonial observers, of course, delighted in reporting western bhikkhus drinking; but it seems clear that they often did. (Whether, as Dhammaloka's own autobiography suggests, some became Buddhist *in response* to the bottle, is something that cannot at present be established.) Ritual poverty and renunciation, of course, could follow from actual poverty and perhaps make it bearable—or give a new status among Asian Buddhists which would not attach to a western ex-alcoholic.

Western Buddhists, monastics or otherwise, then, often inhabited an uncertain borderland in which the inherent challenge to respectable white behaviour entailed in adopting a 'native' religion (and, for bhikkhus, native dress, bare feet, shaved head and begging) was often compounded in the eyes of their betters by previous social failings of various kinds. Of course, this very class issue may have meant that in many cases there was nothing left to lose. Either way, this situation renders them harder to research. Those whose voices had the status to be published at the time, preserved subsequently and digitized or otherwise made available today (three filters in which class, power, race and location played and still play a central role) tended at best to trivialize and at worst to ignore those who fell short of respectable whiteness in both these dimensions, of class and religion.

'Going native', race, and Asian agency

> It is not desirable in the interests of the British Government to have distressed white men on the beach in these colonies. It brings the white race into discredit. (House of Commons 1910, 3)

The late nineteenth and early twentieth century was in many ways a highpoint in the colonial policing of boundaries of colour and religion. *Colour* because the imperial high tide had drastically reduced the number of native states and so the need even to pretend to equality; but also because the direct administration of so much of the world's population (as opposed to working through local comprador elites) placed a premium on cultural tools of deference, aspiration and so on to enforce a social order where the number of soldiers available was always far less than the number of those who might conceivably object to imperial power. *Religion* because the rise of popular movements in Europe, in particular after 1848, had led to an increased need to justify imperial adventures and expenditures. Christian missionising provided one widely-accepted justification, which found its practical expression in the often unwilling opening-up by colonial officials to religious missions of various kinds, despite the risk of 'disturbing the natives'.

In this world where boundaries increasingly had to be constructed and enforced rather than arising automatically from people's own background and socioeconomic position, poor whites were a source of deep anxiety because of their mobility, propensity to drink in unacceptable ways, begging, crime and promiscuity. In other words, they represented a classed threat to white superiority which could be, and at times was, escalated into a personal transgression of establishment efforts to create barriers.

'Going native', then, was from a colonial point of view the ultimate expression of a trajectory of behaviour unworthy of a European in Asia. However, while there is a substantial literature on 'going native' in North America and the Caribbean (Colley 2000, 173–174), there is relatively little on Asia except in relation to *imagined* transitions in fiction (*Kim, The road to Mandalay*, etc.). In this literature, which represents the process from the viewpoint of white elites, the class aspect is largely assumed and what is particularly thematized is loyalty to Asia or England, religious affiliation and gender and sexuality. 'Going native', for those who did not, was understood not only as a fascinating and reprehensible form of sexual and family transgression, but also as the adoption of new religious identities which in turn implied an abandonment of one's national loyalties. In both *Kim* and *Mandalay*, Irish characters have to resolve the tension between their Buddhist loyalties and British military authority, which is represented as without easy solution.

In the first instance, however, 'going native' was of course a practical matter, dependent on the ability to learn the new language effectively. As Colley notes, 'European plebeians stationed in different parts of the world during the course of military or naval service had the opportunity to acquire a variety of spoken languages; and this accomplishment could be the essential passport and temptation to changing who and what they were' (2000, 186).

Dhammaloka, for example, claimed to be able to speak eight languages; although standards were different to those of the present day, Harry Franck witnessed him concluding a theological argument in Hindustani (Hindi-Urdu), indicating that this went well beyond knowing how to say hello (Franck 1910, 366). Franck also records Dhammaloka's friend Askins as being fluent 'in half the dialects of the East, from the clicking Kaffir to the guttural tongue of Kabul' (1910, 254). As a sailor or migrant worker, of course, a good ear for languages was always helpful—and in turn made it possible to 'go native' in ways that were not purely rhetorical.

'... white men who have got into distress in Singapore and Colombo...'

In the early modern period, the key focus of European worries about 'going native' was brutally practical: Europeans working for native rulers transmitted technical and military expertise as well as an understanding of how western power structures worked, all of which could be used against western interests.

By the late nineteenth century, however, the primary meanings of 'going native' were on the one hand having too much sympathy for 'natives' as a western civil servant, or issues related to sex and above all kinship (marrying Asians, or in the case of men, failing to abandon their Asian relationships when the opportunity came to return 'home'). In both cases these represented threats to the elite solidarity of colonial whites.

Going native was proportionately more attractive for plebeians, who had fewer opportunities to return home and for whom white solidarity had less to offer. If, like *Kim's* fictional father, a retired sergeant working on the railways (not an uncommon Irish fate: Cook 1987, 509), such whites married local women and started families, their children would slip down the social scale. Racial categories were shifting, but children whose parents could not afford to send them 'home' for their education or who had one Asian parent might become respectively 'domiciled Europeans' or 'Eurasians' (Mizutani 2006) and would have fewer or no opportunities in the white world. The role of religion in such families has not yet been studied but might throw up more *lay* Buddhists:

> Unlike the middle-class whites who desperately remained in touch with the metropolitan centre, the domiciled were characterised for their immersion in the social and cultural influences of the colonial periphery. (Mizutani 2006, 7)

European bhikkhus and colour lines

> It was often mentioned with indignation in the Police reports that the vagrants wore 'native dress' or 'went about barefooted.' (Fischer-Tiné 2005, 315)
>
> ... any representation of the 'other' within the missionary discourse of civilising ... was to some degree racialised and classed *simultaneously*. (Mizutani 2006, 12)

Poor whites and Eurasians had fewer reasons (and resources) for maintaining the cultural barriers separating them from local culture, and clothing was one crucial marker of the attempt to do so. Dhammaloka's 'shoe incident' (Turner 2010, 154–156) highlights this boundary in reverse, and the particular role which religion played. In the shoe incident, he challenged an off-duty Indian police officer who entered the ritual boundaries of the symbolically important Shwedagon pagoda in Rangoon, wearing shoes. The white gentry were not expected to take their shoes off, but they were expected to use the European mode of removing one's hat as a sign of respect. Some Asians wore shoes, but the point of challenging an Indian (other than the general resentment felt towards their role as police) was that Indians might wear shoes, but would remove them on entering *Indian* temples, so that this was a clear sign of disrespect towards Burmese Buddhism.

Western bhikkhus were at the opposite end of this spectrum, travelling barefoot, shaven-headed and wearing distinctly 'native dress' even at a period when some Asian middle classes were adopting western clothing, shoes and hairstyle. This of course had roots in a ritual poverty marked out on the body (the loss of hair), clothing (symbolically associated with graveyards) and ritualized begging which stood counter to everything white solidarity expected and meant.[5] The latter, in its equally ritualized aspects ('proper' clothing, Christian religious observance, socializing only with Europeans) was intended to mark out a cultural superiority which in this period of direct rule and the need to justify empire 'at home' also entailed claims to a civilising mission, whether spoken in terms of modernization or Christianity (Siddiqi 2008, 76).

Fischer-Tiné notes that alongside the many other sins against empire committed by European loafers—mobility, drinking, begging, crime—conversion was a particularly serious offence. He discusses a series of cases of conversion to Islam in our period (1870–1917) and notes

> A shifting of religious camps was outright provocation [to authorities]. (Fischer-Tiné 2005, 314)

In the European bhikkhu, then, all the problematic aspects of the poor white 'loafer', the 'domiciled European' and 'going native' came together in a highly symbolic challenge to a social order which itself depended massively on the symbolism of racial and cultural oppositions.

Asian agency and Buddhist revival

We should mention one final way in which European bhikkhus challenged the power relations of empire, namely in relation to *Asian* agency. The sangha was, of course, a local institution and ordination required subordination to a series of demanding relationships, even if some latitude was often granted to western monks. Nonetheless, just like Charles Pfoundes as an officer in the Siamese navy (Bocking 2013), Dhammaloka as European bhikkhu was ultimately responsible to Asian superiors.

Ordination was a complex matter, and subjected European bhikkhus to local considerations which they may not have understood or in some cases even been aware of. For example, in our research on Dhammaloka we have found evidence of a series of Europeans refused ordination in Ceylon (presumably because of the caste affiliations of the different nikayas) and who were apparently directed to Burma.

Conversely, if Dhammaloka was not respectable as European, he had a different status as bhikkhu. Thus, in Burma, he was ordained by a number of senior monks; in Japan he was given a robe and an honorary title, apparently by a Shingon dignitary; and his monastic superiors tolerated or turned a blind eye not only to his institutions such as the Buddhist Tract Society, operated from the Tavoy monastery in Rangoon, or the bilingual school which he operated from Wat Ban Thawai in Bangkok—but also to his ordination of over a dozen westerners as monks, only a few years after his own ordination.

Patronage was another important matter: even 'gentleman scholars' like Ananda Metteyya required Asian patrons, but poorer western monks were completely dependent on those who were willing to fund their activities. Thus Turner's (2011b) research on Dhammaloka's patron networks, Bocking's (2010) discussion of the relative Japanese reluctance to work with Dhammaloka, or Choompolpaisal's research (2013) on the ethnic politics of Wat Ban Thawai all point to agendas, opportunities and constraints which must have weighed heavily on western monks.

An unusually clear example is given by the contested politics of Dhammaloka's 1909 Ceylon tour. This was promoted by Anagarika Dharmapala, who brought out a special issue of his *Sinhala Bauddhaya* devoted to Dhammaloka's talks, while the local Young Men's Buddhist Association (YMBA) dissociated itself publicly from the tour, for reasons which are as yet unclear.[6]

Thus, whether we are discussing ordination itself, sangha discipline, financial support or the organizing of tours, to operate as a western bhikkhu meant securing the support of Asian actors. No doubt in many cases—where a bhikkhu lacked either linguistic competence or local political understanding—the agency and strategy was primarily on the Asian side, and the western bhikkhu was little more than a front man. In other cases, relations may have been more equal.

In other words, crossing colour lines submerged European monks more fully within the politics of Buddhist revival, and raises wider questions about Asian agency and power relations in early 'western' Buddhism. As this issue shows, early Buddhist modernists (Asian or European) were very often relatively marginal to begin with, and sometimes 'ahead of their time'. For example, it was to take another 15 years before the shoe question raised by Dhammaloka became a strategic issue for the young Burmese nationalists. (On his recent visit to Burma, US President Barack Obama was photographed on the Shwedagon, barefoot and of course hatless.)[7]

Another way of phrasing this is to say that the Buddhist revival, and Buddhist modernism, *became* central when sangha hierarchies and lay organizations started to adopt themes, strategies and methods which had often been experimented, put on the agenda or discussed by the early networks discussed in this issue. For early *western* bhikkhus, then, it was a question of either convincing local sanghas, sponsors and organizers to take a risk on them—or of being selected as likely candidates for locally-determined roles.

Observing Dhammaloka's Burmese careers between 1900—1902, for example, it is hard to avoid the impression that elements of the Burmese sangha thought it would be useful to have a white bhikkhu who might raise the flag of opposition to Christianity. Such a figure might perhaps be given more leeway within the sangha than could have been allowed to a Burmese-born bhikkhu; if things went wrong, he could more easily be disavowed or disrobe; and he might be expected to have a better sense of how to engage in the new form of religious conflict—as indeed Dhammaloka did, importing for the purpose perhaps both an atheist repertoire of anti-Christian arguments and an *Irish* repertoire of contention, to which I now turn.

Dissident Orientalisms and Irish identifications

Can you bear to see sacrilegious hands deface or destroy our holy inheritance? The star-like Buddhas are calling upon you . . . (U Dhammaloka, 1900)[8]

It is commonly held, following Said (2003), that Orientalism is a gesture of power/knowledge and of course this is often true, including some forms of western Buddhism and Buddhology. It is not, however, the full story. As Clarke (1997) observes, we can also speak of *dissident* Orientalisms—those which, in his accounts, use Asian vantage points to critique their own society or, in the cases we are exploring, feature westerners who converted to a pan-Asian religion in opposition to key elements (Christianity, racial hierarchies) of European society.

Lennon's (2004) text highlights the particular situation here of Irish Orientalism as a form of fantasy identification with other colonized nations, enabling long-distance relationships with Sinhala, Burmese, Indian and Japanese nationalisms. These were often reciprocated in Asian interest in the Irish experience of anti-colonial activism, reaching a highpoint between Irish independence in the 1920s and independence in South and Southeast Asian countries in the 1940s and 1950s.

Thus western or Irish Buddhisms were not only (or mainly) power grabs over Asian knowledge but also (or mostly) arguments against Christianity, (British) empire, and indeed local colonial power holders, as in the case of Dhammaloka, a 'terror to evil-doers' who among many other things sought to bring corrupt officials to book.[9]

> If missionaries appraise you that they have brought to you what they call western civilization . . . do not hesitate a moment to reply that you would rather call it . . . religion of bloodshed. (U Dhammaloka, 1901[10])

As in Ireland, so in Asia?

> 'Ireland?' he cried, tremulously. 'Then you are not a Buddhist! Irishmen are Christians. All sahibs are Christians,' and he glanced nervously at the grinning Burmese about us. (Indian Christian convert, 1905 [cited in Franck 1910, 365])

It was a feature of imperial power that both colonial officials and nationalists drew on analogies between different colonial situations (Nagai 2006). For their part, Irish people in Asia routinely interpreted imperial and colonial relationships through their own varied interpretation of *Irish* situations (Cox 2013). Thus the British consul in Tokyo, an Irishman, saw the Irish Buddhist sympathiser Lafcadio Hearn as a nationalist 'in the most extreme sense of the term' (Murray 1993, 285–286), and indeed Hearn supported the Boers against the British and the Japanese against the Russians.

Just as Irish figures in India such as Annie Besant, James and Margaret Cousins or Sister Nivedita (Margaret Noble) combined conversion to Hinduism with active engagement in Indian-led organizations, so too Irish Buddhists often found themselves employed by Asian organizations, Buddhist and otherwise

(Cox 2010, 2013). Often (not always) they pursued wider visions of a future without empire, whether these were framed in a universalist language or in terms of mutual respect between different cultures. A few examples can show the variety involved.

Some early Irish Buddhist strategies[11]

The ex-Anglican priest John Bowles Daly, principal of a Buddhist school in Ceylon in the early 1890s, pursued his long-standing belief in modernization through secular education in the Buddhist Theosophical Society school movement which aimed at challenging missionary-run schools, not by a revival of traditional temple-based education but by lay-controlled Buddhist schools following a modern curriculum.

Lafcadio Hearn, working in the modernizing Japanese education system, adopted a Yeatsian celebration of peasant life and legend as being the true repositories of national authenticity. This seeming paradox is one that would have been familiar to the many Irish teachers and academics of the period who adopted romantic forms of cultural nationalism that valorized the far west.

Captain Pfoundes (Bocking 2013) held in the 1890s an official position as a representative of the Buddhist Propagation Society in London and, subsequently, served as an anti-missionary agitator in Japan; his talks were translated and published in Japan. Like Hearn he stressed the value of Japanese culture against that of the West.

Another Irish Buddhist monk, U Visuddha, working with the Tamil nationalist Sakya Buddhist Society in Madras, carried out at least one mass conversion ceremony among the dalit goldminers of Marikuppam in 1907, in a strategy which much later became widely popular under B. S. Ambedkar (Jhondale and Beltz 2004).

Dhammaloka, for his part, followed what seems in one respect a straightforward translation or importation of the long-standing Irish nationalist repertoire of contention to Buddhist Asia. Since the Catholic Emancipation movement under Daniel O'Connell in the 1820s and 1830s, Irish national identity had been increasingly identified with a politicized Catholicism. This strategy had the major advantage—following the bloody suppression of the 1798 uprising—that there were limits by the nineteenth century (and even more so following the Indian Revolt of 1857) to exactly how far the colonial power could repress 'native religion', and it is not hard to interpret Dhammaloka's early adoption of this strategy in Burma as a translation from the Irish.

Conclusion: early western Buddhists and the limits of empire

U Dhammaloka's particularly dramatic—and, for this reason, relatively well-documented—experience is in some ways paradigmatic of that of wider groups, created and needed by the new capitalist world-system, who defected from its class, racial and religious hierarchies to 'go native' in ways that were deeply problematic to those whose cultural power depended on maintaining those same hierarchies. If we recall that within half a century of Dhammaloka's ordination most of those empires had been dramatically overthrown in Asia, we can see that the sneers and alarm calls of missionaries, journalists and colonial officials perhaps had substance as responses to the real threat implied by challenges to white superiority.

In the Asian context, conversion to Buddhism and ordination could be acts of solidarity across racial/ethnic boundaries and pioneering, creative responses to these classed and raced structures. Outsider converts were able both to transmit 'repertoires of contention' from one context to another—Irish religious nationalism, Anglophone freethinking arguments, the culture of radical plebeian publishing—but also to bolster new strategies evolved by local actors.

This Asian agency of sangha, sponsors and organizers cannot be ignored in understanding early western Buddhists, who necessarily depended on these structures for practical purposes, although the purposes intended by the former are often harder to recover than those overtly proclaimed by western activists and the power relationships are not always obvious. Here too, Dhammaloka is perhaps paradigmatic: we know him to have been active in Burma, Singapore and other Straits Settlements, Siam, Ceylon and Japan, along with less well-researched activities in Nepal, India and Cambodia (leaving aside Australia, China and Tibet where the situation is too unclear to make confident statements.) As Bocking (2010) shows, and Dhammaloka's unexpected collaboration with Christians in Siam indicates (Choompolpaisal 2013), he adopted different strategies with varying degrees of success in different Asian contexts.

Another way of putting this is to say that, as an ex-migrant worker and ex-sailor, Dhammaloka was happy to arrive in a new country, try to identify a possible sangha context and potential lay sponsors and/or organizations, and see what tasks (preaching, education, publishing, public debate etc.) he could pursue along what lines. At times, as evidently in Burma, Singapore and Siam, there was a meeting of minds or at least of agendas, and he flourished. Elsewhere, as in Japan and perhaps Ceylon, the relationship was not so successful.

If Dhammaloka provides a window into other worlds, those worlds include that of poor whites, loafers and beachcombers; of those who 'went native', including Buddhist converts and western bhikkhus; and of the emerging *Asian* Buddhist networks which employed, resisted, collaborated with, invited or distanced themselves from this highly visible figure in their attempts to shape the future of Buddhist Asia.

Like his older contemporary Hearn—who similarly started out as an Irish migrant worker, adopted strongly anti-Christian and anti-western views and was attracted to local Buddhist culture rather than philosophy or meditation—Dhammaloka's early and public identification with Asian culture *mattered*. As the Irish civil servant and Burmese nationalist Maurice Collis wrote of his friend Gordon Luce, who 'went native' by marrying a Burmese woman,

In point of fact, Luce was one of the sanest men in Burma. What he nourished and advanced, has prospered; what his detractors upheld has withered away. (Collis 1953, 44)

ACKNOWLEDGEMENTS

The initial version of this paper was presented at the Conference SE Asia as a Crossroads for Buddhist Exchange: *Pioneer European Buddhists and Asian Buddhist Networks 1860–1960* hosted by the Study of Religions Department, University College Cork, Ireland, 13–15 September 2012 and funded by the Dhammakaya International Society of the United Kingdom as part of the 2012 postdoctoral fellowship 'Continuities and Transitions in Early Modern Thai Buddhism'. Many thanks are due to Brian Bocking, Alicia Turner and Kate Crosby for their comments on earlier versions of this piece. I wish to acknowledge the support of the Irish Research Council in relation to this research.

NOTES

1. The conversion of a European to Buddhism in Bangkok, *Straits Times*, August 10, 1878.
2. Alicia Turner (pers. comm.) notes that the implication here is that the Thai king had restricted certain positions to former monks because of their assumed education and status.
3. *Times of Burma*, July 19, 1905; *Ceylon Observer*, September 4, 1909.
4. See also http://www.payer.de/budlink.htm under 'Materialien zum Neobuddhismus' for some ground-breaking work in this direction.
5. See also Elleray (2005, 169) on European clothing as a visible and controllable index of less tangible aspects of 'metropolitan orders of being'.
6. The Irish Buddhist priest, *Ceylon Observer*, September 11, 1909; Correspondence, *Ceylon Observer* September 14, 1909.
7. http://buddhism.about.com/b/2012/11/22/the-president-and-the-buddha.htm
8. Warning to Buddhists, *Times of Burma,* January 9, 1901.
9. From Catholic priest to Buddhist monk, *Englishman* (Calcutta), April 11, 1912.
10. 'Christianity' in Burma, *Deseret Evening News*, August 24, 1901.
11. The cases mentioned here are discussed in greater detail in Cox (2013).

REFERENCES

'A SAILOR'. 1928. How I Became a Buddhist. *British Buddhist* 2: 7–8.

ALMOND, P. 1988. *The British Discovery of Buddhism*. Cambridge: CUP.

BOCKING, B. 2010. A Man of Work and Few Words? *Contemporary Buddhism* 11 (2): 229–80.

BOCKING, BRIAN. 2013. Flagging up Buddhism: Charles Pfoundes (Omoie Tetzunostzuke) among the International Congresses and Expositions, 1893–1905. *Contemporary Buddhism* 14 (1): 17–37.

CHOOMPOLPAISAL, PHIBUL. 2013. Tai-Burmese-Lao Buddhisms in the 'Modernizing' of Ban Thawai (Bangkok): The Dynamic Interaction between Ethnic Minority Religion and British–Siamese Centralization in the late Nineteenth/Early Twentieth Centuries. *Contemporary Buddhism* 14 (1): 94–115.

CLARKE, J. J. 1997. *Oriental Enlightenment*. London: Routledge.

COLLEY, L. 2000. Going Native, Telling Tales. *Past and present* 168: 170–93.

COLLIS, M. 1953. *Into Hidden Burma*. London: Faber and Faber.

COOK, S. 1987. The Irish Raj. *Journal of Social History* 20: 507–29.

COX, L. 2010. Plebeian Freethought and the Politics of Anti-colonial Solidarity. In *Fifteenth international Conference on Alternative Futures and Popular Protest*, edited by Colin Barker and Mike Tyldesley. Manchester: Manchester Metropolitan University (CD-ROM).

COX, L. 2013. *Buddhism and Ireland*. London: Equinox.

DESLIPPE, PHILIP. 2013. Brooklyn Bhikkhu: How Salvatore Cioffi Became The Venerable Lokanatha. *Contemporary Buddhism* 14 (1): 169–186.

DIANI, M., and D. DELLA PORTA. 1999. *Social Movements*. New York: Wiley.

ELLERAY, M. 2005. Crossing the Beach. *Victorian Studies* 47 (2): 164–73.

FISCHER-TINÉ, H. 2005. Britain's Other Civilizing Mission. *Indian Economic Social History Review* 42: 295–338.

FOUCAULT, M. 1991. *Discipline and Punish*. London: Penguin.

FRANCK, H. 1910. *A Vagabond Journey Around the World*. New York: The Century Co.

GANACHARI, A. 2002. White Man's Embarrassment. *Economic and Political Weekly* 37 (25): 2477–85.

GHOSH, D. 2011. Under the Radar of Empire. *Journal of Social History* 45 (2): 497–514.

GOVERNMENT OF INDIA. 1881. *General Report of the Maritime Survey of India*. Calcutta: Government Press.

HALL, T. 2000. World-Systems Analysis. *A World-Systems Reader*., 3–28. Boulder: Rowman and Littlefeld.

HARRIS, ELIZABETHJ. 2013. Ananda Metteyya: Controversial Networker, Passionate Critic. *Contemporary Buddhism* 14 (1): 78–93.

HERVEY, H. 1913. *The European in India*. London: Stanley Paul.

HOUSE OF COMMONS. 1910. *Committee on Distressed Colonial and Indian Subjects*. London: HM Stationery Office.

HUDSON, G. F. 1954. Marco Polo. *Geographical Journal* 120 (3): 299–311.

JHONDALE, S., and J. BELTZ. 2004. *Reconstructing the World*. Oxford: Oxford University Press.

KHANTIPALO, BHIKKHU. 1979. *Banner of the Arahants*. Kandy: Buddhist Publication Society.

LENNON, J. 2004. *Irish Orientalism*. Syracuse: Syracuse University Press.

LOPEZ, D. 1998. *Prisoners of Shangri-la*. Chicago: University of Chicago Press.

MIZUTANI, S. 2006. Historicising Whiteness. *ACRAWSA e-journal* 2 (1): 1–15.

MURRAY, P. 1993. *A Fantastic Journey*. Folkestone: Japan Library/Curzon.

NAGAI, K. 2006. *Empire of Analogies*. Cork: Cork University Press.

SAID, E. 2003. *Orientalism*. 2nd ed. London: Penguin.

SCAMMELL, G. V. 1992. European Exiles, Renegades and Outlaws. *Modern Asian Studies* 26 (4): 641–61.

SIDDIQI, Y. 2008. *Anxieties of Empire and the Fiction of Intrigue*. New York: Columbia University Press.

SNYDER, G. 2000. *The Gary Snyder Reader*. Washington: Counterpoint.

SUTIN, L. 2006. *All is Change*. New York: Little, Brown.

THOMPSON, E. P. 1963. *The Making of the English Working Class*. London: Gollancz.

TONKINSON, C., ed. 1995. *Big Sky Mind*. New York: Putnam's.

TURNER, A. 2010. The Irish Pongyi in Colonial Burma. *Contemporary Buddhism* 11 (2): 149–71.

TURNER, A. 2011a. Narratives of Nation, Questions of Community. *Journal of Burma Studies* 15 (2): 263–82.

TURNER, A. 2011b. Buddhism Across Colonial Contexts with an Irish Ally. Paper to Association for Asian Studies/ICAS conference, Hawaii.

TURNER, A., L. COX, and B. BOCKING. 2010. Beachcombing, Going Native and Freethinking. *Contemporary Buddhism* 11 (2): 125–47.

TWEED, T. 2010. Towards the Study of Vernacular Intellectualism. *Contemporary Buddhism* 11 (2): 281–6.

'LIKE EMBERS HIDDEN IN ASHES, OR JEWELS ENCRUSTED IN STONE': RĀHUL SĀṄKṚTYĀYAN, DHARMĀNAND KOSAMBĪ AND BUDDHIST ACTIVITY IN COLONIAL INDIA

Douglas Ober

Two of the most important modern Indian Buddhist pioneers are the polyglot explorer and Marxist revolutionary, Rāhul Sāṅkṛtyāyan (1893–1963), and the Pali scholar and Gandhian nationalist, Dharmānand Kosambī (1876–1947). Although best known as scholars of Buddhism, it is their lesser-known personal lives—namely, their political involvement in anti-colonial efforts, social reform projects, and travels abroad—that are of primary focus in this study. Through an examination of their activities and writings, this essay reveals the methods they employed and the networks of support they utilized in order to propagate Buddhism. In particular, it focuses on two features common to both of their lives: first, their relations with transnational Buddhist organizations and Euro-American and other Asian intellectuals, and second, their collaborative efforts with Indian elites whom they shared similar social, educational and national concerns. These two factors, I argue, were essential to their reconfiguration of a modern Indian Buddhism that was relevant to contemporary Indian concerns.

Studies of the rebirth of Buddhism in colonial India have largely focused on two major social developments. First among these is the European 'discovery' of Buddhism affiliated with the archaeological excavations and Orientalist scholarship of the colonial period. The second major development concerns the efforts of the Ceylonese reformer, Anagārika Dharmapāla (1864–1933), and the activities of the Mahā Bodhi Society more widely. While both of these developments are pivotal to understanding the spread of Buddhism in modern India, the emphasis on them has oversimplified the diversity and neglected the vitality of other Indian Buddhist figures and movements active during the same period. In fact, the voices of Indian Buddhists in this reawakening, with the exception of Dr. B. R. Ambedkar (1891–1956), are glaringly absent from western scholarship.[1]

This essay fills some of these gaps through a brief analysis of two of the most important pioneers of colonial era Buddhism in north India: the polyglot explorer and Marxist revolutionary, Rāhul Sāṅkṛtyāyan (1893–1963), and the Pali scholar and Gandhian nationalist, Dharmānand Kosambī (1876–1947). Although best known in western scholarship for their scholarly contributions to the fields of Indology and Buddhist studies, their personal lives, which combined a dedication to Buddhism with an astonishing array of political, social, and educational activities, reveal important, but little-understood dimensions of the significant but subtle role that Buddhism played in colonial India. These include the distinct interest in Buddhism among India's nationalist elite; the growing emphasis on the Buddha's humanity and rationality; and the natural affinities many Indians saw between Buddhism, socialism and Marxism.

While space here does not allow for a comprehensive discussion of all of these factors, by narrowing in our focus on the lives of Sāṅkṛtyāyan and Kosambī, I hope to bring to light the larger networks that came to shape this modern Indian Buddhist discourse. In particular, the paper focuses on two dimensions of their lives: first, their relations with transnational Buddhist organizations and Euro-American and other Asian intellectuals; and second, their capacity to gain support from Indian elites who, while only minimally interested in reviving Buddhism as a distinct tradition, shared similar social, educational and national concerns. These two factors, I suggest, were instrumental in their ability to reinvent a modern Indian Buddhism in the vernacular that was culturally appealing, internationally respectable and relevant to contemporary Indian concerns.

Conditions for the rebirth of Buddhism in colonial India

By the second half of the nineteenth century, Buddhism in India, with the important exceptions of the border areas of the Himalayas and Chittagong Hill tracts, was largely in a moribund state. It was, in other words, a topic of discussion reserved more for a small, but growing class of English-educated Indian elites fascinated by the latest archaeological finds than it was for actual practitioners seeking refuge in the Triple Gem. This was also a period, however, in which the influences and interests of this small Indian elite expanded considerably. Due to advances in communication and transportation technologies—especially printing presses, railways, and steamships—and the growing centrality of voluntary associations and societies (sabhā, samāj) in urban life, the elite interest in Buddhism took on wider dimensions. By the end of the century, there was an unprecedented expansion in the volume of communication and travel between urban centres in India and across the globe, and it was in this context that Buddhism—as history, philosophy and religion—regained a following in the Indian marketplace.

The premier Buddhist organization in India for spreading Buddhism at this time was the Mahā Bodhi Society (MBS), founded by Dharmapāla and

Henry Olcott in 1891. The headquarters of the MBS in Calcutta and its many branches throughout India served as major physical conduits for Buddhists and non-Buddhists to establish intellectual and economic relationships and exchange ideas. With the help of several extremely wealthy financiers, the MBS did a tremendous amount to promote knowledge of Buddhism inside India through the regular publication of journals, texts, translations, pamphlets and guidebooks, and the creation of an expansive network of pilgrims' rest houses (*dharamśālā*) at all the major ancient Indian sites. Although the MBS was not, strictly speaking, a missionary society in the sense of seeking Indian converts (Zelliot 1979, 392), its broader interpretation of 'original' Buddhism as scientific, humanist, rationalist, and egalitarian appealed to a diverse group of Indian elites. In other words, for many Indians, supporting Indian Buddhist efforts did not mean that one had to necessarily cease being a Hindu, Muslim, atheist, or secularist.[2]

Indeed, as Buddhism became more resurgent in the Indian public sphere, it was frequently interpreted through the dominant Brahmanical discourse that the Buddha was an *avatar* of Vishnu and his doctrine was an *upadharma*, or subordinate dharma (Joshi 1983). While there were certainly a number of variations on this theme, three brief examples here will suffice to capture the popular public discourse. For Swāmī Vivekānanda (1863–1902), one of the most towering religious intellectuals at the turn of the century, the Buddha was praised as the 'ideal karma yogi' and 'the first great reformer the world has seen' (Vivekananda 1962, Vol. I, 117). At the same time, however, he added that the Buddha 'came to preach nothing new... [his doctrine was] the logical development of the religion of the Hindus' (Vivekananda 1962, Vol. I, 21). By the 1920s, racially-inspired conceptions of the Buddha were articulated by one of the 'founding fathers' of Hindu nationalism, V. D. Sāvarkar (1883–1966). In his seminal text, *Hindutva: Who is a Hindu?* (1923), he declared: 'the Buddha—the Dharma—the Sangha. *They are all ours*' (Sāvarkar 1938, 27, italics mine). By 1956, in a government publication celebrating the anniversary of 2500 years of the Buddha's enlightenment, India's Vice-President (and later, second President), Sarvepalli Radhakrishnan (1888–1975) would declare, 'The Buddha did not feel that he was announcing a new religion. He was born, grew up and died a Hindu' (Radhakrishnan 1956, ix).

This kind of rhetoric provided both opportunities and challenges for those Indians who hoped to revive Buddhism on Indian soil. In the decades following the MBS's creation, several other like-minded Buddhist organizations formed across India. Due to the limited knowledge we have about the particulars of all these organizations, it is, at this point, premature to make any grand claims about their wider implementation. Nonetheless, a list of just some of them is illustrative of the wider geographical interest in Buddhism at this time: the Bengal Buddhist Association of Calcutta (1892); Sakya Buddhist Society of Madras (1898); General Buddhist Association in Darjeeling (1907); Bombay Buddhist Society (1922); Indian Buddhist Society of Lucknow (1916); the Kashmiri Raj Maha Bodhi Society of Srinagar (1931); Ladakh Buddhist Education Society (1933).

While this pan-Indian enthusiasm for the Buddha as a historical figure and social reformer meant there was a wide range of support for reviving knowledge of his teaching, there were limits to the kind of Buddhism that could be articulated. Those Indians and organizations that professed the view that his teaching was distinct from, or in resistance to Hindu tenets, faced different degrees of resistance, discrimination, or even violence. In South India, for instance, where a lower-caste, conversion-based Buddhist movement developed, Indian Buddhists were 'accused of godlessness, anti-religion, customs and tradition, defiance of Vedas and Vedic authorities and, in general, of abetting anarchy and chaos in society' (Aloysius 1998, 60). For these Buddhists, of whom Sāṅkṛtyāyan and Kosambī were representative, the ability to navigate these internal tensions while simultaneously exploiting wider national and international support was integral to their success.

Dharmānand Kosambī (1876–1947)

By the time of his death at Gandhi's ashram in 1947, Dharmānand Kosambī had become one of India's most distinguished scholars, earning a Ph.D. from Harvard in 1929 and publishing more than 30 books on Buddhism and Indian history, and dozens of articles on a variety of topics in Marathi, Gujarati and English. Although he is primarily known today as a scholar of Pali language and Buddhist studies, he was also active in the Gandhian Non-Cooperation Movement, leading several *satyagraha* protests against British rule—two of which he was jailed for—and was an ardent social reformer who attempted to eradicate caste-based discrimination among the mill workers of Bombay through the spread of Buddhism and socialism.

Kosambī was born into a Gauḍ Sārasvat Brāhmaṇ family in the Portuguese colony of Goa, the youngest of seven siblings. His enthusiasm for Buddhism was ignited by his reading of a popular account of the Buddha in the Marathi children's magazine, *Bālbodh*, and later, a Marathi translation of Sir Edwin Arnold's *The Light of Asia*. Life in the village was increasingly unsatisfying, however, and his memoir voices frequent frustration at the prevalence of caste-based disputes (*grāmaṇya*), prostitution and the Hindu worship of 'Lady Liquor' (D. Kosambī, [1924] 2010, 64). At the age of 23 years old, Kosambī abandoned his wife and child for Pune and Benares, where utilizing his connections as a Gauḍ Sārasvat Brāhmaṇ he began studying Sanskrit with the renowned Sanskritist and social reformer, Dr. R. G. Bhandarkar (1837–1925). Kosambī's ultimate goal, he professed, was knowledge of Buddhism (D. Kosambī, [1924] 2010, 73–74) After two years, in which he faced constant criticism for his interest in Buddhism, he journeyed onwards to Nepal and eventually to Bodhgaya, where his life took a significant turn when he encountered a Burmese monk affiliated with the MBS.

During the next six years, Kosambī's circle of friends and knowledge of Buddhist scripture and practice grew exponentially as he travelled a Buddhist network shaped by his connection with the MBS. In 1902, he took the vows of a *śrāmaṇera* at the Vidyodaya Piriveṇa in Colombo under the Venerable Hikkaḍuvē Sumangala, and a year later, he became a *bhikkhu* in Burma. Kosambī's affinity for

Buddhism and the Pali language exposed him to a variety of figures, ideologies and practices, as he trained in meditation practice at Sagaing Hill in Burma alongside the German convert, Nyanātiloka Mahathera (1878–1957), studied comparative religion with the Tamil Buddhist apologist, P. Lakshmi Narasu (1861–1934) in Madras, and took over the management of the newly constructed Buddhist vihara at Kuśinagar.

By 1906, this phase of Buddhist practice and study in Kosambī's life entered a new stage when he arrived in Calcutta, determined 'to make some effort to propagate knowledge of Buddhism' (D. Kosambī, [1924] 2010, 186). His reputation as an expert in Pali language came to the attention of a number of politically influential Bengali *bābūs* whose wider interests in educational reform and Indian history made them sympathetic to the introduction of the Pali language at university level. By the end of the year, Kosambī held positions as a Pali language instructor at both the University of Calcutta and National College. This was the beginning of a decades-long teaching career that would take him to universities in Calcutta, Bombay, Sarnath, Pune, Benares, Leningrad, Baroda, and Boston.

While in Calcutta, he also came under the personal support of the famed progressive social reformer and patron of educational projects, Sayajirao Gaikwad, the Maharaja of Baroda (1863–1939). Following Sayajirao back to western India, Kosambī began working on a number of books on Indian history and Buddhism. This also reconnected him with Bhandarkar and several prominent members of the Prārthanā Samāj (Prayer Society), an ecumenical society composed of well-educated Maharashtrian social reformers. With their popular influence (and intellectual and financial support), Kosambī's skills in Pali language came to the attention of the Harvard Sanskritist James Woods (1864–1935), who brought Kosambī to Harvard in 1910 to work on a critical edition of the *Visuddhimagga*.[3]

Kosambī's writing career began in 1909 with Marathi translations of Aśokan inscriptions and the *Sīgāla Sūtta*, but quickly proceeded into more diverging topics and mediums by 1910.[4] In his first essay for the Marathi-language journal *Kesarī*, of the radical Lokamānya Tilak group, Kosambī contended that the idea of democratic-socialist governance was founded by the early Buddhist sangha, and was not of European origin (D. Kosambī, [1910] 2010, 314). Despite frequent forays into current social affairs and critical editions of Pali texts, the bulk of his writings remained focused on the popularization of Buddhism in Marathi. By the end of his life, he had even written a play of Gautama's life (*Bodhisatva: Nāṭak*, 1949), in which the Buddha-to-be finds suffering not only in the physicality of the world but in its social affairs.[5] While exploring these new literary mediums, he also published multiple books, the most well-known of which, *Bhagavān Buddh* (1940), was translated into more than 13 languages (M. Kosambi 2010, 35).[6] Based entirely on primary sources, *Bhagavān Buddh* is a rationalist retelling of the Buddha's life that, in addition to discussing scholarly affairs such as the dating and reliability of certain sources, also critiqued several popular Indian views of Buddhism.[7]

Kosambī's choice to write almost entirely in Marathi can be understood on two different fronts. On the one hand, it demonstrates his larger efforts to democratize and vernacularize Buddhist knowledge. It is quite clear that his audience was not just the English-educated elite, but a wider population of Maharashtrians. Second, his focus on the vernacular coincided with his desire to implement social and educational reform among the lowest classes. His efforts in this regard must be understood as part of the larger colonial-era concern with downward social mobility. Throughout the late nineteenth and early twentieth centuries, there was an unprecedented targeting of lower class and caste communities by Christian missionaries and Hindu, Parsi, and Islamic reformists. It was not until 1910, however, when Kosambī was on his way to Harvard that he believed he had discovered the missing ingredient in his recipe for achieving genuine social reform (*sevā*). From this period onwards, his writings and activities demonstrate a clear trajectory towards the fusion of Buddhism and socialism (M. Kosambi 2010, 8).

The idea of implementing a socialist style of governance into the current Indian political system appealed to him, but as the decade wore on and the violent dimensions of Marxist revolution unfolded in Russia, Kosambī found Marxism difficult to reconcile with his Buddhist faith. His text, *Hindī Sāṃkṛtī āṇī Ahiṃsā* (*Indian Civilization and Non-Violence*), published in 1935, elaborates on earlier arguments supporting the merits of Marxist thought, but incorporates this thinking within a Gandhian and Buddhist framework. He admonishes Marx for replacing the hostility between nations with a hostility between bourgeoisie and workers, comparing it to a strategy of 'removing a thorn with another thorn' (D. Kosambī, [1935] 2010, 356). A better solution, he advocates, is to balance Marxist thinking with the non-violence (*ahiṃsā*) of the Buddha. This, he argues, has been best put into practice by figures like Tolstoy and Gandhi:

> If all the workers in Western countries had similarly refused to fight [literally, done satyagraha] at the beginning of the world war, the war would have ended within a week... only if non-violence is accompanied by the wisdom of socialists will this current turn in the right direction, and lead to the welfare of mankind (D. Kosambī, [1935] 2010, 356–357).[8]

Non-violence, which in Kosambī's eyes was quintessentially Buddhist, had a unique and important contribution to the progressive agenda of socialist nations. As a rational system of thought, Kosambī argued that Buddhism, coupled with socialism's economic insights, had the potential to remove the stains of political violence and social divisions that had befallen not only India but also the globe.

His definitive attempt at putting this philosophy into practice occurred in the mill workers' area of Parel in Bombay in 1936. To do so, he enlisted the support of the philanthropist-industrialist and Gandhian nationalist, J. K. Birla (1884–1967), whom he knew through Gandhi and the MBS.[9] In 1936, Kosambī inaugurated a Buddhist temple (*Buddh Mandir*) to help educate low-caste workers, end caste discrimination, and spread Buddhist and socialist thought. While Kosambī stayed at the temple for three years, this early experiment in Indian Buddhist socialism ultimately failed on terms that are suggestive of the larger social attitude towards

Buddhism. In the months just prior to the temple's inauguration, the Maharashtrian Congressman B. G. Kher—whom Gandhi had asked to oversee Birla's donations to the temple—sent a letter to Gandhi declaring that he could not work on the temple after its completion: "How am I to work on a Buddhist Vihar committee? Are they all going to become Buddhists? Where is the need?" (Gandhi 1999, Vol. 69, 318, fn2).

Gandhi's reply to Kher was adamant that there was to be no proselytizing: 'There is no question of anyone becoming a Buddhist.' Taking it one step further, Gandhi then framed the temple's status not as a tradition distinct from Hinduism, but rather part of it, telling Kher that 'at the most it is to be a Hindu temple of an advanced type' (Gandhi 1999, Vol. 69, 318–319). Four months later during the temple's inauguration, Gandhi would publicly repeat this very proclamation in the *Bombay Chronicle*, describing the *Buddh Mandir* 'as part of the Hindu revival movement that is going on in our midst' (Gandhi 1999, Vol. 70, 272). Judging by the series of heated debates Kosambī had with Indian intellectuals over why Buddhism was not just another Hindu sect,[10] there is little doubt that he would have been angered by Gandhi's characterization. By 1939, these tensions resurfaced once again when Kosambī learned that Birla had expressed negative views of Kosambī's interpretation of Hinduism in *Hindī Sāṃkṛtī āṇī Ahiṃsā* (M. Kosambi 2010, 29–30; Zelliot 1979, 392–393). Disgruntled, the obstinate Kosambī resigned his position as the temple keeper and returned to teaching Buddhist literature in Sarnath. Although the temple was taken over by the MBS to pursue 'a somewhat less ambitious encouragement of Buddhist ideas' (Zelliot 1979, 393), Kosambī did not sever his connections with Gandhi or Birla altogether, and he remained steadfast in his support of Gandhi's political leadership, eventually dying in 1947 at Gandhi's ashram in Sevagram.

Rāhul Sāṅkṛtyāyan (1893–1963)

Rāhul Sāṅkṛtyāyan, like Kosambī, crisscrossed the growing networks of Buddhist activity in colonial India, as an outstanding scholar and popular writer. Although best known in Buddhist circles for his recovery of 'lost' Sanskrit manuscripts in Tibet,[11] the well-travelled explorer was also active in the nationalist movement, first with the Gandhi-led Congress and then with the Kisān Sabhā or Peasant's Movements, and spent a total of six years in British prisons between 1920–1942.

Born Kedārnāth Pāṇḍe to an orthodox Brahman family in what is today the state of Uttar Pradesh, he received his first education in the village *pāṭhśālā*, where he studied Urdu and Sanskrit. At the age of 10 years old, he moved to Benares to continue studies in Sanskrit and became a Vaiṣṇava sādhu, adopting the name Baba Rāmodār Dās. The experience of reciting mantras and performing rituals, however, turned him away from Hindu orthodoxy, and by 1914, fed up with the ritual purity (*śauc-snān*) of the temples, he became a travelling missionary (*prachārak*) for the Hindu reformist organization, the Ārya Samāj. While honing his skills in proving one's case (*mandan*) and refuting other ideologies (*khandan*)—the basis of Ārya Samāji missionary work—Sāṅkṛtyāyan gained greater exposure to Buddhism, first as text and then tradition. The central text of the Samāj, the *Satyārth Prakāś (Light of Truth)* (1875), which Samājis were required to master, contained a special chapter dedicated to refuting the 'heterodox' schools of Indian philosophy, among which Buddhism was included. While working in Lucknow in 1917, Sāṅkṛtyāyan encountered the Indian Buddhist Society, an organization composed largely of Baruas and founded by the Bengali Buddhist monk, Bhadant Bodhānanda Mahāsthavir (1874 – 1952). Impressed by Bodhānanda's character and presentation of Buddhism, Sāṅkṛtyāyan began what can be truly marked as the beginning of his life-long engagement with Buddhism.[12]

What Sāṅkṛtyāyan discovered in Buddhist doctrine was an atheist humanism (*nāstik mānavīyatā*), social egalitarianism, and a system of reason (*buddhi*) compatible with the modern world. Like many other Buddhist modernists of the twentieth century, he was particularly impressed by those texts, such as the Kālāma Sūtta, which as David McMahan (2008, 64) notes, are 'widely interpreted today as exemplifying a [sic] empiricist spirit of free inquiry and self-determination.' Sāṅkṛtyāyan's reading of this text and the *Majjhima Nikāya* mirrors this kind of interpretation:

> When in the *Kālāmas*, I discovered the Buddha's teaching—do not accept the teaching of any book, any tradition, out of concern for your elders, always decide for yourself before you take it on principle—my heart suddenly said, listen, here is a man whose unswerving faith in truth [*satya*] understood the strength of man's independent reason [*buddhi*] . . . when, in the *Majjhima Nikāya*, I read: the teachings of the *dharma* that I have given are like rafts, to carry you to the other side, not to be carried like burdens upon your head; only then I realized, that the thing which I had been seeking for so many days, had been found (Sāṅkṛtyāyan 1950, 8).

For Sāṅkṛtyāyan, the words of the Buddha were 'like embers hidden in ashes, or jewels encrusted in stone,' and despite being spoken 2500 years ago were still relevant to the modern mind and worthy of recovery and propagation (1950, 7).

It was not just the progressive and modern feel of these texts that stood out however. For Sāṅkṛtyāyan, and many other scholars rediscovering India's Buddhist past, there was a sense that 'authentic' religion must somehow be tied to empirically verifiable history. The scholars who discovered Kuśinagar and the other sacred sites of the Buddha in India were engaged in a specific quest to locate the 'truth' of the Buddha in India (Allen 2002). This historical interpretation of religion, which by no means was restricted to Buddhism, can also be seen as part of the humanization of ordinary life, which as Charles Taylor (1992, 266 – 304) suggests, is central to the transformation of social consciousness in the modern world. Recovering this forgotten history and revitalizing it in the Indian present is what Sāṅkṛtyāyan described in later years as his 'compulsion':

> ... by bringing prominently the efforts made in the past towards progress, one can arouse the impulse for ideals in the head and heart of the readers. It is not essential to take much trouble for finding out points of propaganda in my novels and stories, because in using them my objects [sic] has been to inspire the readers with some ideals ... therefore, what is called propaganda by my friends, I consider it to be my compulsion (quoted in Ram 1994, 51).

An ardent nationalist, Sāṅkṛtyāyan hoped to impart revolutionary ideas among the masses not just through his writings, but through his activities as well. He was active in the Gandhian Non-Cooperation Movement in Bihar, and in between two and a half years of jail terms from 1921–1925 he was elected as the Secretary of the District Congress in Saran. One of his primary tasks during this period was to serve on the committee for the Mahā Bodhi Temple case. Campaigning on behalf of the MBS's interests, he formed close, lifetime relationships with several influential figures and associations sympathetic to the propagation of Buddhist knowledge in India.[13] Through these connections, Sāṅkṛtyāyan then travelled to Ceylon in 1927 where he taught Sanskrit and studied Pali literature at the Vidyālankāra Pirivena. Following his first major trip to Tibet from 1929–1930, he became a *bhikṣu*. Accepting an offer from the MBS, he then began conducting missionary work (*dharmaduta*) for Dharmapāla's London Buddhist Mission in Europe from 1932–1933. It was during this time that he shared the exploits of his Sanskrit manuscript collection with several European scholars, one of whom—the renowned Orientalist Sylvain Lévi (1863–1935) — was so impressed with Sāṅkṛtyāyan's research that he had two of his articles translated into French and published in the *Journal Asiatique* (Sāṅkṛtyāyan 1934). While Sāṅkṛtyāyan was already well established in Indian journals, these publications helped cement his standing as a Buddhist scholar and historian of international merit.

Upon his return to India, he earned the support of the Bihar Research Society and again returned to Tibet to search for Sanskrit manuscripts. This also marked the beginning of his collaborative work with the Tibetan intellectual Gedun Chophel (dge 'dun choe 'phel) (1903–1951) and the Russian Buddhologist, George Roerich (1902–1960).[14] With the combined support of European scholars, the MBS, the Bihar Research Society, and sympathetic Indian nationalists, Sāṅkṛtyāyan achieved a public legitimacy and position of authority among Indian elites that gave his otherwise unorthodox Buddhist identity serious weight.

Unlike Kosambī, however, whose main point of departure was almost always in Marathi, Sāṅkṛtyāyan's message was delivered in the supra-regional idiom of Hindi. Seeking to gain a wider audience, he experimented with a variety of new literary forms, such as prose essays, adventure tales, travelogues, short children's stories, and historical fiction.[15] The sheer scope and depth of these writings merits further attention but, like Kosambī's works, they were provocative in nature, challenging the economic clout of landholding classes, the orthodoxy of Brahmin priests, and urging women to travel freely and peasants to rise up against their masters. From the early- to mid-1930s onwards, there is also a clear movement in his writings towards the synthesis of Buddhism with Marxism.

The compatibility of Buddhism with Marxism, he contended, rested in the socially egalitarian doctrine of 'bahujana hitāya, bahujana sukhāya,' or 'the good of many, the happiness of many.' Yet, while arguing this to be theoretically congruent with Marxism, he rebuked the Buddha for having 'confined his [socioeconomic] efforts to the monastic communes alone' (Sāṅkṛtyāyan 1970, 2). This was the reason why Buddhism failed to remove the 'basic foundation of casteism' in the distinction between the 'haves' and the 'have-nots' (Sāṅkṛtyāyan 1970, 3). Buddhism, in other words, had retained a tradition of the status quo. In an evocative passage, Sāṅkṛtyāyan outlined what he clearly felt was a more appropriate modern application of the Four Noble Truths:

> Suffering is to be found in the world; it caused by exploitation; suffering will cease to exist if exploitation is done away with, that is, [the] road to communism is followed; and communism is the way to the cessation of suffering (quoted in R. Bhattacharya 1994, 119).

Gradually, Sāṅkṛtyāyan's personal commitment to Buddhist doctrine, particularly its inward, meditation-based aspects, was submerged by a materialistic interpretation of the world that saw Buddhist practice alone as incapable of enacting social change.[16]

By 1938, Sāṅkṛtyāyan had disrobed, and as he threw himself into the Kisān Sabhā, or Peasant's Movements—he spent the majority of 1939–1942 in Hazaribagh jail and the Deoli detention camp—his Marxist view became even more pronounced. In 1942, he published *Bauddh-Darśan*, which was his attempt at linking the development of Buddhist thought with a materialist interpretation of history (N. Bhattacharyya 1981, 82). At this same time, Sāṅkṛtyāyan's passion for Marxist revolution also appears to have made him more dismissive, or at the very least, impatient with the political utility of non-violence. Some of his writings were vitriolic, attacking Gandhi and the Congress party as 'an agent of Big Business,' an 'utopian believer in non-violence,' and 'an obstacle to the revolution' (cf. Machwe 1978, 49; Sāṅkṛtyāyan 1943, 362). In his most famous work of historical-fiction *Volgāse Gaṅgā (From the Volga to the Ganges)*, the protagonist, Safdar, ridicules Gandhi's use of non-violence as an 'unfailing weapon' (*amogh-kamogh hathiyār*) and boldly proclaims, 'in this world, animals which can't fight fall victim to others' (Sāṅkṛtyāyan 1943, 362). Despite his waning faith in the use of Buddhism as a method for economic and political reform, Sāṅkṛtyāyan continued to promote Buddhism until the end of his life through translations and texts, as well as teaching appointments in Russia and Sri Lanka.

The Buddhist path in colonial India

As relentless campaigners for Buddhism, social equality and political freedom, Kosambī and Sāṅkṛtyāyan shared a tremendous amount in common in their social strategies, networks, and sources of knowledge and inspiration. Each pioneered a novel interpretation of Buddhism, and significantly, both chose to contribute to the intellectual reconfiguration of Buddhism through modern Indian vernaculars. Buddhism's rationality, closeness to socialist thought, and its potential to eradicate caste and liberate socially marginalized communities from religious dogma was central to both of their visions. By drawing on their traditional knowledge of Buddhist scripture and history alongside their knowledge of the new (*naī vidyā*)—an idiom that contained everything from Darwinian science to socialist thought—they were able to shape a modern Buddhism that spoke to the India of the colonial period.

During the first decades of the twentieth century in which Sāṅkṛtyāyan and Kosambī sought to gain knowledge of Buddhism and later, spread it, they participated in what Richard Jaffe (2004, 67) has described more generally as 'the emergence of a tightly linked global Buddhist culture' composed of 'diverse "complex global loops" through which ideas were transmitted.' This culture was, in large part, a creation of several well-known Buddhist reformers, pilgrims and globetrotters, who not only saw the nineteenth and twentieth centuries as a period of colonial interference, but also an opportunity for expansion and growth facilitated by empire and modern technologies. Kosambī and Sāṅkṛtyāyan both shaped and were shaped by this global Buddhist sphere, as they utilized new technologies and literary forms to travel further distances, reach wider audiences and establish relationships with figures and organizations in North America, Europe and Asia. Their wide circle of friends and sympathizers across the globe—American, Ceylonese, Tibetan, Russian, and so on—were integral to their success. While this international support was paramount, it by no means stood alone.

Inside India, Sāṅkṛtyāyan's and Kosambī's ability to draw on elite social formations—national universities, princely classes, research societies, and the nation's most influential politicians—were crucial to their national recognition and success. While the access to power and knowledge they had was typical of those in their class, their unorthodox opinions on the social and political issues of the day created a distance between the social groups they were born into and affiliated with. What helped them form a bond with other Indian elites that did not necessarily share the same interest in reviving Buddhism was their common ground in anti-British nationalist activities, educational concerns for recovering India's past and wider regard for social reform and assistance (*sevā*).

The contradictions in their positions and synthesis of various ideologies—Buddhist modernism, socialism, Marxism, Indian nationalism, to name a few—allowed for a creative tension that reached far beyond their own circles but was also perhaps too eclectic to have any singular, sudden impact. However, the discourse around Buddhism that they shaped, while threatening to some, continued to attract a wide range of Indians throughout the final years of the colonial period, coalescing in the stitching of the *Aśokan dhammacakra* on the Indian national flag in 1947, and later, the mass conversions of *dalits* or former untouchables led by Dr Ambedkar in 1956. Although our understanding of colonial-era Indian Buddhism is still fragmentary, the lives of Kosambī and Sāṅkṛtyāyan reveal the prominence—and arguably, even triumph— of a particular kind of Buddhism based on not just humanity and reason, but also revolution. That is, for many Indians, the Buddha was not only a social reformer and rational, empirical thinker whose ancient sangha founded the ideals of socialist democratic governance. He—and his humanity, not divinity, was of importance here—was also a social revolutionary who rebelled against the dogma and tyranny of the status quo. This was, of course, similar to the many ways in which India's nationalists and social reformers imagined themselves.

NOTES

1. There are, however, some exceptions to this trend, the most notable of which are Zelliot (1979), Aloysius (1998), and Ahir (1989).
2. There are numerous examples of figures with a wide variety of non-Buddhist religious affiliations supporting Buddhist activity in India at this time. See Ahir (1989, 159–163).
3. This was eventually published in 1950 in the Harvard Oriental Series with Henry Clarke Warren.
4. M. Kosambi (2010) has translated a selection of his works into English. A complete bibliography of Kosambī's works is also available in M. Kosambi (2010, 413–417).
5. An English translation of this play is found in M. Kosambi (2010, 358–408).
6. English, however, was not one of these.
7. For instance, Kosambī contended that the Buddhist stress on non-violence was *not* responsible for India's downfall (this was a popular position at the time), that the Buddha (and Mahavira) was *not* a vegetarian, and that the driving force behind Gautama's renunciation was *not* the Four Passing Sights, but his disenchantment with political violence (M. Kosambi, 2010, 33–36).
8. I am grateful to Laurence Cox for pointing out that this kind of political critique was in fashion at the time among those figures who eventually founded the third communist International and later started revolutions in Russia and Germany.
9. Birla, who was an orthodox Hindu, financed the construction and restoration of multiple MBS Buddhist viharas across India. It is important to note, however, that Birla conceived of a Buddhist revival in India as part of a Hindu renaissance, and not as a distinct tradition.
10. Throughout the 1920s and 1930s, Kosambī wrote a series of essays strongly criticizing Rajendra Prasad's (later, the first President of India) and the Indian historian, Dr S. V. Ketkar's views of Buddhism (for brief discussions of these debates, see M. Kosambi, 2010, 16–17, 32–33).
11. Sāṅkṛtyāyan visited Tibet four times (1929–1930, 1934, 1936, 1938) in search of manuscripts relevant to the study of Indian history. Amongst his most important

discoveries there were a large number of Sanskrit manuscripts dating from the eleventh to thirteenth century CE, some of which he was able to photograph or copy by hand. These included the complete manuscripts of the *Pramāṅavārt-tika-bhāṣā*, a subcommentary on Dharmakīrti's work on logic and Asaṅga's *Yogācārabhūmi*. According to Andrew Skilton (personal communication, February 13, 2013), photographic negatives of around half of Sāṅkṛtyāyan's collection is currently housed in Patna. Also noteworthy was what was then one of the oldest known versions of Saraha's *Dohakośa* (composed in Apabhraṃśa) and the biography of Dharmasvāmin (Chag lo-ts-ba Chos-rje-dpal), a Tibetan pilgrim who visited India during the thirteenth century. Numerous translations and critical editions of these manuscripts based on Sāṅkṛtyāyan's collection have since been published by the Bihar and Orissa Research Society and K. P. Jayaswal Research Institute. Although Sāṅkṛtyāyan also published extensively on a variety of Buddhist topics (see Ram, 1994), very few of his works are available in English. A notable exception is *Sāṅkṛtyāyan* (1984).

12. On Bodhānanda, see Ahir (1989, 65–67).
13. The most important of these friendships were with the Bihari lawyer, Rajendra Prasad (1884–1963), later to become the first President of India; the Indologist K. P. Jayaswal (1881–1937), who was the director of the Bihar Research Society; and the Venerable Devapriya Valinsinha (1904–1968), who later became the General Secretary of the MBS from 1933–1968.
14. On the interactions between these figures, with a central focus on Chophel, see Stoddard (1985, chap. 6).
15. Bhaṭṭācārya (2005, 205–215), has identified 148 books and 71 articles credited to Sāṅkṛtyāyan.
16. According to one of his disciples, the Indian Buddhist monk, Jagdiś Kāśyap (1908–1976), Sāṅkṛtyāyan had dismissed Kāśyap's interest in meditation as something best to be done in old age whereas the present was better spent in missionary work (Kāśyap 1961, 8).

REFERENCES

AHIR, D. C. 1989. *The Pioneers of Buddhist Revival in India*. Delhi: Sri Satguru Publications.

ALLEN, C. 2002. *The Buddha and the Sahibs: The Men Who Discovered India's Lost Religion*. London: John Murray.

ALOYSIUS, G. 1998. *Religion as Emancipatory Identity: A Buddhist Movement Among the Tamils Under Colonialism*. New Delhi: Christian Institute for the Study of Religion and Society.

BHAṬṬĀCĀRYA, A. 2005. *Mahāpaṃdita Rāhula Sāṅkrityāyan ke vyaktitvāntaraṇ kī prakriya. [Mahapandit Rāhul Sāṅkṛtyāyan's Science of Transcending the Individual]*. Kolkātā: Ānaṇda Prakāśan.

BHATTACHARYYA, N. N. 1981. *History of Researches of Indian Buddhism*. New Delhi: Munshiram Manoharlal Publishers.

BHATTACHARYA, R. 1994. From Buddha to Marx. In *Essays on Indology: Birth centenary tribute to Mahapandita Rahula Sankrityayana*, edited by Alaka Chattopadhyaya, 118–21. Calcutta: Manisha Granthalaya.

GANDHI, M. K. 1999. *The Collected Works of Mahatma Gandhi* (electronic book). New Delhi: Publications Division Government of India, 1999, Vol. 69–70. http://www.gandhiserve.org/cwmg/cwmg.html

JAFFE, R. M. 2004. Seeking Sakyamuni: Travel and the Reconstruction of Japanese Buddhism. *The Journal of Japanese Studies* 30 (1): 65–96.

JOSHI, L. M. 1983. *Discerning the Buddha: A Study of Buddhism and of the Brahmanical Hindu Attitude to It*. New Delhi: Munshiram Manoharlal.

KAŚYAP, J. 1961. Rāhuljī: Mere Gurubhaī. *Journal of the Bihar Research Society* 47: 7–10.

KOSAMBĪ, D. 1949. *Bodhisatva: Natak*. Mumbai: Dharmanand Smarak Trust.

KOSAMBĪ, D. [1910] 2010. The Oligarchic Kingdom of the Vajjis. In *Dharmanand Kosambī: The Essential Writings*. edited and translated by Meera Kosambī, 312–5. Ranikhet: Permanent Black.

KOSAMBĪ, D. [1924] 2010. *Nivedan* [A Narrative], 1912–1924. In *Dharmanand Kosambī: The Essential Writings*. edited and translated by Meera Kosambī, 53–219. Ranikhet: Permanent Black.

KOSAMBĪ, D. [1935] 2010. Civilization and Non-Violence. In *Dharmanand Kosambī: The Essential Writings*. edited and translated by Meera Kosambī, 327–57. Ranikhet: Permanent Black.

KOSAMBI, M. 2010. Introduction: Situating Dharmanand Kosambī. In *Dharmanand Kosambī: The Essential Writings*. edited and translated by Meera Kosambī, 1–53. Ranikhet: Permanent Black.

MACHWE, P. B. 1978. *Rahul Sankrityayan*. New Delhi: Sahitya Akademi.

MCMAHAN, D. L. 2008. *The Making of Buddhist Modernism*. Oxford: Oxford University Press.

RADHAKRISHNAN, S. 1956. Foreword. In *2500 Years of Buddhism*, edited by P. V. Bapat, i–xvi. New Delhi: Ministry of Information and Broadcasting.

RAM, R. 1994. Contribution of Rahula to the Indian Buddhist Studies. In *Mahapandita Rahula Sankrityayana Birth Centenary Volume*, edited by H. B. Chowdhury, 43–55. Calcutta: Bauddha Dharmankur Sabha.

SĀṄKṚTYĀYAN, R. 1934. Recherches Bouddhiques, par le Bhiksu Rahula Sāṅkṛtyāyana (de Benares). *Journal Asiatique* CCXXV: 195–230.

SĀṄKṚTYĀYAN, R. 1943. *Volgāse Gaṅgā*. [From the Volga to the Ganges]. Ilāhābād: Kitāb Mahal.

SĀṄKṚTYĀYAN, R. 1950. *Merī jīvan yātrā*. [My Life Journey]. Vol. II. Ilāhābād: Kitāb Mahal.

SĀṄKṚTYĀYAN, R. 1970. Buddhist Dialectics. In *Buddhism: The Marxist Approach*. New Delhi: People's Publishing House.

SĀṄKṚTYĀYAN, R. 1984. *Selected Essays of Rahul Sankrityayan*. New Delhi: People's Publishing House.

SĀVARKAR, V. D. 1938. *Hindutva: Who is a Hindu?* New Delhi: Central Hindu Yuvak Sabhā.

STODDARD, H. 1985. *Le Mendiant de l'Amdo*. Recherches sur la Haute Asie 9 Paris: Société d'Ethnographie.

TAYLOR, C. 1992. *Sources of the Self: The Making of the Modern Identity*. Cambridge: Harvard University Press.

VIVEKANANDA, S. 1962. *The Complete Works of Swami Vivekananda*. Vol. I. Calcutta: Advaita Ashrama.

ZELLIOT, E. 1979. The Indian Rediscovery of Buddhism, 1855–1956. In *Studies in Pali and Buddhism: A Memorial Volume in Honor of Bhikkhu Jagdish Kashyap*, edited by A. K. Narain, 389–406. Delhi: B.R. Publishing Company.

ELECTIVE AFFINITIES: THE RECONSTRUCTION OF A FORGOTTEN EPISODE IN THE SHARED HISTORY OF THAI AND BRITISH BUDDHISM – KAPILAVAḌḌHO AND WAT PAKNAM

Andrew Skilton

The article discusses the first attempt to establish an independent bhikkhu-saṅgha in England in 1956 and the reasons that this initial attempt failed. The account draws on testimony from George Blake, one of the monks ordained under this initiative. After a short contextualization of the situation in which Blake met with Buddhism in London, there follows a further discussion of two issues on which his evidence sheds fresh light: the falling out of the British monk Kapilavaḍḍho with Luang Por Sodh (Phra Mongkolthepmuni), the abbot of Wat Paknam in Bangkok; and the move away from the teaching of the soḷasakāya meditation at the English Sangha Trust in London.

Introduction

By the 1950s, Buddhism had been known and practised to varying degrees by a widening circle of interested parties in the West. A major focus of such activity in England was the Buddhist Society, founded in 1924 under the presidency of the barrister, and later judge, Christmas Humphreys and based at that time in Great Russell Street in Bloomsbury (see Yoshinaga 2013). In addition, a number of Asian Buddhist monastic emissaries had come to the UK to teach and run Buddhist activities. While a number of westerners had already travelled to Asia, to seek ordination, there were also those who supported the idea of creating an independent *bhikkhu-saṅgha* resident in England. In the middle of the decade an attempt was made to do just this, with the ordination of four men from England at Wat Paknam in Thailand. To support their monastic life and work once they returned to England, the English Sangha Trust was created in 1956—and yet this Thai project failed. Within a few months of their ordination, two of the four had disrobed, their leader following suit by May 1957, and the future of the whole plan looked bleak. While the English Sangha Trust (EST) carried on its work, eventually successfully supporting the transmission of the Thai Forest Sangha of Ajahn Chah to the UK, the fate of that original scheme passed into obscurity with virtually no comment in the published records. An unexpected inheritance of the situation was a prejudice against the Wat Paknam meditation method (the *soḷasakāya* meditation pioneered by Sodh from c. 1914) in EST circles.

The present article seeks to shed some light on the events that led to this initial setback, drawing on the direct testimony of one of those remarkable young men who had become monks in 1956—B. George Blake. He had met with Buddhism in 1951 while working for the London County Council after being demobilized from wartime service in the RAF. It seems from this distance that, despite rumours and half-truths that have obscured what happened at the time, the EST plan was ultimately foiled by the intersection of conflicting concepts of loyalty and cultural expectation, fatefully admixed with personality traits, that may have made the outcome inevitable. Dr Blake, now a retired clinical psychologist in his 80s, graciously agreed to meet the author for an extended interview in 2010 in which the events that are the focus of this article were covered in some detail.

The creation of the English Sangha Trust

The English Sangha Trust could be seen as a natural consequence of the activities of a number of now quite well known individual men from the British Isles, who had travelled to Asia where they underwent ordination and lived a Buddhist life as monks. It is probably inevitable that sooner or later the will to create an independent native British *bhikkhu-saṅgha*, consisting of British monks with the authority to teach and to ordain as a quorate *nikāya*, would emerge. By the early 1950s, this ambition had become focussed around William Purfurst, a charismatic, forceful character attending activities, by this time, at the Buddhist Society in London and teaching both there and around the country, including Manchester. Purfurst had met U Ṭhittila, a Burmese monk who was librarian at the Buddhist Society, studied with him and eventally in 1952 received from him his lower ordination, *pabbajjā*, and thereby had become a *sāmaṇera*. Keen to follow U Ṭhittila to Burma (whence the latter had returned in that same year to take up an academic post in Rangoon) in order to receive his higher ordination and become a full *bhikkhu*, Purfurst's plans were foiled when his application for a visa was turned down.

It was therefore a fateful coincidence that in the same period Luang Por Sodh (Phra Mongkolthepmuni), the abbot of Wat Paknam in Bangkok, had conceived the ambition to spread his teaching, particularly of his *soḷasakāya* meditation practice, beyond Thailand. He sent an emissary monk to London, the capital of the greatest contemporary colonial power and unexpected victor in the recent World War. Phra Ṭhitavedo arrived in London from Wat Paknam in 1953 where he made contact with the Buddhist Society and quickly understood the potential for mutual fulfillment in the ambitions of Purfurst.[1] He assisted Purfurst in obtaining a visa for Thailand in order to seek ordination there.

In February 1954, Purfurst travelled to Bangkok with Ṭhitavedo, in May receiving his *upasampadā* and the name Kapilavaḍḍho at the hands of Sodh himself. Purfurst's own report claims that this was a national event, attended by an audience of 10,000—after all, Purfurst was thought to be the first Englishman to be ordained in Thailand (Randall 1990, 74).[2] Over the coming months Kapilavaḍḍho was put to various tests—recorded in vivid detail in his memoir (Randall 1990)—and once he had demonstrated his competence, was sent, under protest, back to the UK by Sodh in November of the same year to proselytize the *soḷasakāya* meditation there.

By 1955 Kapilavaḍḍho, clearly a strenuous activist, had gathered suitable recruits—three young men who under his guidance became *sāmaṇeras* at the Sri Lankan London Buddhist Vihara—Peter Morgan, Robert Albison and George Blake. (Blake received his *pabbajjā* in October.) The inaugural meeting of the EST, to establish a financial basis for an independent English *bhikkhu-saṅgha*, was held in November of the same year (Webb, n.d., 1). By December, Kapilavaḍḍho and his three trainees were received at Wat Paknam, and the *sāmaṇeras* had undergone their higher ordination there in January 1956. Peter Morgan became Paññāvaḍḍho, Robert Albison Saddhāvaḍḍho, and George Blake Vijjāvaḍḍho. (Kapilavaḍḍho had been honoured by Sodh making him their *anusāsanācariya* 'junior examining monk' for the ordinations [Randall 1990, 192]. One might see this as part of Sodh's preparation of Kapilavaḍḍho for his anticipated role in creating a Wat Paknam [and Mahā Nikāya] sponsored British *bhikkhu-saṅgha*.)[3] No comment is made in any English language sources on the strange fact that the new monks appear to have moved quickly from Wat Paknam to Wat Thathong. Moreover, leaving his trainee monks behind, Purfurst shortly returned to London where he hurriedly set about working with supporters there to bring the EST into being. Saddhāvaḍḍho/Albison had also returned but quickly disrobed. Funding was raised, accommodation found, a constitution agreed and the Trust incorporated in May 1956 (Shine 2009, 40; Webb, n.d., 1), but Kapilavaḍḍho was 'called back' to Bangkok in June to assist Blake/Vijjāvaḍḍho who in some sources is described as having become 'ill'. By August Kapilavaḍḍho, Vijjāvaḍḍho/Blake and Paññāvaḍḍho/Morgan were all back in London, and Vijjāvaḍḍho had disrobed. By the same time in the following year, Kapilavaḍḍho himself had disrobed, claiming physical overwork, and Paññāvaḍḍho, the only one of the original four monks still in robes and a *bhikkhu* of but 16 months standing, was left at this point to take over leadership of the EST.

By any standards, this is not a tale of success—three out of four founding monks had disrobed within a year, including, crucially, Purfurst. As a plan it looks like a drastic failure, although most printed sources on the matter write as if this broken trajectory were unremarkable.

The falling out with Sodh

Published sources on these events are few and far between. Most treatments of this period of development of British Buddhism say little or less about them. Both Terry Shine (2009, 44), in his monograph on the history of the EST and Theravada in the UK (offered as a tribute to Kapilavaḍḍho), and Purfurst himself in his memoir of these three years in his life (Randall 1990, 193–194), says nothing at all—merely mentioning the trip to assist Vijjāvaḍḍho—as does Bluck (2006, 9–10).[4] The personal testimony of George Blake is therefore all the more illuminating in offering evidence that for the first time begins to make these events more intelligible in terms of their inner dynamics.

However, his is not the only voice that speaks about the hasty return of the UK monks and what may have been involved. A modern anonymous biography of Sodh, *The Life and Times of Luang Phaw Wat Paknam* (hereafter *Life and Times)*, has recorded for us an account of events that took place in Wat Paknam and appear to be about a serious 'falling out' between Kapilavaḍḍho and Sodh (*The Life and Times* 2010, 130–131; cited in Mackenzie 2007, 37). It explains that the UK monks were given a number of special privileges, but that the special treatment offered to the newcomers went to their heads and they forgot their junior status. Through an interpreter they asked for further privileges while in a plenary meeting at the temple and then, unaccountably, walked out on Sodh—a grave insult towards him as abbot and preceptor (*upajjhāya*). The author comments, 'Unfortunately, the translator made no attempt to remedy the situation', and cites Sodh's determination that such insubordination should be curtailed for the good of Buddhist discipline as a whole.

This account describes a breakdown of communication, which is a matter of both decorum and discipline, occuring at a temple meeting. He emphasizes the conflict between Sodh's desire to spread the dhamma but not to tolerate Western insubordination. From this perspective the problem is the usurping of monastic hierarchy, and how to manage disrespect. However, there is no explanatory content to the account, other than the suggestion that the junior monks have lost the sense of where they belong, and their subsequent actions do not really make sense.

The author goes on to explain that shortly after this incident in 1956, Sodh fell ill and could not therefore receive the ill-mannered British monks. In February 1959, Sodh died. In Bangkok a connection came to be made between the 'Kapilavaḍḍho debacle' and Sodh's demise—a connection clearly alluded to in the *Life and Times* account.

George Blake's account

Blake vividly recalls the events of this period.[5] They were indeed treated from the start with kindness and privilege. They were provided with a specially built *kuṭi* which even housed a flush toilet, on the expectation that Westerners would need one. Their living arrangements contrasted greatly with the living conditions of fellow Thai monks at Wat Paknam. They were also dependent on Ṭhitavedo, who was their advocate, administrative contact and interpreter (confirmed by Purfurst; Randall 1990, 192). Ṭhitavedo too was residing with them in the special *kuṭi*. Kapilavaḍḍho felt a very close bond with Ṭhitavedo—even claiming that 'they had been brothers in a previous lifetime'—but one night, Blake remembers, Ṭhitavedo simply vanished from their *kuṭi*.[6] No explanation of this disappearance was offered to Blake or the other new monks, then or later.

A few days later, the UK contingent were summoned to a plenary meeting in the pagoda, at which, the new monks seated before the abbot, Sodh said through his own interpreter that he needed to explain to them 'the business with Ṭhitavedo'. At this point Kapilavaḍḍho, apparently assuming some kind of bad news, interrupted the abbot and said, 'I don't want to hear anything against my brother!' Sodh: 'No, it's important that you hear what has happened.' Kapilavaḍḍho (interrupting again): 'If you insist, I will leave!' For a third time, Sodh tried to explain, at which Kapilavaḍḍho stood up and walked out as Sodh was speaking.[7] Saddhāvaḍḍho immediately followed Kapilavaḍḍho; then Paññāvaḍḍho likewise followed. Blake/Vijjāvaḍḍho, in an acute crisis of loyalties, decided he, too, had to go, but grasped Sodh's feet in a gesture of respect before moving to follow the person whom he saw as his immediate teacher—Kapilavaḍḍho.

Blake sees their behaviour as 'a gesture of insult', and feels embarrassed by the memory. The two parties remained unreconciled, and during the interview Blake speculated about writing to the present abbot of Wat Paknam to attempt some reconciliation.

Luang Por Sodh's account

While I am not aware of an account of this espisode penned by Sodh himself, the Wat Paknam web pages include one by an anonymous author who had discussed it directly with Sodh at the time and claims to have been personally involved.[8] Following a description of the lavish welcome and support given to the UK monks (including the flush toilet), the falling out is described thus:

> Later on, a misunderstanding occurred. There is no clear evidence which suggests the reasons why things went wrong . . . The Western monks and their interpreter approached Luang Pho [= Sodh] to make a request for some privileges. Luang Pho explained the reasons why such a request could not be fulfilled. These monks [i.e. the Western monks] didn't listen and suddenly left the congregation without respect . . . . The interpreter didn't attempt to help Luang Pho and these Western monks understand each other . . . These monks and the interpreter left the temple . . . Both the interpreter and the Western monks came to see me [the author] in order to inform me that they had left the temple. After having left the temple, these monks didn't return to the temple. Only the interpreter stated clearly that he would come back if the request was fulfilled. Luang Pho insisted on refusing such requests and rejected all the interpreter's proposed stipulations. As the interpreter's request wasn't allowed, he didn't come back to the temple. The Western monks resided in Thailand for a little longer before disrobing and returning to Europe as lay people.[9]

This account has important details to add to our understanding of these events, and it is likely that the same source informed the *Life and Times* version.

An interpretation

These accounts all doubtless contain elements of what happened—some elements that are complementary, but others that are incompatible, particularly the role (if any) of Ṭhitavedo at the plenary meeting. Blake's recollection is that Ṭhitavedo was not there and the meeting was about his absence. Sodh's account politely indicates, by established Thai convention, that he was. He is not named, but his identity is established by the frequent reference to his role as 'the interpreter'. Throughout Kapilavaḍḍho's time in Thailand up to this point, interpreting was one of the main functions that Ṭhitavedo had performed for the UK monk(s). The possibility remains that Blake's recollection misplaces Ṭhitavedo's disappearance to before the meeting rather than afterwards. These accounts, however, are agreed that the foreign monks walked out on Sodh at a plenary meeting at the temple, this usurped normal protocols, and possibly amounted to disciplinary infraction.

Blake emphasized that Kapilavaḍḍho had a charismatic streak, but also tended to be feisty and even confrontational in his manner.[10] For example, he described him as being 'tolerated' in Buddhist Society circles, and thought that his treatment of Sodh in this incident was entirely characteristic of the man. He also recalled that Kapilavaḍḍho retained a strong sense of having been shortchanged in Thailand of the recognition that he thought he, himself, deserved. The *Life and Times* account, which has been approved as 'correct' by senior monks at Wat Paknam who had witnessed the event,[11] is surely also correct in emphasizing the problem of formal hierarchy and decorum raised by Kapilavaḍḍho's behaviour. The Wat Paknam account also emphasizes the issue of insubordination, both in the event itself and as reflected in Sodh's later response.

Both Blake and *Life and Times* mention food. The latter, in a generalizing tone, writes: 'While the newly ordained monks were seated *à table* enjoying a full-blown English breakfast, their seniors had to sit on mats on the ground with only rice soup as their food' (*Life and Times* 2010, 130). While this seems to suggest that this inappropriate scenario was an ongoing problem, it is possible that this might be a reference to one specific incident which Blake recalls vividly.

Blake is adamant that the new monks wanted to be able to integrate with the Thai monks at the appropriate level, that is, as Thai monastic ritual and etiquette demands, at the most junior level. However, on one occasion he thinks that the group may have been 'set up' by Ṭhitavedo. At one meal time, as they took their proper places amongst the junior monks at the lowest level in the food hall, they received a message that they assumed came from Sodh, inviting them to sit at a special table in the centre of the hall. Blake recalls feeling embarrassed and uncomfortable. In retrospect, he thinks the invitation may have been just the work of Ṭhitavedo. For the very reason that Blake felt uncomfortable, so too may senior monks have felt slighted and that proper monastic protocols were being usurped.

All of these components were facets of a more complex situation. To put together the links, albeit in a speculative vein, one can summarize the situation as follows:

(a) As general background, Kapilavaḍḍho was confrontational by temperament and, allegedly, thought he deserved more recognition than he got.

(b) Ṭhitavedo must have accrued some enhanced status arising from his successful mission to the UK to implement Sodh's vision for international expansion. (To have been sent at all suggests he must already have had fairly high status within the community, along with serviceable English.) Within three years of his mission, four UK monks had been ordained by Sodh at Wat Paknam—a great success. It is clear, especially from Purfurst, that Ṭhitavedo was closely associated with the *farang* monks and the success they represented, and even, one suspects, enjoyed (in both senses of this term?) the acclaim that the converts attracted. We should bear in mind that this acclaim was national, not just restricted to Wat Paknam. The film of the ordination shows Ṭhitavedo alongside the westerners seated in state in western chairs at the centre of attention the night before the ordination, and the anonymous commentary introduces him as 'a very famous *bhikkhu*, Ṭhitavedo *bhikkhu*,' in contrast to Sodh, the abbot, who is just 'a famous teaching *bhikkhu* in Thailand'![12]

(c) The realization of the ambitions of each man, Kapilavaḍḍho and Ṭhitavedo, lay in different hands. While Kapilavaḍḍho felt considerable loyalty to his mentor, Ṭhitavedo, the latter did not necessarily reciprocate this in the same way or to the same degree. Kapilavaḍḍho's ambitions for ordination had been facilitated by Ṭhitavedo on whom he was significantly dependent (Randall 1990, 9, 80, 112, 140), but ultimately lay in London where he had been for some years enacting a leading Buddhist role. The evidence of his memoir suggests that Purfurst found great fulfillment and satisfaction in his Thai idyll (present author's term) but this was clearly a time-limited option, since his hosts had other plans for him (Randall 1990, 177–178).

(d) An inappropriate and presumptuous eating arrangement was enacted at a mealtime on at least one occasion, which clearly left senior monks feeling slighted since it is remembered over 50 years later.

(e) What is extraordinary, however, is the evidence from Sodh's account that indicates that 'the translator', who could have been no-one other than Ṭhitavedo, actually took sides with the foreign monks in making demands that were, by the rules of monastic protocol, undeliverable without significant cost to Sodh's status and to monastic discipline at Wat Paknam. There is no indication of what these demands might have been, unless we infer that the food incident was related. (Blake's testimony is that neither he nor Paññāvaḍḍho had any problems with the climate, food or conditions in Bangkok, both having been born to similar climates, cuisines and cultural practices—Blake as a village Jamaican and Morgan as an Anglo-Indian. Blake does recall Saddhāvaḍḍho being challenged by the local conditions. Kapilavaḍḍho's memoir indicates no major cultural problems on his own part.) Surely, fulfillment of Ṭhitavedo's ambitions, whatever they may have been, lay with Sodh? While Ṭhitavedo probably felt genuine friendship towards Kapilavaḍḍho, his interests ultimately lay at Wat Paknam, not with the Englishman, and yet it seems that he was moved to compromise his relations with Sodh, as Kapilavaḍḍho was to do. Ṭhitavedo left the temple. It appears that Ṭhitavedo linked his monastic fate to a demand on behalf of the foreign monks, but this 'ransom' was simply not sufficient for Sodh to risk the disciplinary structure of Wat Paknam. There is no evidence that he kept up contact with Kapilavaḍḍho after the denoument, and the present author infers that this re-alliance was not based on personal friendship on Ṭhitavedo's part—even though from the point of view of Western sentiment, one would expect it to have been. One wonders if Ṭhitavedo in fact tried to use his connection to the foreigners as leverage to improve his own position/status at Wat Paknam—a strategic move that, in this case, failed.

(f) It seems that Ṭhitavedo simply left Wat Paknam. His position there would clearly have become untenable after pitching his own position against the authority of the abbot.[13] Blake's recollection that Ṭhitavedo had disappeared before the walkout from the plenary meeting possibly indicates some retrospective conflation or telescoping of events on both sides. A possible reconciliation of Blake's and the Wat Paknam account is to understand that Ṭhitavedo's challenge to Sodh's authority happened at an earlier plenary meeting, and his mysterious disappearance as recalled by Blake was the result of having effectively talked himself out of his own monastery through his challenge to the abbot's authority. The foreign monks were then summoned a day or so later to a second plenary meeting so that Sodh could explain what had happened to their interpreter and mentor, and it was at this point that Kapilavaḍḍho walked out, it seems, in a gesture of solidarity to someone he regarded as a close friend. This personal loyalty is described in a letter by Paññāvaḍḍho.[14]

> We were from the start put under the charge of Bhikkhu Thitavedo allied with Kapi [Kapilavaḍḍho]. This because we spoke no Thai, but Thitavedo spoke quite good English. We didn't realise however that Thitavedo was somewhat of a rogue. Eventually he had to disrobe but I don't know the full story of what happened. The people at Wat Paknam kept telling Kapi about Thitavedo but for some time he chose not to listen. Eventually an English resident and some reliable Thai people impressed on Kapi that the situation was not good and it was decided to move to Wat That Tong (without Thitavedo of course). Then Kapi having shed the load and feeling content with the situation, went off to England.

Presumably Kapilavaḍḍho's touchiness at this stage was also informed by the issue of the 'demands', which were about to be publicly refused. It seems unlikely that Ṭhitavedo would have ventured his own future on a set of demands which were completely unknown to the intended beneficiary. Kapilavaḍḍho was also effectively pre-empting his own public humiliation by walking away and not allowing his abbot to exercise his legitimate authority. These unmet demands could also have been the basis for Kapilavaḍḍho's sense of lack of recognition alleged by Blake.

(g) Kapilavaḍḍho sealed the demise of the relationship with Sodh and, thereby, with Wat Paknam tradition and practices, by impetuously walking out on his preceptor and abbot. Worse still, the affront was performed in front of the entire monastery, with every monk in attendance from the most senior to the most junior. It was a very public insult of major proportions in Thai eyes, a usurping of monastic discipline, and one that could not but have major repercussions. There is only one conceivable way for the junior party to recover from such a situation—apology and submission to formal disciplinary procedures. Yet this was an unlikely path for a man of Kapilavaḍḍho's character to take.

(h) Sodh himself was left in a most difficult position. He could not retract anything—neither the ordinations nor the time invested in this attempt to establish his teaching outside of Thailand. Nor could he ignore the insult, even if he was personally disposed to be magnanimous. As abbot he could not afford to lose face, and indeed the preservation of monastic discipline is an irreducible necessity. Moreover, the establishing of proper discipline at the temple is an important part of the narrative of Sodh's transformation of Wat Paknam after his appointment as abbot there in 1916 (*The Life and Times 2010*, 55ff.). Therefore, it begs the question of whether or not Sodh resorted to monastic disciplinary procedures to bring the UK monks back into line. Of the range of disciplinary options open to the abbot, those which most simply correspond with subsequent events are that Kapilavaḍḍho had either received a 'dismissal' (*paṇāmanā*) from Sodh or, more seriously, been served a 'banishment order' (*pabbājaniya-kamma*) by Sodh. A dismissal is a more personal action initiated by an *upajjhāya* (preceptor) towards a pupil monk in his tutelage, and dissolves the link between the two by means of a simple statement such as, 'I dismiss you'. The enacting of a banishment order is a communal act and would be consistent with the plenary gathering(s), and would have required the relocation of the miscreant(s) to another temple where they would be obliged to live under a number of restrictions. It is 'a sort of temporary removal from the monastery where [one] is normally residing' (Upasak 1975, s.v. *pabbājaniya-kamma*) combined with a reduced status. Both can be enacted as a penalty for, amongst other things, rude or insubordinate behaviour such as Kapilavaḍḍho's, albeit for different degrees of seriousness, although both are also formal conditions from which it is possible—with due acknowledgement by the refractory monk—to be released. Indeed, there is an obligation on the part of an *upajjhāya* who issues a dismissal to accept a genuine apology from his former pupil. To decline it would be for the *upajjhāya* to incur a *dukkata* offence himself.[15]

However, it is quite possible that far from being dismissed or banished, the UK monks debunked under their own initiative. Perhaps a formal disciplinary course of action would have, in the context, invited public, national interest in the internal business of Wat Paknam and drawn attention to the lack of control that Sodh could exercise over his new and prestigious foreign monks. The UK monks could, and eventually did, slip away back to England, having demonstrated that they were not fully obedient to Thai monastic protocols. As it was, they 'slipped away' even while in Bangkok, a development to which we shall come shortly. It is, therefore, quite possible that an expedient and effective response to this *impasse* was to become diplomatically unwell, so that he 'could not' receive the problematic westerners and thereby not give fuel to the contentious situation, nor appear to condone bad behaviour. The Wat Paknam web account confirms the strategic component of this interpretation: paradoxically, it offers two parallel and unreconciled reasons for Sodh's conduct at this point: (i) that Sodh was just ill; but (ii) that Sodh was simply not prepared to be seen to endorse such gross indiscipline as Kapilavaḍḍho had exhibited, and also described the latter as a 'necessary' position, a position he confided personally to the author of that account:

> At that time, Luang Pho (LP) was seriously ill so could not meet Kapillavattho [sic]. There was a rumor that the main reason for LP's illness was due to his disappointment with the foreign monks. But in fact he was ill before the dispute... LP explained to me [the web page author] that he didn't meet Kapillavattho again as Kapillavattho should not have left the congregation in that rude manner lacking in respect, adding that LP wouldn't be able to support anyone who didn't respect others... According to LP, LP's refusal was necessary as he expected to teach the foreign monks what should be done and what should not. (Wat Paknam. Accessed December 11, 2012, translated by Choompolpaisal. http://www.watpaknam.org/content.php?op = teacher_psodh_pp_0)

This strategic withdrawal from the situation only then came to be connected with the actual illness leading to his death a few years later, and the local tradition that the behaviour of the UK monks led to his death was born. The assumption that the illness was the *result* of this major disappointment in relation to the foreign monks was irksome to Sodh who explicitly denied the link.

Aftermath

After the disastrous walkout, what happened? According to Blake, Kapilavaḍḍho asked a Thai lay supporter to find the UK contingent new accommodation away from Wat Paknam. They moved from the Mahā Nikāya Wat Paknam to a Dhammayutika Nikāya temple, Wat Thathong. At that time Wat Thathong was some way outside the city, as indeed was Wat Paknam—the two on opposite sides of the city. At this remove how should we understand what it meant in Thai eyes for the new monks, who had attracted so much national attention, to relocate to a temple from another *nikāya*? Doubtless the prestige of the exotic foreign monks was sufficient to ensure new accommodation, but we should also be aware of the further possibility that they had been 'poached' by representatives of the Dhammayutika order—an action that makes sense when one understands the ongoing tension between the royally sponsored Dhammayutika reform tradition and the unreformed Mahā Nikāya (see Choompolpaisal 2013).

In fact, the period from the establishment of democracy in 1932, with its attendant loss of autonomous royal power and patronage (hitherto directed mainly at the Dhammayutika Nikāya), had witnessed an increasingly intense competition for power and patronage between the Dhammayutika and Mahā Nikāyas, which at its peak involved the persecution and, in 1962, the arrest and attempted defrocking of the high-ranking Mahā Nikāya monk Pimonlatham.[16] The UK monks appeared on the scene at the height of this period of competition and there can be no doubt that their movement from Wat Paknam to Wat Thathong was a move from a Mahā Nikāya to a Dhammayutika Nikāya sphere of influence, a move replete with sectarian meaning on the Thai side. The happenstance appropriation of the high-profile foreign monks, taking advantage of their fallout with Sodh, would then have made them unwitting booty within national monastic power relations which predated their arrival on the scene by many decades and of which they were probably oblivious.

Shortly afterwards, in late March, Kapilavaḍḍho returned to the UK, apparently responding to demands from there, and Saddhāvaḍḍho followed in April.[17] In his memoir he makes the seemingly disingenuous claim that all the new monks remained at Wat Paknam, where: 'Judging by their behaviour they were extremely happy in their new surroundings' (Randall 1990, 193). Left behind, Blake/ Vijjāvaḍḍho and Paññāvaḍḍho settled into a routine in the new monastery which involved receiving much attention from Thai visitors including on one occasion, Blake recalls, the King's mother. Having attracted national attention while at Wat Paknam, one wonders if in fact they were now 'on display' in their new Dhammayutika Nikāya residence, attracting even royal attention, and Blake recalls that they were subject to so much sightseeing by Thai visitors that it was difficult to maintain their meditation practice. Blake was also visited every day by a young monk from Wat Paknam, allegedly to practise his English, and they usually discussed meditation. The UK monks also visited Wat Vivekārām in Chonburi (Shine 2009, 86), southeast of Bangkok and also Dhammayutika, to find better conditions to continue their meditation.

However, in this period, Blake also started to force his meditation practice too intensively, and got himself, in his words, into 'such a mess'. Friendly Thais concerned for his welfare repeatedly told him to take the pressure off himself, but he ignored everyone. He also suspects now that the junior monk visiting from Wat Paknam had, in fact, been sent by Sodh to help him moderate his unbalanced efforts (Blake 2012, 137). (We might also consider that if the UK monks were undergoing a banishment from Wat Paknam, then the daily visitor may also have been checking their compliance with its rules.)

Eventually Blake arrived at a crisis point. Retrospectively, he refers to it as involving personal egotism and some kind of aggrandisement—interestingly a theme which also cropped up repeatedly in his discussion of his professional mental health work. It is relevant here to understand that the *soḷasakāya* meditation was not practised outside Wat Paknam, especially not in Dhammayutika Nikāya monasteries in Thailand. The Dhammayutika Nikāya had rejected techniques similar to the *soḷasakāya* meditation as a part of their own reformist agenda.[18] Only 20 years before this time a Dhammayutika monk, Jai Yasotharāt, had been commissioned to review and confirm the reform order's position on this type of meditation—a review that underlay Yasotharāt's volume of 1936. The new monks were therefore committed to a technical practice which requires regular support from a qualified teacher, but for which they were receiving none. Kapilavaḍḍho, as Blake's teacher, the man whom he had chosen to follow out of the fateful meeting in the temple, eventually returned to Bangkok in June, and brought the two new monks home to the UK in July.

On the Thai side, Kapilavaḍḍho's return to Thailand at this stage was interpreted as a trip made for the purpose of delivering an apology to his preceptor. Sodh put on record his 'refusal' to meet with him and so no apology could be made.[19] It is not clear whether any such approach was made, nor that Kapilavaḍḍho even had any such intention. This perception on the part of the Thai monks indicates such an approach was possible, even expected, and perhaps that formal monastic penalties were involved. It is reasonable to assume that the refractory monk will prefer reconciliation and thereby revived access to his home temple and rehabilitated status. Sodh's insistence that he would not receive Kapilavaḍḍho, inconsistent as it appears to be with the protocol of dismissal as a technical penalty, may be a retrospective stance to save face. For Sodh to decline a genuine apology from Kapilavaḍḍho for either possible offence (if one were offered) seems a very unlikely action for him to have taken—especially with what was at stake in broader Thai religio-political terms. His apparent unwillingness to 'receive' Kapilavaḍḍho subsequently may indicate that a non-formal 'penalty' for the bad behaviour had been incurred, or that Kapilavaḍḍho was not observing the conditions of a banishment order, and/or perhaps even some degree of intransigence on Sodh's behalf.

On the circumstantial evidence available it seems most likely that Kapilavaḍḍho could have received a *pabbājaniya-kamma*: this would be consistent with the formal meeting of the sangha, the move to another residence, and notably the position of Sodh in not receiving him, given that the rescinding of such an order was a matter of formal and collective responsibility, not a personal one between individuals (unlike a dismissal).

The *soḷasakāya* meditation in the UK

Both Paññāvaḍḍho (Shine 2009, 42) and Blake recall that Kapilavaḍḍho continued to practice and teach the *soḷasakāya* method from Wat Paknam immediately after his return to the UK and up to his own disrobing in 1957.

However, it becomes apparent that Kapilavaḍḍho eventually moved to a position from which he was critical, even dismissive, of the method, even though it was the one by which he had achieved extensive insights and had seemingly realized the deepest truths of Buddhist teaching (Randall 1990, 131 – 132). By 1967 a Dr M. Clark, a pupil of Kapilavaḍḍho's, was explaining the latter's view that 'the Wat Paknam method could have an adverse effect on people's minds' (Shine 2009, 43). (It seems likely that this claim can only have been made on the basis of Blake's experience. Kapilavaḍḍho reports no such reservation in his memoir, which discusses his meditation experience in some detail.) It is for this reason, it appears, that Kapilavaḍḍho instead began to teach Burmese *vipassanā* meditation—a method 'evangelically' promoted by Ānanda Bodhi (Sangharakshita 2003, 38), the incumbent at the EST in the early 1960s. This switch of methods was facilitated by the sudden global spread of Burmese *vipassanā* meditation in the 1950s following Burma's independence (see Crosby, 2013, chap. 6).

However, the person to whom the meditation crisis happened, who subsequently pursued a successful career as a clinical psychologist, now looks back on this episode and sees the crisis that he experienced as just a general 'danger' of engaging in intense Buddhist practice without a cultural context or the close support of a teacher. Blake does not see it as connected to the specific form of meditation practised at Wat Paknam. Indeed, after his retirement he has once again taken up practice of the *soḷasakāya* method (Blake 2012, 197).

More interpretation

To understand this critical characterization of the *soḷasakāya* method emerging from Kapilavaḍḍho's circle in the 1960s, we need to see it in the context of his relationship to Wat Paknam. Each party to that falling out needed to find a resolution to a somewhat intractable and painful situation—the link between preceptor and monk had been severely damaged, but all parties were under pressure not to expose this.

Sodh, I have suggested, dealt with this crisis by becoming 'ill' and thereby no longer needing to deal personally with the refractory monks. However, the pressure on the UK monks had a different significance. It is perhaps difficult to identify now with the idealism that doubtless motivated the three young monks and their leader, Kapilavaḍḍho. How were they to cope with their own intense spiritual aspirations in the face of the breakdown of the institutional mechanisms by which they had expected to realize them? Blake, possibly in a spirit of 'enlightenment or bust', intensified his meditation to crisis point. Beyond this point it led to his clinical interest in the mind (a transitional activity mediating his exploration of mental states in a non-monastic setting?). Saddhāvaḍḍho simply disrobed almost as soon as possible. Paññāvaḍḍho, once free from the EST duties that were to fall upon him as 'the last man standing', was to disrobe and re-ordain under another teacher in a different Thai tradition.

Back in England, Kapilavaḍḍho had participated in the formal creation of the EST on the strength of having a quorate *bhikkhu-saṅgha* in the Wat Paknam *nikāya* (lineage). While he continued to practise and teach *soḷasakāya* meditation at the EST on his return to the UK, within 14 months of the debacle he too had disrobed on the basis of physical ill health—but was this the only way for him to cope with the irresolvable conflict that had arisen in Bangkok?

However that may have been, it surely became necessary for Kapilavaḍḍho to justify his sudden distance from Sodh and Wat Paknam. He could not go back there—Sodh would not see him if he did. He had left London something of a pioneering hero, only to return having had an unreported but cataclysmic breakdown of communication with his Thai preceptor and abbot. One suspects that the best way forward became to critique the meditation method taught there—characterizing it as 'dangerous'—thereby having a circumstantial justification for no longer pursuing the path of formal meditation practice which he had, formerly, so publicly advocated, and to support which he had garnered the willing support of others in the creation of the EST. In this respect, while Purfurst's own health difficulties appeared to arise from physical over-exertion, Blake's crisis in Thailand seemingly sufficed as a quasi-medical incident which allowed Kapilavaḍḍho to claim that this method was injurious to health. Teaching a different meditation technique, originating in Burma, re-oriented the perceived focus of Kapilavaḍḍho's spiritual lineage away from Wat Paknam. Kapilavaḍḍho's disrobing and re-ordination in a different tradition severed that link altogether.

Subsequent lives

The latter activities of Robert Albison/Saddhāvaḍḍho are, at present, unknown and he has died in recent years.[20] Kapilavaḍḍho, having disrobed in 1957, reordained at the invitation of EST in 1967 at Wat Buddhapadipa, East Sheen. He died shortly after disrobing, and marrying for the third time, in December 1971. Blake/Vijjāvaḍḍho disrobed and moved to Edinburgh to study psychology and later trained to be a clinical psychologist specializing in addictive behaviours, moving to Canada in 1966. Ṭhitavedo 'eventually ... had to disrobe'.

After the departure of Kapilavaḍḍho, Paññāvaḍḍho had to run the EST for four years, but then returned to Thailand, where he disrobed, re-ordained and retrained in the Dhammayutika Nikāya with the famous *dhūtaṅga* monk Ajahn Maha Boowa, with whom he subsequently visited the UK in 1974 (Shine 2009, 64). Why did Paññāvaḍḍho re-ordain at this point? He had been a validly ordained monk for five years, had that period of seniority (a consideration in traditional monastic terms), had been practising, teaching and managing

Buddhist activities in England in good faith throughout that time. In fact, Paññāvaḍḍho returned to Thailand at the height of Dhammayutika persecution of Mahā Nikāya monks. By going to study with Mahā Boowa, he was in fact *required* to disrobe since Dhammayutika monks did not recognize the equal validity of a Mahā Nikāya ordination, and Paññāvaḍḍho thus lost his five years of seniority and was reduced to 'starting again' at the most junior status. All this could have been avoided had he returned to Wat Paknam, where he had been ordained. We can only conclude that this option was not open to him. By this time Sodh had died and the local rumours of the UK monks' deleterious effect on his health were already in circulation (despite Sodh's denials). There may not have been a warm reception waiting for him there, but maybe also he himself still felt the conflict arising from the original breakdown of relations with his *upajjhāya*. Perhaps also a monastic penalty towards the UK monks (or just Kapilavaḍḍho) was still in force. On the other hand, the primary motivation for ordination on the part of westerners has often been the prospect of personal transformation offered by meditation, since the traditional, social, educational and status aspects within Thai Buddhism that inspire local young men to take ordination are less, if at all, relevant to westerners. The Forest Dhamma Organisation's biography of Paññāvaḍḍho records of his London period that, 'He deeply felt the lack of a reliable mentor, a good teacher who could assure him that the noble goals of the Buddha's teaching were still attainable in the modern era.' When he returned to Thailand in 1961 to: 'look for a good teacher, one who could command his full trust,' he stayed initially at Wat Chonlaprathan, moving only in 1963 to Mahā Boowa's Wat Pa Baan Taad where he was to live for the rest of his life (Forest Dhamma, accessed February 6, 2013. http://www.forestdhamma.org/about/panya/).

Mahā Boowa was also the teacher of Ajahn Chah, who was to bring his own western disciple, Sumedho, to the UK in 1977 to lead the successful establishment of the Dhammayutika Nikāya Thai forest monk tradition at Chithurst. Paññāvaḍḍho lived for another 40 years in Thailand, and died in 2004, a revered teacher.

Conclusion

One might say that this whole narrative begins with an unacknowledged gap in the record, a silence. The overall intention has been to breathe some life into otherwise unexamined events. The unintentional pull of this type of narrative exegesis is to imbue every event and action with the aura of conscious intent, as if every action has been 'thought through' in the manner that one is now 'thinking it through', but there is the everpresent possibility that decisions were made without this, that they sometimes unfolded 'on the back foot'.

The events described revolve around three types of ambition: for the international expansion of Wat Paknam; to create an English *bhikkhu-saṅgha*; and possibly the desire of an individual monk to advance his own career. These ambitions intersected in 1953 when Ṭhitavedo arrived in London and met Bill Purfurst. The next steps, and possibly the eventual outcome, may have been inevitable.

The uncomfortable falling out described here was subsequently downplayed by both sides, although it appears that it was only discussed publicly at all on the Thai side. Even there it was minimized, and the UK monks are described as disrobing prior to leaving Thailand—presumably invoking, implicitly, the model of temporary ordination popular in that country. The fact was that all the monks concerned returned to the UK as monks. Both 'sides' presumably downplayed events in order to reduce the discomfort of acknowledging the poor judgements made. More was at risk for the UK monks, whose legitimacy as members of a living monastic community was at stake (possibly at a formal level, but also in their own minds), and this perhaps explains the silence on their part and even their eventual disrobing.

If a monastic penalty was involved, we might see Kapilavaḍḍho's seeming unwillingness to reconcile not just as an expression of his temperament, but also as a function of his outsider status which meant that he had another 'life' to which he could return when relations in Bangkok soured, and this may be a characteristic dynamic of western interactions with the Asian *bhikkhu-saṅgha* in general. We can also see that as outsiders the UK monks were, from the Thai perspective, relatively transient exotica that became useful pawns in national religio-politics. It seems unlikely that any of them were ever aware of this dimension of the events that unfolded, focused as they were on their individual spiritual aspirations.

Both sides were guided by loyalty: in Thailand, by loyalty to the monastic institution and possibly legal protocol; in the UK by loyalty to personal friends and companions. Ṭhitavedo appears to transgress this otherwise neat distinction. In this divergence perhaps we can also see being worked out the 'subjective turn' that has characterized changed attitudes to religion in the West during the twentieth century. The UK monks would then be representatives of what Heelas and Woodhead (Heelas and Woodhead 2005, 6) call the 'subjective-life', the orientation to spirituality, which emphasizes 'inner sources of significance and authority', crossing cultural boundaries to seek spiritual fulfillment and placing a high value on personal sentiment and forging one's own life path, often at the expense of duty and expectation; whereas the Thais, including Thitavedo, would represent the 'life-as' religious orientation with its emphasis on external, socially instantiated sources of significance and authority, and in which conformity to established roles and tradition is a primary requirement.

The personalities involved, the misunderstandings and the resulting need to justify intractable positions gave rise in the respective communities to vaguely symmetrical 'justificatory' myths concerning illness: (i) in Bangkok, the UK monks had demanded overweening privileges, were disrespectful and, implicitly, they precipitated Sodh's demise and death; (ii) in EST circles in the UK, *soḷasakaya* meditation (and, implicitly, Wat Paknam?) came to be seen as dangerous to one's mental health and to be avoided.

However disastrous the events may have seemed at the time to those involved, we can discern the threads of eventual success running via Paññāvaḍḍho, Ajahn Mahā Boowa and Ajahn Chah. The EST ambition for a native British *bhikkhu-saṅgha* was eventually to blossom at Chithurst in 1979—an undoubted success story.

Finally, had events been otherwise, the *soḷasakāya* meditation method, seen as somewhat marginal in its Thai context, might have become mainstream in the UK. As it is, it has been veiled by obscurity in the UK (even though it has been practised here throughout), despite its crucial historical role in the development of a native British *bhikkhu-saṅgha*.

ACKNOWLEDGEMENTS

I gratefully acknowledge the assistance of Phibul Choompolpaisal, Kate Crosby, Terry Shine and Russell Webb in developing this article.

NOTES

1. Ṭhitavedo is variously spelt Thiṭavedho, Ṭhittavedho, Thiṭavaḍḍho, Thiṭavedo and Thitavedo in sources.
2. After disrobing in 1957, Purfurst changed his secular name to Richard Randall and his memoir was published posthumously under this new name. Thus, the same historical figure is denominated William/Bill Purfurst, Kapilavaḍḍho and Richard Randall in various parts of this narrative.
3. A film was made of the ordination and (parts of ?) it can be viewed online. http://www.youtube.com/watch?v = HS8kZyrrvOg&list = PLBD6E7C3674739EB4&index = 4 (accessed February 10, 2013.). All actors in this narrative can be seen there. On the Mahā Nikāya dimension, see 'aftermath' below.
4. Other sources say nothing at all: e.g. Snelling (1998, 262), Waterhouse (1997, 74) and *Exemplary Conduct of the Principal Teachers of Vijja Dhammakaya* (2010, 54–55).
5. What follows is from my record of Blake's recollections. Passages in quotation marks are taken verbatim from the interview.
6. Kapilavaḍḍho/Randall does not mention any of this event in his memoir. He repeatedly emphasizes his close personal relationship to Ṭhitavedo (Randall 1990, 38, 46, 89, 104, 189).
7. The Buddhist rhetorical trope of three may be in operation here.
8. I am indebted to Phibul Choompolpaisal who located this source and translated it for me. The translation here is his.

9. Other records indicate that all but one disrobed once back in the UK.
10. Purfurst/Randall freely admits the latter qualities in his own memoir (1990, 4, 5, 62), in the pages of which one can also easily detect his personal charisma and candour.
11. Personal communication from the author (September 10, 2012).
12. The commentary was apparently recorded afterwards by Kapilavaḍḍho himself (Shine, personal communication, February 12, 2013)—which means that he was commenting after the falling out had occured. He also does give Sodh's titles and explains that he is head of the monastery but, in this directly comparable descriptive comment, he seems to give greater emphasis to Ṭhitavedo.
13. An unconfirmed accusation of financial irregularities in relation to temple funds on the part of Ṭhitavedo was also reported to the present author by personal communication. Like accusations of sexual irregularities, it is very difficult to assess such easy accusations when they are made against monks. (Also Ṭhitavedo is the only participant in these events who does not speak to posterity with his own voice, and it is easy for him to be cast as the 'fall guy' for what, instead, is really a collective failure.) Accusations concerning sex and money are powerful slurs against monks in Asia (the former involving a betrayal of the *vinaya* and the latter of the donating lay community) and while easily made are almost impossible to disprove. The present author treats both with extreme caution and has ignored them where they have surfaced in other parts of this narrative. An interesting analysis of the rise of the political use of accusations of sexual misconduct against monks in Thailand in the nineteenth to twentieth centuries is outlined in Choompolpaisal (2011, 272).
14. Email to Terry Shine (July 1, 2002). The persuasion that led to their relocation presumably only worked after the confrontation with Sodh.
15. A further consideration is that the formal meeting from which Kapilavaḍḍho walked away was a disciplinary meeting in relation to Ṭhitavedo. Readers wanting to understand better the formal legal underpinnings of these monastic penalties are referred to the *Mahāvagga* I.27.1-8 (re dismissal) and *Cūlavagga* I.13-17 (re banishment) of the Pali Vinaya (Rhys Davids and Oldenberg 1982 I, 165–168; 1982 II, 347ff.).
16. These developments are analysed in Choompolpaisal (2011).
17. These dates are from Shine (2009, 86). Blake recalls Kapilavaḍḍho taking Saddhāvaḍḍho with him.
18. The *soḷasakāya* meditation is a contemporary survival of pre-reform meditation techniques which can be broadly labelled *borān-yogāvacara* and are the subject of ongoing research, which is changing our views of the history of Theravāda in Asia. See for example Crosby, Skilton and Gunasena (2012).
19. See Wat Paknam web page, http://www.watpaknam.org/content.php?op=teacher_psodh_pp_0 Accessed 11 December 2012.
20. Personal communication, Terry Shine (January 20, 2013).

REFERENCES

BLAKE, B. GEORGE. 2012. *By-Passing the Ego*. Online: Lulu.com.

BLUCK, ROBERT. 2006. *British Buddhism Teachings, Practice and Development*. Abingdon: Routledge.

CHOOMPOLPAISAL, P. 2011. *Reassessing Modern Thai Political Buddhism: A Critical Study of Sociological Literature from Weber to Keyes*, PhD diss. SOAS, University of London.

CHOOMPOLPAISAL, PHIBUL. 2013. Tai-Burmese-Lao Buddhisms in the 'Modernizing' of Ban Thawai (Bangkok): The Dynamic Interaction between Ethnic Minority Religion and British–Siamese Centralization in the Late Nineteenth/Early Twentieth Centuries. *Contemporary Buddhism* 14 (1): 94–115.

CROSBY, KATE, with ANDREW SKILTON, and AMAL GUNASENA. 2012. The Sutta on Understanding Death in the Transmission of *Borān* Meditation from Siam to the Kandyan Court. *Journal of Indian Philosophy* 40 (2): 177–98.

CROSBY, K. 2013. *Theravada Buddhism: Continuity, Diversity, and Identity*. Oxford: Wiley-Blackwell.

EXEMPLARY CONDUCT OF THE PRINCIPAL TEACHERS OF VIJJA DHAMMAKAYA—THE LIFE HISTORY OF THE MOST VENERABLE PHRAMONKOLTHEPMUNI, (SODH CANDASARO), THE DISCOVERER OF VIJJA DHAMMAKAYA. 2010. Translated by Dr Anunya Methmanus. Dhammakaya Open University, California.

HEELAS, PAUL, and LINDA WOODHEAD. 2005. *The Spiritual Revolution: Why Religion is Giving Way to Spirituality*. Oxford: Blackwell Publishing.

MACKENZIE, RORY. 2007. *New Buddhist Movements in Thailand: Towards an Understanding of Wat Phra Dhammakāya and Santi Asoke*. Abingdon: Routledge.

RANDALL, RICHARD. 1990. *Life as a Siamese Monk*. Bradford on Avon: Aukana Publising.

RHYS DAVIDS, T. W., and HERMANN OLDENBERG. 1982. *Vinaya Texts*. Parts I & II. Delhi: Motilal Banarsidass, [Original publication, 1885. Oxford: Oxford University Press].

SANGHARAKSHITA. 2003. *Moving Against the Stream*. Birmingham: Windhorse.

SHINE, TERRY. 2009. *Honour Thy Fathers A Tribute to the Venerable Kapilavaḍḍho*. www.aimwell.org. www.buddhanet.net

SNELLING, JOHN. 1998. *The Buddhist Handbook*. London: Rider [Originally published 1987].

THE LIFE AND TIMES OF LUANG PHAW WAT PAKNAM. 2010. 4th rev. ed. Bangkok: Dhammakaya Foundation.

WATERHOUSE, HELEN. 1997. *Buddhism in Bath: Adaptation and Authority*. Leeds: Community Religions Project, University of Leeds.

UPASAK, C. S. 1975. *Dictionary of Early Buddhist Monastic Terms*. Varanasi: Bharati Prakashan.

WEBB, RUSSELL. n.d. Hampstead Buddhist Vihara. Unpublished historical review.

YASOTHARAT, PHRAMAHA CHOTIPANYO[JAI]. ยโสธรัตน์, (พระมหาโชติปัญโญ) ใจ. 1936 CE [2478 BE]. *Book of Phuttha Rangsi Thrisadiyan Relating to Samatha and Vipassana Meditation Covering the Four Eras* หนังสือพุทธรังษีธฤษดีญาณ

ว่าด้วย สมถและวิปัสสนากัมมัฏฐาน 4 ยุค [*Nangsue Phuttha Rangsi Thrisadiyan Wa duay Samatha Lae Vipassana Kammatthan See Yuk*]. Bangkok: No publisher details.

YOSHINAGA, SHIN'ICHI. 2013. Three Boys on a Great Vehicle: 'Mahayana Buddhism' and A Trans-National Network. *Contemporary Buddhism* 14 (1): 52–65.

BROOKLYN BHIKKHU: HOW SALVATORE CIOFFI BECAME THE VENERABLE LOKANATHA

Philip Deslippe

This article provides a biographical overview of the life of the Venerable Lokanatha (1897–1966), who was born in Italy as Salvatore Cioffi and raised in Brooklyn, New York. After converting to Buddhism in his late-twenties, Lokanatha travelled to Burma, took ordination as a monk, and began a remarkable 40 year career as a writer, lecturer, organizer, and Buddhist missionary throughout South Asia and the world. Beyond biography, Lokanatha and the various responses to him are contextualized within the different cultural spheres in which he operated, from the anti-colonial Buddhist revival in Burma to the mocking indifference Lokanatha found in the United States. Scholarship on modern Buddhism, particularly recent work on U Dhammaloka, is used to situate Lokanatha's life and its facets of conservative reformer and transnational actor. Finally, an account of the source material used to reconstruct the life of Lokanatha is employed to offer practical methodological explanations for his absence from conventional narratives of modern Buddhism and what his inclusion along with other figures might mean in the future.

Introduction

His life could read as a Buddhist tale from centuries or even millennia ago. A young man leaves his family and home behind, and after travelling across the world by boat and foot, becomes a monk. After years of traditional practice and austerities, he receives the patronage of a king to preach the Dharma in the land of its birth.

His life could also be read as decidedly modern. A trained chemist from the metropolis of New York is drawn to Buddhism and sees it as a scientific truth far ahead of the twentieth century's technological innovations. Using international media and emerging social networks, he travels for decades as a missionary to affirm the modern relevance of Buddhism to the world.

The Venerable Lokanatha exists somewhere inbetween the categories and narratives that are commonly used within the history of modern Buddhism. He was both Eastern and Western, traditionalist and reformer, outsider and insider.

Yet despite being one of the most unusual and influential Buddhist figures of the twentieth century, as well as the catalyst for one of the largest religious mass-conversions in history, Lokanatha is conspicuously absent from histories of modern Buddhism.

This article will serve three main functions. It will provide an abbreviated, but comprehensive, biography of Ven. Lokanatha with an emphasis on his influence on the conversion of Dr Ambedkar to Buddhism. Secondly, it will place Lokanatha within the cultural and historical contexts in which he operated, particularly in America during his mission in the late 1940s. Finally, Lokanatha will be analysed as an interstitial figure that can partially be understood by historical context and scholarly categories, but ultimately problematizes those same taxonomies.

'How strange, this incarnation!': the life of Lokanatha

The man who would be remembered eventually as the Venerable Lokanatha was born as Salvatore Cioffi in Cervinara, Italy on the day after Christmas in 1897, and emigrated from Naples to the United States at the age of four years.[1] Salvatore grew up in Brooklyn, New York with five sisters and three brothers in a large and devoutly Catholic family. We can find hints in records to suggest that despite the large size of his family, they grew up well-educated and in relative comfort. Cioffi knew French in addition to English and Italian, and he was adept at the violin.[2]

FIGURE 1
The senior portrait of Salvatore Cioffi from the 1922 Cooper Union Cable yearbook. Courtesy of The Cooper Union.

In his early-twenties Salvatore Cioffi enrolled at Cooper Union in Manhattan, and in 1922 he graduated with a degree in chemistry (Figure 1). Although the yearbook listings for his classmates were littered with playful jokes and affiliations with fraternities, the space dedicated to Cioffi was downright sombre. 'Sally' claimed to be a stoic, and with philosophy listed as 'the breath of his life,' he chose as his personal quote the melancholic line from *Hamlet*, 'How weary, stale, flat and unprofitable seem to me all the uses of this world.'[3] It was during his time at Cooper Union that Salvatore chanced upon a copy of the *Dhammapada*. Thirty years later he would look back and say that: 'It was the Dhammapada which completely changed my life. I became a Buddhist by reading the Dhammapada' (Lokanatha 1952, 66). After his graduation, Cioffi worked for a time as an analyst at the Crucible Steel Company of America and then Procter & Gamble.[4] It became his routine during this period to commute from his job on Staten Island to the New York Public Library and read about Buddhism.[5]

After a few years of work, Cioffi returned to school and entered the College of Physicians and Surgeons at Columbia. The program required dissecting and etherizing of cats and frogs which horrified him, and a staunch vegetarianism would later become a hallmark of his teaching and conception of Buddhism. His vegetarianism, philosophical searching, and ever-deepening interest in Buddhism all combined and reached their tipping point when Salvatore Cioffi converted to Buddhism by himself at the age of 27 years old. Leaving a note for his family saying that he was 'dying to the world for the sake of Supreme Perfection,' he headed east on a swift ocean liner, the R.M.S. Mauretania.[6]

Salvatore Cioffi was ordained as a Buddhist monk in Rangoon, Burma in 1925. At present, we have little information as to what brought Cioffi specifically to Burma, the circumstances of his ordination there, or if he took a new name upon becoming a monk. It is possible that Cioffi initially tested the waters before making the leap into monastic vows. An Italian magazine article suggests that inbetween his old life in America and ordination in Burma, Cioffi was a participant in a group tour of Americans visiting Buddhist holy sites in India (Pardo 1984).

Six months after becoming a monk, Salvatore Cioffi returned to his birth country of Italy. Some accounts attribute the move to a serious bout of dysentery and an attempt to recover in the care of relatives there.[7] More hagiographic accounts place him in Italy with a convert's zeal to sway the Italians (including the Pope) towards Buddhism and leaving when he found the climate unripe for missionary activity (Profumo 1997, 54; Soni 1966, 177). Several sources agree that the return journey from Italy to India was long and extraordinary, mostly conducted on foot.

In India, Cioffi stayed for a half-decade in monasteries, caves, and forests in the foothills of the Himalayas and at Buddhist sites including Bodh Gaya. There he devoted himself to intense dharmic study and practice. He read Buddhist texts, spent rainy seasons in silent meditation, and incorporated the 13 ascetic practices, or *dhutangas*, that regulated how he ate, travelled, and slept, including the practice of sleeping in a seated position which he rigidly adhered to. An obituary written four decades later noted that after this period in India, 'only in his death he lay on his back' (Soni 1966, 177).

It was from this period that Salvatore Cioffi emerged, in name and in spirit, as Lokanatha. A visiting monk from Sri Lanka had given him the name Lokanatha, which Cioffi noted had the same meaning as his Italian birth name of Salvatore: saviour. When he left India for Burma in 1932, Lokanatha was described as having a 'spiritual radiance around him' that belied his short height and soft, round face, and one traveller to Burma in the 1980s heard stories that Lokanatha was 'admired for his psychic powers and his faith' (Soni 1966, 177; Del Boca 1989, 58).

Lokanatha then launched missionary expeditions in three successive years in 1933, 1934, and 1935 respectively from Burma, Thailand and Ceylon. His method and goal was the same in each: gather up 'lion-hearted monks' from various countries and then travel to Bodh-Gaya in India so that the group could be trained, educated, and fortified to act as a type of monastic shock troop to bring about a revival of Buddhism in India and ultimately mass-conversions to Buddhism throughout the world.[8] The first constitutional monarch of Thailand, King Prachatipok, gave patronage and paid for passport fees for 100 monks on one of these expeditions. The participants included Ajahn Panya, who would become a prominent Thai Buddhist preacher (Tiyavanich 2007, 5–6). After an initial enthusiastic gathering of participants, these trips all eventually found their numbers drop and seemingly dissolved into failure for a variety of reasons including the weather, sickness and disease, changes in culture from one country to the next, and Lokanatha's insistence on exacting standards for travel and personal conduct.

In the initial stages of gathering recruits in Burma on the first expedition of 1933, Lokanatha met a Punjabi medical doctor named R. L. Soni in Paungde. Lokanatha stayed up all night answering Soni's questions underneath a Bo tree, and within a week Lokanatha counted him as his 'first important convert' (Soni 1951).[9] Eventually the group shrank from nearly 100 to just 14 by the time of the rainy season and arrived in Benares all in poor health with two of the monks requiring care in a nearby hospital.[10] A fascinating side note to this first trip is the fact that none other than Aung San, the key figure in the creation of modern independent Burma, was one of the many young admirers of Lokanatha during the beginning stages of this first mission. Aung San went so far as to ask his mother if he might be able to join the Italian monk and his troupe (Houtman 1999, 245).

Undeterred by the first mission's failure, Lokanatha made plans for the next mission to be even larger. His aspiration for the trip in 1934 was that it would contain 1000 Buddhist monks who would travel from India to Rome on foot, spreading the Dharma and preaching vegetarianism along the route.[11] Lokanatha spoke to reporters about the trip and said that he hoped to convert Mussolini. He would not rule out preaching in Vatican City and hoped that the group would eventually arrive in the United States, but none of those hopes would be realized. The following and final trip, however, would indirectly plant seeds for mass conversions to Buddhism that would rival Lokanatha's lofty imagination.

In October 1935, the Indian political leader Dr Bhimrao Ramji Ambedkar made the bold statement at a conference in Yeola that he had decided to leave Hinduism, and wanted his large number of followers in the lower castes to join him, since he saw no possibility of equality or justice for them within the Hindu-fold. Numerous faiths saw an incredible opportunity to fill their ranks and made attempts to court Ambedkar, including Sikhism and Christianity. After a 'feeble attempt' by the Maha Bodhi Society, Lokanatha abandoned everything and went to Mumbai to directly make the case for Buddhism to Ambedkar (Ahir 1990, 146). Lokanatha followed up the visit by writing a pamphlet titled 'Buddhism Will Make You Free!!!' where he told readers that 'Brahminism, not Buddhism, is the cause of the downfall of India' (Ahir 1990, 147). Again, in June 1936, Lokanatha went to Ambedkar to continue to persuade him to embrace Buddhism, meeting him at his residence in Dadar (Keer 1954, 276). After leaving Dadar for Sri Lanka, Lokanatha began corresponding with Ambedkar, writing him a letter from Colombo in July and another from Panadura in August (Ahir 1990, 147).

A few years later during the start of the Second World War, Lokanatha was held as a prisoner of war by the British and interred in a series of camps. His Italian descent was likely a factor, but Italian-language sources claim a more significant reason. According to them, Lokanatha was the 'spiritual pupil' of U Wisara, a Burmese monk who was jailed by the British for inciting sedition (Del Boca 1989, 58). There are multiple accounts that Lokanatha lobbied for male nurses and separate wards for Buddhist monks in the nation's hospitals, but U Wisara's death in jail in 1930 creates an unlikely window of time for Lokanatha to have studied with him directly (Soni 1958, 12; 1966, 179). It is not clear if Lokanatha opposed the British on political grounds, or rather as an extension of defending Buddhist standards. This is almost the inverse of the Irish monk U Dhammaloka, whose anti-colonial views are certain.

There are corroborating accounts of Lokanatha coming into dramatic conflict with his jailers at the camp in Patna, India. Unable to practice his Buddhism fully to his satisfaction within the camp's rules, Lokanatha sat immobile in the open air during a 96 day hunger strike, returning to the same place each time the soldiers dragged him away. Once the British gave into his demands, Lokanatha stood up and silently returned to his barracks surrounded by the applause of his fellow prisoners (Pardo 1984; Del Boca 1989). Towards the war's end, Lokanatha's younger Burmese friend from an earlier 'lion-hearted monk' missionary trip to India, Karuna Kusalasaya, was reunited with him in the camp at Deoli. While talking through the barbed wire fencing that separated their wings of the camp, Lokanatha described having continued his missionary activities and claimed to have converted several Christians to Buddhism during his internment (Kusalasaya 1991).

Internment and the war derailed Lokanatha's plan for a missionary tour of Europe and America and also resulted in the permanent loss of many of his manuscripts, but the Second World War would have a deeper impact on him. After the war, he saw Buddhism as not just as a matter of personal liberation, but a sorely needed remedy for a conflict-prone world. Lokanatha would frame his lectures and writings on Buddhism in light of the Cold War, and would frequently fast and lead silent meditations in public meetings for the cause of world peace.[12]

On the last day of October 1946, Lokanatha and Dr Soni organized a public meeting in Mandalay for creating a 'world-wide Buddhist movement for promoting peace in the human family,' and the Buddhist Foreign Mission was organized a month later. In the July of the following year, Lokanatha was sent out to travel throughout the globe as the 'first Dhamma-Ambassador to the world in a thousand years' by the Buddhist Foreign Mission after being honoured by five separate Buddhist organizations in Rangoon within sight of Shwedagon Pagoda. Announcing his arrival in America in advance, Lokanatha told the press in Hong Kong that his endeavour would be bringing an 'Atomic Bomb of Love' to the West.[13]

In many respects Lokanatha's year and a half-long tour of America consisted of what would be expected of any visiting missionary: lecturing, teaching, preaching, fund-raising, and trying to generate publicity. Lokanatha gave lectures to students at the University of Michigan, University of Chicago, Northwestern, Hamline University in Minnesota, and lectured to high school students on Good Friday. In northern California, he was hosted by the Japanese community at the Fresno Buddhist Church and gave a lecture in English on 'Buddhism for Americans' in an open meeting for a mixed group of Buddhists and non-Buddhists with a question and answer session afterwards.[14] In southern California, he gave similar lectures to raise funds for Buddhist centres and went on a public fast of several weeks for world peace telling the *Los Angeles Times* that 'each one of us is responsible for war through his thoughts.'[15] In Chicago, he was interviewed on midday radio.[16]

Although Lokanatha's tour of the United States left behind no institutions or groups in its wake, from an article in the *New Yorker*, we do have a detailed glimpse into one of the meetings Lokanatha offered in Manhattan. The author of the short piece describes entering a room in the Cornish Arms Hotel and finding Lokanatha with a dozen men and women sitting in silent meditation for about half an hour with a small alarm clock ticking away the seconds and the monk's begging bowl sitting as an improvised collection plate. After the meditation ended, Lokanatha sat at a table and answered questions from the group about the marks of a master, the status of women in Buddhism, and the date of the next full moon.[17]

Shortly after his arrival in America, in April 1948 he flew to Los Angeles and was greeted at the airport by Gypsy Buys, a socialite with a penchant for the esoteric. Gypsy and her husband Jerry hosted Lokanatha at Falcon Lair, their hilltop mansion and the former residence of Rudolph Valentino (Figure 3). Jerry Buys told people in confidence that he had first met Lokanatha when he 'caught the monk in Tibet' and took it upon himself to stage an event in downtown Los Angeles where in a crude facsimile of a Burmese act of reverence towards an honoured Buddhist, nine American women kneeled before 'the Venerable One' and Lokanatha walked on their hair since 'his feet were too sacred to touch the sidewalks' (Shulman 1967, 457) (Figure 2).

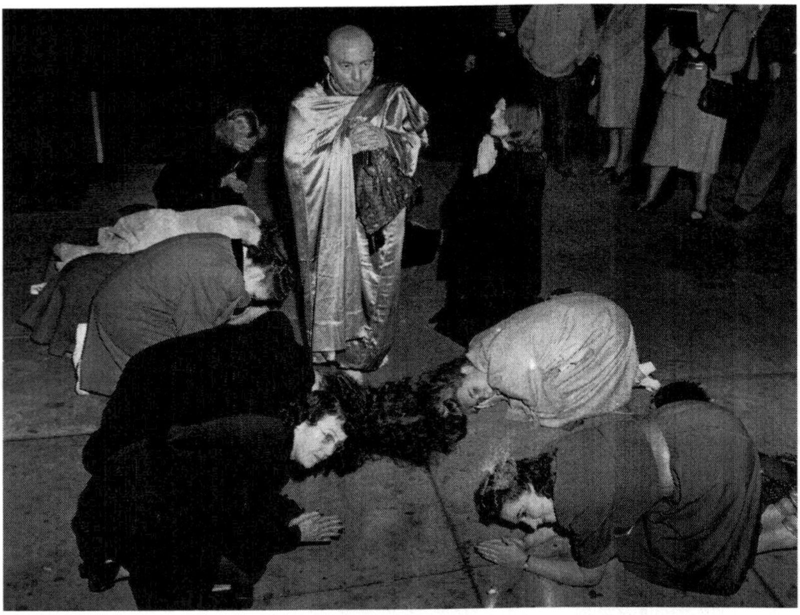

FIGURE 2
One of the many widely circulated wire photos of Lokanatha walking on the hair of kneeling 'girl adherents' in Hollywood. Image by Acme Newsphotos, 1948.

A week later Gypsy and Jerry held a séance at Falcon Liar to contact the late movie star and heartthrob, Rudolph Valentino on his fifty-third birthday. The séance was presided over by 30 spiritualists and mediums and was nothing less than a frenzied circus. There was a sighting of the (then living) film producer Louis B. Mayer on a white horse, someone saw a birthday cake for Valentino, and contact was allegedly made with the star's late pet dog, Kabar. Lokanatha was deferred to as a spiritual authority during the séance, but he was conveniently under a vow of silence at the time, and merely raised his hand a few times in what was alternately interpreted as a blessing or an instruction to quiet down (Shulman 1967, 456–459).

The Los Angeles newspapers reported the two events and once picked up by national wire services they spread like wildfire throughout the country and dwarfed any news of his missionary activities. In sharp contrast to the conventional wisdom that any publicity is good publicity, they became the lasting legacy of Lokanatha's entire American endeavour. The *Stars and Stripes* newspaper summed up Lokanatha's tour of the United States curtly with:

> Last year a Buddhist monk, Brooklyn-born Lokanatha, arrived in Hollywood. His sponsors furnished him with a press agent. Lokanatha attended séances allegedly with Rudolph Valentino's ghost. He departed without establishing any mission.[18]

After passing through England and Europe, Lokanatha stayed for a time in Sri Lanka where he attended and spoke to the inaugural conference of the World Fellowship of Buddhists. Lokanatha then returned to Burma in Spring 1951, where in Mandalay he raised the World Buddhist Flag for the first time in the country. In Burma, Lokanatha travelled throughout the country preaching for a considerable period. One visitor to the country described Lokanatha in a travelogue as 'the leading spirit' of a missionary and reformist Buddhist 'evangelical fervor' he saw sweeping through Rangoon and greater Burma (Lewis 1954, 146). In 1954 he again addressed the Fellowship of Buddhists, this time in Rangoon, and according to Dr Soni, was elected the Spiritual Patron of the 1956 *Mahajayanti* in Pakistan. The real fruits of his preaching, travelling, and organizing activities would come later in the same year.

The conversion of Ambedkar

In March 1948, Lokanatha was quoted in a Californian newspaper as saying that he looked forward to 'a tremendous Buddhist revival in the Buddhist year 2500,' about nine years ahead in the future.[19] The next year he told a reporter in New York that 'In seven years there will be a big swing to Buddhism . . . you have but to wait and see.'[20]

The efforts that Lokanatha had made almost two decades earlier to convert Ambedkar had slowly been gaining momentum. Dr Soni, Lokanatha's 'first important convert' from 1933, had become a close associate of Ambedkar. Four years after Soni's conversion in 1937, Lokanatha, with the help of a recent German-born Buddhist convert, initiated Acharya Ishvardatt Medharthi of Uttar Pradesh to Buddhism. Medharthi became a strong critic of the caste system and also another close contact of Ambedkar who visited Medharthi's school in Buddpuri in the early 1940s (Sadangi 2008. 101; Bhaskar 2009, 149). By 1956, Ambedkar's careful considerations, helped along by Lokanatha's two converts, had reached a conclusion.

On 14 October 1956, shortly after making his initial decision in the home of Dr Soni in Mandalay during a visit to Burma, Ambedkar made his formal conversion to Buddhism and then immediately proceeded to convert nearly half a million of his supporters who had gathered for the event. Ambedkar expressed an interest in having the new masses of converts educated in Buddhist values by the Venerable Lokanatha, and wanted the monk to come to India for that purpose (Kusalasaya 1991, 293). Based on estimates from the 2001 Indian census, the number of Ambedkar Buddhists today is around eight million.

If the ambitious aims of Lokanatha to see 'skyscraper pagodas to world peace' erected in Manhattan, the conversion of Mussolini to Buddhism, or the entire globe reading the Dhammapada seemed naïve and childlike, and if his various missionary tours seemed prone to collapse into disaster and tragicomedy, then his influence on Ambedkar and the resulting Buddhist revival provides a strong counterpoint. Being a catalyst to perhaps the largest mass religious conversion in modern history gives a gravitas to Lokanatha's efforts and underscores how significant a figure he was in the modern history of Buddhism.

In late 1965, four decades after his ordination, Lokanatha developed a sore on his forehead that turned cancerous. He had planned to travel to the United States for treatment, but underwent a local, indigenous treatment that allowed the cancer to spread, and he died in the hill station town of Maymyo on the 25 May 1966, at the age of 69. In slightly confusing testimony from Dr Soni, Lokanatha's body was taken by procession to Shwezigon Monastery where it lay in state for 'all Burma to pay homage.' Soni mourned the passing of his teacher as 'an irreparable loss to the Buddhist world' and upon his own death, his remains were interred alongside those of Lokanatha according to his wishes (Soni 1966, 178).

Situating and contextualizing Lokanatha

Lokanatha was certainly a fascinating and powerful individual, but it would be simplistic to think of him as merely a unique figure that forged his own path through history. While they cannot ultimately encapsulate him in full, many of the categories and narratives used by scholars of modern Buddhism can further our understanding of Lokanatha and his efforts, and, in turn, the inability of Lokanatha to fit definitively into these categories and narratives helps to problematize such categories. Lokanatha operated in specific cultural contexts that in no small measure aided his success, and it is reasonable to assume that Lokanatha, like many others who depended upon patronage, had an appeal to patrons that extended beyond his own charisma.

Although he was very much grounded in Buddhist communities and practices, Lokanatha shares common ground with many of the so-called rational and modern Buddhist individuals from his time. In a 1947 interview with the United Press wire service in Hong Kong, just prior to his departure for the United States, Lokanatha singled out Buddhism as the only 'absolutely scientific' religion and he expressed his desire to share the value of Buddhism with 'free thinkers, rationalists and agnostics' in America. In other places, such as his work 'There is No God and No Soul,' Lokanatha framed his concept of Buddhism as explicitly atheistic. It was perhaps this inroad that helped Lokanatha to convert Dr Soni, the medical doctor who has been described as 'a free thinker' with a previous 'search for something abiding in religion' (Ahir 1992, 45).

Lokanatha's Buddhism was deeply informed by his background as a scientist. Buddhism was defended on scientific grounds and Lokanatha's sermons and writings are filled with references to scientific principles, logical arguments, and ideas such as atomic energy. Lokanatha went so far as to place the Dharma ahead of science, and he described modern science as finally approaching the truths of Buddhism, 'the super science of the atomic age,' after 2,500 years (Lokanatha 1952, 57). An associate of Lokanatha described his strongest appeal as being with 'the moderns of Thailand' (Kusalasaya 1991, 68). A travel writer in Burma placed Lokanatha in the mid-1950s as central to a new wave of scientific and modern presentation of traditional Buddhism (Lewis 1954).

If Buddhism could be aligned with science for Lokanatha, as an individual he is much more difficult to locate. Lokanatha thought of himself, and was referred to by others, as alternately Italian and American. With his travels and his extended stays in Burma, Thailand, India, and Sri Lanka, it was even more difficult to attribute any single, fixed national identity to Lokanatha. Perhaps this was also part of the appeal for so many international Buddhist organizations in placing him front and centre on missionary tours and committees. Being both grounded in science and having no particular national identity allowed Lokanatha to be seen as a universal citizen and a modern, rational representative for Buddhism as a whole. He was a natural fit for those looking to assert Buddhism on the stage of world religions.

Despite both his atheist Buddhism as an adult and abandonment of his Catholic childhood, Lokanatha can be seen in the light of 'Protestant' Buddhist reformers such as those laid out by scholars such as Gombrich and Obeyesekere (1988) and Prothero (1996). While he certainly viewed himself as a Buddhist insider and participant, and not an outside reformer, Lokanatha's aims to reform and correct Buddhism, and restore it to his conception of an earlier, more pristine period are not dissimilar to many Victorian Buddhist reformers such as Henry Olcott. Lokanatha's own conception of his name's meaning of 'saviour,' his desire to spread a pure and original form of Buddhism to Asia and the rest of the world, and his steady production of printed matter, from pamphlets and catechisms to books, attest to his reforming ideals in this vein.

With his tendency to universalize Buddhism, his participation and adaptation to the Buddhist cultures he lived in, and his own background, it is also worth entertaining the thought that Lokanatha could perhaps be seen as something akin to a Catholic Buddhist. As a counterpoint to the figure of the Protestant Buddhist who wanted to strip Buddhism of its cultural contexts, devotional practices, and popular traditions, Lokanatha seemed willing to include local forms of Buddhist practice into his larger conception of the Dharma.

Lokanatha's success in Burma stemmed in part from this type of local adaptation. In Burma, Lokanatha stressed proper behaviour and moral conduct for himself and others through vegetarianism as 'a religious article of faith,' Buddhist scholarship, both in the digestion of ancient texts and in the production of contemporary Buddhist apologetics, and according to Dr Soni, a revival of the practice of meditating in cemeteries (Mannin 1955, 38). Lokanatha also gave a generous donation of 50,000 kyats to the construction of the Sunlun Dhammayone meditation and lecture hall (Soni 1966, 179). Alicia Turner's work on the Buddhist response to British colonial rule in Burma from 1885–1920 helps provide an understanding of Lokanatha's reception. According to Turner, 'Buddhist discourse offered an internal dynamic of decadence and decline that made... inarticulate forces intelligible' (Turner 2009, 1–2). While he came to Burma several years after this period, it is easy to see how his actions aligned so well with the continuing values and efforts that were held by much of Burma as part of stemming the decline of the Buddha's dispensation or sāsana.

As Laurence Cox has suggested, it is worth investigating what Lokanatha had in the way of a 'fixer,' or an agent who would act as a problem-solving buffer between a figure like Lokanatha and the public, both in Asia and in his tours of the West. While there is no evidence of someone playing such a role for Lokanatha (besides his translators in Asia, and Jerry Buys for Lokanatha's short stay in Los Angeles), it is useful to think of the cultures in which Lokanatha operated in terms of an individual fixer. In Buddhist climates such as Burma and Sri Lanka, there would be common norms for regarding Buddhism and treating Buddhist monks that would have shielded Lokanatha from criticism and provided a positive frame for the public to view him through. In post-War America, Lokanatha would have been operating without a similar type of cultural buffer and his engagement with the media in this non-Buddhist culture was decidedly 'unfixed.'

Spooks, screwballs, and Buddhism in early twentieth century America

The treatment of Lokanatha in the American popular media during his tour in the late-forties not only shows the way in which Lokanatha was presented, both visually and in written descriptions, to millions of Americans, but they also provide a window into the popular conceptions and misconceptions that were held in regards to Buddhism. It is reasonable to assume that the popular press, in the business of appealing to and not confronting its readership, would have portrayed Lokanatha in terms that a mass audience would have thought of Lokanatha and the figure of the Buddhist monk.

Most historical scholars of modern Buddhism attempt to locate the origins and precedents of contemporary traditions, or similarly, find figures in the past that are recognizable by the ways they reflect our notions of a Buddhist and Buddhist practice. Lost in these efforts are the popularly held notions of Buddhism among the general public. As Jane Iwamura argued in her book, *Virtual Orientalism* (2011), the icon of 'the Oriental monk' in post-War American popular culture has been charged with not only a romantic otherness, but America's political and racial sense of itself. Buddhists were popularly viewed in early twentieth century America through a similarly ungrounded and confused lens of exoticism. The word Buddhism often preceded the word cult. Bhikkhus were interchangeable with swamis. Vaudeville magicians used statues of the Buddha to create ambiance. Cosmetics and incense manufacturers such as Valmor used images of scantily-clad women encircled by lit candles and incense smoke and prostrating in front of massive Buddha statues to advertise their wares.

True to the period, Lokanatha was viewed as a marginal figure: curious and strange at best, laughable at worst. Lokanatha's suggestions for having Buddhist rituals shown on television were placed by a United Press correspondent alongside a strongman, a woman who dressed up as a giant bird, and a man with a flea circus, as one of several attempts by 'screwballs' to employ the new medium.[21] A syndicated article from years earlier made a similar move with

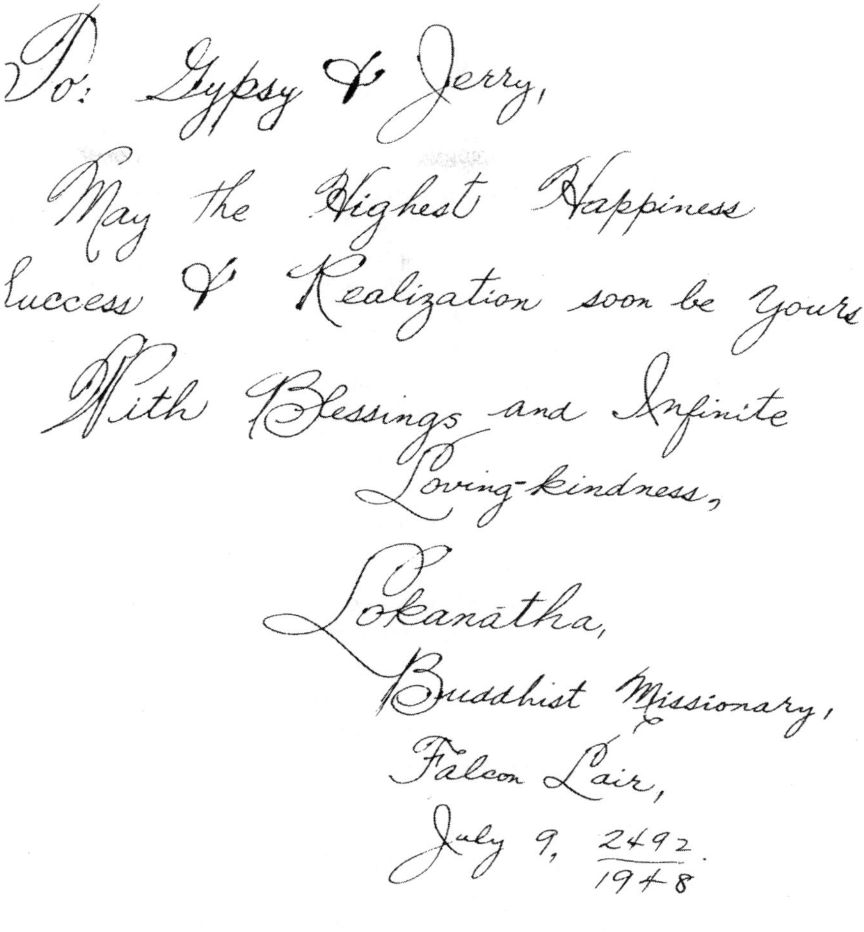
To: Gypsy & Jerry,
May the Highest Happiness
Success & Realization soon be Yours
With Blessings and Infinite
Loving-kindness,
Lokanātha,
Buddhist Missionary,
Fālcon Lair,
July 9, 2492/1948.

FIGURE 3
Inscription on a gifted copy of Irving Babbitt's translation of The Dhammapada given from Lokanatha to Gypsy and Jerry Buys. Collection of the author.

another American convert to Buddhism, placing him in line with hermits and eccentrics who lived semi-naked in shacks with various wild animals.[22]

Lokanatha's status as a celibate monk was also held up for derision. In the wake of his American tour, the *Chicago Tribune* ran a photo feature titled 'Beauty and Buddhist,' with a young woman in a bikini on a beach above a photo of a robe-swaddled Lokanatha standing on a London sidewalk, shortly after his departure from America. In case the presumptive humour of the juxtaposition was missed, the lower caption informed readers that Lokanatha has not even 'slept in a bed for 10 years.'[23]

By being placed in Los Angeles, Lokanatha could be explained by the popular American conceptions of the city's eclectic spiritual climate. In turn, Lokanatha served as another piece of evidence to validate that conception. In the late nineteenth century, Boston was the presumed headquarters for unusual religious experimentation in America, with Christian Science and mental healing. By the turn of the century, 'Pagan Chicago' took on that same role as its charismatic leaders and scandal-plagued occult societies made headlines around the country. In the 1920s, Southern California had assumed the mantle that it still holds to the present day, the assumed home for 'cults, sects, and 'isms' and 'weird things done in the name of God.'[24] In a photo carried far and wide by newspaper wire services, Lokanatha was shown standing in front of Falcon Lair with his begging bowl described as the 'newest addition to Los Angeles' collection of queer cults... gazing mystically into a pottery vase.'[25] With a sceptical qualification at every possible turn, the photo was captioned:

> He calls himself the Venerable Lokanatha, and says he's back from Burma. It turns out he has lived in Brooklyn, New York, since he was four. He's now fasting, he says, until Russian-American relations improve.[26]

This and other similarly uncharitable descriptions of Lokanatha might stem from the common perception that many of the fringe religious groups, particularly in Los Angeles, were scams and fraudulent 'rackets.' Lokanatha's incredible story, with the added twist of a nearly identical brother in Brooklyn who was a monsignor in the Catholic Church, did not help. An earlier 1934 article in *Time* magazine put Lokanatha directly in such dubious company by pairing him with Timothy Lincoln Trebitsch, a Hungarian Lutheran-Anglican-Quaker double agent and convert to Buddhism.

It is also a by-product of a complementary side to Iwamura's central thesis in *Virtual Orientalism*. If Asian religions in America were racialized and inextricably linked to perceptions of their Asian practitioners, and more specifically to ideas of 'the Asian mind,' then, as a European-American convert, Lokanatha would have to be some configuration of an inept and an imposter, missing the mark of being a 'true' Buddhist by either accident or hidden intention. This would explain the similar treatment of Lokanatha in *The New Yorker*, which explained to its readers with a wink and a nod that after leaving Brooklyn, the monk 'wound up the ranking Occidental in the Buddhist hierarchy of Burma' and the earlier line in *Time* magazine that 'abruptly last week the Buddhist religion produced an Italian in Siam.'[27] As Lokanatha's status of an outsider legitimated him in Asia, the qualities that made him an insider in America delegitimized him there during his tour.

Racialized Asian religions in America could also be romanticized or dismissed on the basis of the perceived political and economic power of the countries in which they dominated. Both American admirers and critics of Hinduism and Vedic philosophy in the early twentieth century explained poverty in the country not as a result of colonialism, but a spiritual worldview that prized emptiness and eschewed the material. A column in a Maine newspaper looked back on Lokanatha's tour of

America and patronized the monk, while sarcastically reassuring readers that 'there is no danger that the presence of a few Buddhist monks in this country will be followed by imperialistic demands from Burma . . . [that does] not possess the force necessary to make their views pressing or dangerous.'[28]

Conclusion: the future of Modern Buddhism's historical past

Scholars who have researched U Dhammaloka have uncovered exciting suggestions of numerous other contemporaneous European coverts to Buddhism in Asia. Similarly, this research into Lokanatha has led to the discovery of nearly 20 parallel American converts who took monastic Buddhist vows during the first half of the twentieth century. Some received ordination in the United States from Asian teachers, while others travelled to receive ordination in Japan, China, Sri Lanka, and elsewhere. Some of these Americans remained in Asia, while others returned to the United States to practice in relative isolation, to teach to other Americans, and on several occasions, to minister to immigrant Buddhist communities within the United States.

It may be difficult in the present moment to draw a clear theoretical thread through Lokanatha and this group of early American Buddhist converts. They were unconnected to one another, not held within a single group and, ironically, have unique personal histories and motivations as their most commonly held feature. When taken together they, at the very least, problematize the standard 'Two Buddhisms' model used to analyse American Buddhism and its binaries of so-called cradle and convert Buddhists. When we go deeper and also include the various occult-oriented Buddhist groups in early twentieth century America, taxonomy and terminology become even more complicated. Secretive and nebulous groups such as the Unreformed Buddhist Church, the Udana Karana Order, and those who claimed Buddhism as a form of 'True Freemasonry' make the use of even basic Buddhist terms such as ordination, sangha, and practice difficult.

Once figures like the Venerable Lokanatha become visible, it is hard to unsee them. When Thomas Tweed and Stephen Prothero refer to Alan Watts as 'perhaps the most influential populariser of Asian religions of his generation,' an awareness of Lokanatha and the millions of Ambedkar Buddhists forces us to reconsider many of the underlying assumptions we make about modern Buddhism and Buddhism's transmission to the West (Tweed and Prothero 1999, 229). Are Western Buddhists presumed to have more import than those in historically Buddhist countries, and do thousands of Beat and Hippie Buddhists somehow count for more than millions of Burmese and Indian Buddhists? Do texts and individual meditative practices point to a more 'real' Buddhism than traditional monastic codes of conduct and devotional practices carried across multiple generations? How much are we in the West invested in a romantic narrative of a smooth procession of authentic Buddhism moving from the East to the West? Does that imagined narrative make us hesitant to engage with figures and movements that complicate such ideals as Rick Fields' (1992) 'swans coming to the lake'? As scholars like Joseph Cheah (2011) and Sharon Suh have noted, many of our assumptions about normative and authentic Buddhist practice are fraught with problematic notions of race and gender.

Like recent work on U Dhammaloka, the materials that were used to create the narrative of Lokanatha's life in this article were very much dependent on contemporary archives and research methods. The historical newspaper accounts, mentions in periodicals, accounts in memoires, and primary historical documents that were stitched together came through avenues that would only be feasible through the internet of the last few years: commercial and academic databases, ongoing digitization projects, keyword searches in various online catalogues, instant translations via Google Translate, and communication across the globe with archives and fellow scholars. It would be hard to conceive of doing such work on Lokanatha even five years ago.

An historian's work is naturally limited by the available archive. Figures like Lokanatha and Dhammaloka, who frequently courted and interacted with the media, give a scholar more documents that are preserved and accessible, and thus more of a chance to engage with them in detail. However, as digitization projects expand, a host of passenger manifests and small local newspapers from around the world will become as accessible as canonized monographs. The scope of possible research will only continue to widen and obscure figures who avoided press coverage might soon be able to be seen in depth as well. The next several years may see a new subfield in Buddhist Studies as once hidden subjects from the late nineteenth and early twentieth century are revealed by new digital sources. The terms and narratives we are comfortable using to describing modern Buddhism will serve us less, and to modify the phrase of Philip Deloria, in the wake of scholarship on Lokanatha and Dhammaloka, we should start expecting to find Buddhists in unexpected places.

ACKNOWLEDGEMENTS

An earlier draft of this paper was given in September 2012 at the conference: *Southeast Asia as a Crossroads for Buddhist Exchange: Pioneer European Buddhists and Asian Buddhist Networks 1860–1960* at University College Cork, Ireland. The author would like to thank the hosts and sponsors of the conference for providing such a platform for exchange, and especially the conference participants for their helpful and ongoing suggestions and support. The Reverend Monsignor Ronald T. Marino, Angelo Marchese, and the Archives at the Cooper Union Library, are also appreciated for their help and efforts.

NOTES

1. Passenger manifest of alien immigrants arriving from Naples on the S.S. Trave, dated 2 September 1902. Many of the basic facts of Lokanatha's life vary

between different accounts, and there is several periods in his life where there currently seems to be no information. The confusion seems even greater in recent online mentions of him and in the conflict between historical records and sources that want to create a hagiography of Lokanatha. This article relies on primary documents and direct interviews with Lokanatha when possible, and memoirs of Lokanatha's associates when those were not available, particularly Dr R. L. Soni and Karuna Kusalasaya.

2. His ability to speak French is noted in a passenger manifest for the S.S. Matsonia that departed Honolulu on 24 January 1948. A recital by Cioffi on the violin was broadcast on the radio in the summer of 1922, when Cioffi would have been 24, and his classmates mentioned his playing in the Cooper Union yearbook of 1922.
3. Cooper Union Yearbook for 1922, 51.
4. Lokanatha, *The New Yorker*, March 5, 1949.
5. Orient 'Atomic Bomb of Love' Offered U.S. As Cure for Ills, *The Dothan Eagle* (Alabama), October 16, 1947.
6. Lokanatha, *The New Yorker*, March, 5, 1949.
7. Lokanatha, *The New Yorker*, March 5, 1949.
8. Lion Hearted, *Middletown Times Herald*, April 16, 1934.
9. Lokanatha writes about this encounter in the introduction to Dr Soni's pamphlet 'A Glimpse of Buddhism.'
10. Climatic Conditions and Buddhist Monks, *Times of India*, July 7, 1933.
11. Religion: Bhikkhu & Chao Rung, *Time*, April 23, 1934.
12. Fasting Buddhist Monk Here to Aid Fund-Raising Drive, *Los Angeles Times*, April 16, 1948.
13. 'Atomic Bomb of Love' From Orient Offered to US as Cure for Ills, *Logansport Pharos Tribune*, October 20, 1947.
14. Buddhist Principles Will Be Explained, *Fresno Bee Republican*, March 23, 1948.
15. Fasting Buddhist Monk Here to Aid Fund-Raising Drive, *Los Angeles Times*, April 16, 1948.
16. Listener's Choice Special Events, *Chicago Tribune*, May 16, 1949.
17. Lokanatha, *The New Yorker*, March 5, 1949.
18. Sects Abound in Sunshine of California, *Stars and Stripes (Europe, Mediterranean, and North Africa edition)*. September 6, 1949.
19. Buddhist Principles Will Be Explained, *Fresno Bee Republican*, March 23, 1948.
20. Lokanatha, *The New Yorker*, March, 5, 1949, 24.
21. Aline Mosby (1948) The Screwballs Are Generous With Notions for Television. *The Washington Post*, September 19, TV10.
22. Americans Get Away From It All, *Emporia Daily Gazette* (Kansas), September 5, 1940.
23. Beauty and Buddhist, *Chicago Daily Tribune*, September 18, 1949.
24. Bob White (1936) Weird Things, *Los Angeles Times*, March 1.
25. Buddha from Brooklyn, *Indiana Evening Gazette* (Indiana, Pennsylvania), July 28, 1948.

26. Sects Abound in Sunshine of California, *Stars and Stripes (Europe, Mediterranean, and North Africa edition)*, September 6, 1949.

27. Lokanatha, *The New Yorker*, March 5, 1949, 23; Religion: Bikkhu & Chao Rung, *Time*, April 23, 1934.

28. The 'Venerable Lokanatha', *Bar Harbor Times*, September 1, 1949.

REFERENCES

AHIR, D. C. 1990. *The Legacy of Dr Ambedkar*. Delhi: B.R. Publishing Corporation.

AHIR, D. C. 1992. *Dr Ambedkar and Punjab*. Delhi: B.R. Publishing Corporation.

BHASKAR, V. S. 2009. *Faith and Philosophy of Buddhism*. Delhi: Kalpaz Publications.

CHEAH, JOSEPH. 2011. *Race and Religion in American Buddhism: White Supremacy and Immigrant Adaptation*. New York: Oxford University Press.

DEL BOCA, BERNADINO. 1989. *Birmania: un paese da amare*. Torino: L'Età dell'Acquario.

FIELDS, RICK. 1992. *How The Swans Came to the Lake: A Narrative History of Buddhism in America*. Boston: Shambala.

GOMBRICH, RICHARD, and GANANATH OBEYESEKERE. 1988. *Buddhism Transformed: Religious Change in Sri Lanka*. Delhi: Motilal Banarsidass.

HOUTMAN, GUSTAAF. 1999. *Mental Culture in Burmese Crisis Politics: Aung San Suu Kyi and the National League for Democracy*. Tokyo: ILCAA.

IWAMURA, JANE. 2011. *Virtual Orientalism: Asian Religions and American Popular Culture*. New York: Oxford University Press.

KEER, DHANANJAY. 1954. *Dr Ambedkar: Life and Mission*. Mumbai: Popular Prakashan.

KUSALASAYA, KARUNA. 1991. *Life Without a Choice*. Bangkok: Sathirakoses-Nagapradipa Foundation.

LEWIS, NORMAN. 1954. *Golden Earth: Travels in Burma*. London: Readers Union.

Lokanatha. 1952. A Sermon to Students at Rangoon University. *The Light of the Dhamma* 1 (1): 57–70.

MANNIN, ETHEL. 1955. *Land of the Crested Lion*. London: The Travel Book Club.

PARDO, PAOLO. 1984. Il bonzo Napoletano. *L'Espresso*, April 4, 50–58.

PROFUMO, EDOARDO. 1997. *Viaggio in Birmania: alla ricerca della meditazione vipassana*. Valencia: Promolibri.

PROTHERO, STEPHEN. 1996. *The White Buddhist: The Asian Odyssey of Henry Steel Olcott*. Bloomington: University of Indiana Press.

SADANGI, HIMANSU CHARAN. 2008. *Dalit: The Downtrodden of India*. Delhi: ISHA Books.

SHULMAN, IRVING. 1967. *Valentino*. New York: Trident Press.

SONI, R. L. 1951. *A Glimpse of Buddhism*. Mandalay: Institute of Buddhist Culture.

SONI, R. L. 1958. A Decade of World-Wide Buddhist Revival. *The Light of Buddha* 3 (1): 12–16.

SONI, R. L. 1966. The Venerable Lokanatha. *The Maha-Bodhi*, July–August: 177–179.

TIYAVANICH, KAMALA. 2007. *Sons of the Buddha: The Early Lives of Three Extraordinary Thai Masters*. Boston: Wisdom Publications.

TURNER, ALICIA. 2009. Buddhism, Colonialism and the Boundaries of Religion: Theravada Buddhism in Burma 1885–1920. Ph.D. diss., The University of Chicago.

TWEED, THOMAS, and PROTHERO, STEPHEN, eds. 1999. *Asian Religions in America: A Documentary History*. New York: Oxford University Press.

Appendix: bibliography of Lokanatha

1932. *Celestial India, by an Italian Buddhist Monk*. Patna City.

1932. *The Finest Religion in the World by an Italian Buddhist Monk*, pamphlet. Calcutta: Gouranga Press.

1936. *Buddhism Will Make You Free!!!* Pamphlet. Panadura: The Harijan Publishing Society.

1947. *The Light of Truth: Sermons Delivered by the Ven. Lokanatha in Singapore*. Singapore: Ngai Seong Press.

1951. *A Glimpse of Buddhism*, written by R. L. Soni with an introduction by Lokanatha. Mandalay: Institute of Buddhist Culture.

Unknown. *The Crime of Killing*, unpublished pamphlet.

Unknown. *Girdling the Globe with Truth*.

Unknown. *The Incomparable University*.

Unknown- *There Is No God and No Soul*.

Note

1. This list contains every mentioned title written by Lokanatha that was come across during the course of researching this article, although it is likely that Lokanatha's written output, especially in pamphlets, was much greater. The information given was often sparse and contradictory, and the very existence of many titles differs from source to source. *Girdling the Globe with Truth*, for example, is praised in one account and described as lost without any surviving copies in another. The bibliography provided here is given in the hope that it might allow for some of these texts to be brought out into the open and assist further research on Lokanatha.

Index

Note: Page numbers in **bold** type refer tofigures
Page numbers followed by 'n' refer to notes

Ajahn Chah 162–4
Ajahn Maha Boowa 161–2, 164
Ajahn Panya 171
Albison, R. 150; and EST 150; as Sadhāvaḍḍho 150–4, 158, 161; subsequent life 161–2
Amarapura Nikaya 41
Ambedkar, Dr B. 8, 45, 128, 134, 181; conversion 172, 175–6
American Pacific Exposition and Oriental Fair 26
Anagarika Dharmapala *see* Dharmapala, Anagarika
Ānanda Bodhi 160
Ananda Metteyya 77–92, 118, 121, 125; anti-missionary agenda 85–6; as *bhikkhu* 77–81; Buddhist education opportunities 85–6; Buddhist networks 82–5; controversial figure 79; fighting speech 79; founding of *Buddhasāsana Samāgama* 82, 85; *Handbook to Buddhism* 79; illness and poverty 80, 89n; images 77–8, **78**; and imperialism 87–8; and Tibet 83
Anglo-Thai Company 100
anti-colonialism 5, 65–74
Anuradhapura monasteries 39–40, 47n; Abhayagirivihara 39; Mahavihara 39–40, 45; superiority struggle 39
Arnold, E. 80, 83, 136
Asian networks 3–16; data collection 10–13; empirical findings 8–10
Asoka, Mauryan King 37–39
Assumption College 99–100; bilingual school 99
Aung San 44

Bālbodh (Marathi children's magazine) 136
Bangkok, Ban Thawai area 7, 93–114; migration 100–1; population (1894) 100–1, 110n; schools 106–8; and Siamese-British-French treaty jurisdiction 7–8, 97–8; urban landscape transformation 99–100; Wat Ban Thawai monastery 8, 99
Bauddh-Darśan (Sāñkṛtyāyan) 142
Bechert, H. 43
Bengal Buddhist Association (Calcutta) 135
Bennett, Allan 7; biography 80–2; unmarked grave 79, 82, *see also* Ananda Metteyya
Besant, A. 52, 66, 127
Bhagavān Buddh (Kosambī) 137
Bhandarkar, R.G. 136–7
bhikkus 77–8, 81, 85–6, 136; early Western 121–6; ordination 125–6; *sañgha* 163–4, *see also* EST
Bigelow, W.S. 51
Bihar Research Society 141
Bijou of Asia 56
Birla, J.K. 138, 144n
Blackburn, A. 9
Blake, George 8; and EST 150; Kapilavaḍḍho and Sodh disagreement 151–7; subsequent life 161–2; as Vijjāvaḍḍho 8, 148–61
Blavatsky, Madame 66
Bluck, R. 151
Bocking, B. 6, 9, 16–36, 118, 125; Turner, A. and Cox, L. 1–16
Bombay Buddhist Society 135
Bombay Burmah Trading 100, 110n
Bombay Chronicle 139
Bowring Treaty (1855) 97–8; Article VI 98; Articles IV and VIII 97–8; freedom of religion promotion 98
British Borneo 100
Brunton, P. 80–2

Buddh Mandir 139
Buddha 135; as ideal karma yogi 135; Jayanti 45; as Vishnu avatar 135
Buddhagosa 40–1, 46n
Buddhism: An Illustrated Review (ed by Metteyya) 82–7; international focus 84
Buddhist Crossroads conference (Cork, 2012) 13
Buddhist Foreign Mission 173
Buddhist Mission (Singapore) 17
Buddhist Propagation Society 128
Buddhist Review 22, 56, 82
Buddhist Society of Great Britain and Ireland 77–82, 86–8; and EST 148, 153; Housing Fund donation 79; Liverpool Branch 81
Buddhist Society for the Promotion of Asia 52
Buddhist Theosophical Society 128
Buddhist Tract Society 125
Burma 9–10, 44; Buddhist Head *thathanabaing* 87; Department of Religious Affairs 45; reformist fraternities 41; stone library 42–6; and Tai-Lao Buddhisms 93–111; tooth relic copy 42–3; treaties 97–8; urban landscape transformation 99–100; World Peace Pagoda 44
Burris, J.P. 22–3, 33n
Burton, A. 65
Buys, Gipsy and Jerry 173–4, 178; copy of *Dhammapada* given by Lokanatha 179; séance to contact Rudolph Valentino 173–4

Cai Dai religion (Vietnam) 52
Carus, P. 20, 55, 83
Catholic Emancipation movement 128
Ceylon 10, 84
Ceylon Friend, The (Wesleyan journal) 84
Chakrabarty, D. 66
Chamberlain, B.H. 19
Chatterjee, P. 66
Chatthasanghayana edition creation (Burma) 45
Cheah, J. 182
Chicago 6, 20, 29; Centennial Congress 25; White City and Columbian Exposition 23–4; World's Parliament of Religions (1893) 6, 20, 23–4, 28
Chicago Tribune 179
Choompolpaisal, P. 7–10, 13, 125
Chophel, G. 141
Christian Science 180
Christianity 9, 20; alternatives 9; anti-missionary agenda 85–6; critique and harms 72–4, 77; as drunken religion 68–74; missionaries impact 98
Chulalongkorn, King of Siam 38, 43, 96–7; Buddhist canon recitation and edit 43; defender of faith role 43; marriages 101–2
Cioffi, Salvatore 8; and Ambedkar's conversion 175–6; biography 169–5, **169**; living in wild 170–1; as Lokanatha 8, 168–84, **174**; ordained in Rangoon 170
Clark, Dr M. 160
Clarke, J. 117
Cohen, G. 100
College of Physicians and Surgeons (Columbia) 170
Colley, L. 114, 123
Collis, M. 29
colonialism 8; anti- 5, 65–74; British and Burma/Siamese centralization 95–7; critique 66–8; and Dhammaloka's denunciation 65–74; resistance 65–76; Victorian vegetarianism and homosexual activism 66–7, 74; violence 70, 73
Congress of Orientalists, Hanoi (1902) 16, 24–8; flag 16, 29, 30–1n
Copway, Rev George 70
Cousins, J. 59
Cousins, M. 127
Cox, L. 8, 115–32, 178; Bocking, B. and Turner, A. 1–16
Crow, J. 77, 80–1, 85–6
Crowley, Aleister 81
Crucible Steel Company of America 170

Daly, J.B. 128
Darwin, Charles 87, 143
De la Courneuve, M. 121
Deloria, P. 182
Der Buddhist 86
Deslippe, P. 8–10, 121, 168–85
dhamma 38–41, 44–5; authoritative version agreement 38–41; transmission to Sri Lanka 39, *see also* synods
Dhammakaya International Society of UK (DISUK) 13
Dhammaloka 4–12, 25, 29–30, 34n, 84–5, 88, 105, 109, 168, 181; Bible, bottle and knife 7, 68–74; career and activism programme 72–4; death from *beri-beri* 11; first Buddhist bilingual school 7–8, 106; identity change/death fake 120; as Irish Buddhist 17–18, 116–29; and

Lokanatha 172–82; pamphlets use 10; public career as monk 10–11, 68–72; shoe incident 124–6; and Wat Bantawai temple (Bangkok) 93–4, 103–9; as white advocate for Sri Lankan Buddhists 65
Dhammapada 170, 175, 179
Dhammayutika Nikāya monasteries 159–2; monk persecution 162
dharamśālā (pilgrim rest houses) 135
Dharmakāya 57–8
Dharmapala, Anagarika 19, 24, 28, 79, 88, 133; London Buddhist Mission 141
Dipavamsa chronicle 40, 43

early Western Buddhists *see* European-Asian connections
East of Asia Magazine 22
Eastern Buddhist 56
Elam, Caroline 17–19; father (Lt Joseph Elam) 31n; Pfoundes' mother 17
Ellis, H. 20
English Sangha Trust (EST) 148–64; aftermath 157–59; creation and Wat Paknam (Thailand) 148–65; George Blake's account 151–2; gesture of insult disagreement with Sodh 150–7; interpretations 153–7, 160–1; Luang Por Sodh's account 152–3; and *soḷasakāya* meditation 148–50, 159–4, 165n; subsequent lives 161–2; unsuccessful outcome 150; and Wat Paknam (Bangkok) 148–65
Esoteric Buddhists 24, 27–8
European-Asian connections 7; bhikkus 121–5; and Dhammaloka 116–29; dissident Orientalism and Irish identities 126–8; early Western Buddhists 115–32; going native 122–6; Irish 127–8; and limits of empire 128–29; Marco Polo 116; patronage 125–6, 129; pauper lunatics and beachcombers 117–22, 129; Phr'a Kow Tow 115; poor whites/loafers 119–2, 129; race and agency 122–6; respectability issues 121–5
Everett, R. 61
Exhibiting religion (Burris) 22–3

Fausböll, V. 83
Fellowship of the New Life 20
Fields, R. 181–2
Fischer-Tiné, H. 119–20, 125
Fisher, A. 77–8
Folklore Society 19
Forest Dhamma Organization 162
Franck, H. 123
Franco-Indo-China Colonial Empire 25
Frasch, T. 6, 9, 37–50
From Volga to the Ganges (Sāñkṛtyāyan) 142
Fuehrer, A. 121
Fuso-mimi-bukuro: A Budget of Japanese Notes 19

Gandhi, Leela 66–7, 74
Gandhi, Mahatma 136–39, 142; Non-Cooperation Movement 136, 141
Gandhi, Mohandas 66
General Buddhist Association (Darjeeling) 135
Ghosh, D. 119
Gloucester Citizen 25
Gombrich, R.: and Obeyeseker, G. 177
Gotama Buddha (fourth) 38–39; *parinibbana* 38, 44
Great Britain 18
Greenstock, Rev. W. 105
Gueth, Anton 84; as Nyāṇatiloka 84–5, 88, 118

Hadani, Ryōtai 55–7
Hansei Zasshi 56
Harris, E. 7, 77–92, 121
Harris Park Treaty (1856) 98
Hearn, L. 127–29
Hecker, H.: and Nyanatusita, B. 85
Heelas, P.: and Woodhead, L. 163
Heian Middle School 54–6
Hermetic Order of the Golden Dawn 80, 89n; Allan Bennett as *Iehi Aour* 81
Hewavitarana, Dr 79, 82, 89n
Hibino, Setti Line 60, 63n
Hill, L. 19
Hill, R.A. 19, 32n
Hindutva: Who is a Hindu (Sāvarkar) 135
Hirai Kinza 54
Hollywood High School 51; College Preparatory Course 59
Hong Kong: United Press wire service 176
Hong Kong Daily Press 17
Humphreys, C. 59–1, 79, 148

Ideal Form of Monotheism (Hadani) 57
identity checks 9–10
imperialism 87–8
India 8–9, 41; *Aśokan dhammacakra* on national flag 143; birthplace of Buddhism 9; Buddhist pioneers 8; colonial Buddhist

activity 133–47; Revolt (1857) 3, 116–19; Untouchables religion 45
Indian Buddhist Society (Lucknow) 135, 140
Indian Civilization and Non-Violence (Kosambī) 138–39
International Order of Good Templars (IOGT) 72
International Parliament of Religions 28
International Union of Orientalists 28
internationalism 6
Introduction to Mahayana Buddhi (McGovern) 57
Islam 54
Iwamura, J. 178

Jaffe, R. 2, 143
Jai Yasotharāt 159
Japan 7; art treasure sale 18–19; Buddhology 20–2; emerging shipping industry 18; swastika emblem 30–1n
Japan Mail 19
Japanese Art Treasures catalogue 20
Japanese Mail and Transport Steam Ship service 18
Jōdo sect 17; *Kaigai senkyōkai* missionary society 20; *Kyōkai Ichiran* journal 54; Nishi Honganji temples 52–5, 59–1; Shinshū 51–4
Johnstone, Capt J.C. 69
Journal Asiatique 141
Junjirō, Takakusu 20

Kakuzō, Okakura 24
Kālāma Sūtta 140
Kama Sutra translator 60
Kapilavaḍḍho 148–65; banishment order 156–59; disagreement with Sodh 150–7; disrobing and re-ordination 161, 164n; ordination ambitions 154; temperament 154
Kashmiri Raj Maha Bodhi Society (Srinagar) 135
Kesarī (Marathi-language journal) 137
Keyes, C. 97
Kher, B.G. 139
Kirby, M.T. 4, 7, 11, 51, 55–6; biography 54–5; as Shaku Sōgaku 54
Kosambī, Dharmānand 8, 133–45; as *bhikkhu* 136–7; biography 136–39; born as a Gauḍ Sārasvat Brāhmaṇ 136; death (1947) 139; non-violence and Marxism 138–39, 144n; writing career 137–39
Krotona Institute of Theosophy 53, 59
Kyandaw Monastery 84

Ladakh Buddhist Education Society 135
Ladies Bazaar Association 98
Lamp, The 20
lay movements 5; and ordination 51, 54
Leadbetter, C.W. 84
Lees, E. 20
Lévi, S. 141
Lewis and Clark Centennial Exposition (1905) 18, 24–29; Congress of Orientalists 18
Lewis, Samuel L. 55; as Sufi Ahmed Murad Chisti 55
Life and Times of Luang Phaw Wat Paknam (Anon) 151–3
Light of Asia 80, 136
Light of Dharma 56
Light of Truth (central Samāj text) 140
Lim Pagoda 16
Lokamānya Tilak group 137
Lokanatha 4, 168–84; atheistic concept of Buddhism 176–8; conversion of Ambedkar 169–4, 175–6, 181; death (1966) 176; and Dhammaloka 174–82; homage at Shwezigon Monastery 176; as *Mahajayanti* Spiritual Patron 175; meditation hall construction 177; missionary expeditions 171–3; perceptions and treatment in America 173–81; prisoner of war 172; psychic powers 171, 174; situating and contextualizing 176–8; and vegetarianism 171, 177
London Theosophists 20
Los Angeles Times 173
Le Lotus 20
Louis T. Leonowens (teak trader) 100
Lovelorn Ghost and the Magical Monk, The (McDaniel) 4
Luang Por Sadh *see* Sodh, Luang Por
Luce, G. 129–130
Lucifer 20

McDaniel, J. 4
Macdonald, Ramsey 20
McFarland, G.B. 98
McGovern, J. 53, 56
McGovern, W. 4, 7, 51–5, 59; biography 52–4; kikyō-shiki (lay ordination) 54; as Shaku Shidō 54
McKechnie, J.F. 81; as Ven Sīlācara 84–6
McMahan, D. 140
Maddox, R. 79

Maha Bodhi Society 10, 37, 44, 120, 133–8, 141, 172; *British Buddhist* 120; temple case 141
Mahanikay sect 97
Mahasena, King of Sri Lanka 39
Mahathera, Nyanātiloka 137
Mahayana Association 7, 51–2, 55–6; Lodge and scholars 58–61; Order of Star in the East 60–1
Mahayanist journal 52–8; members and contributors list 55–7; similarity/difference points-Christianity and Buddhism 57
Majjhima Nikāya 140
Maoria (Johnstone) 69
Marco Polo 116
Markwald 101
Marxism 138–39, 142–43
Matsutarō, Matsuyama 19
Mayer, Louis B. 174
Medharthi, Acharya Ishvardatt 175
Meiji Restoration (1868) 18
Mettayya, Ananda *see* Ananda Mettayya
Metteya Buddha (fifth) 39–1, 44–5; failure to appear 40
migration 100–1; Ban Thawai (1880's-1900) 101
millenarian thinking 40–1; and calendar end date 41
Mindon Min, King of Burma 38, 42–5; stone copy of Buddhist canon 42–6
missionaries 37, 105; Christian organizations 43; hostility 118
Mongkut, King of Siam 97–8; marriage relations 101
monks: non-conformist 38–39, 44
Morgan, P. 150; and EST 150; as Paññāvaḍḍho 150–4, 158–64; subsequent life 161–2
Müller, Max 20

Naasu, P.L. 137
Nanthapho, K. 97
Narasingha, Swami B.H. 30–1n
Nature of Buddhist Trinity (McGovern) 57–8
New York Public Library 170
New Yorker, The 180
newspapers and media 10–11
Noble, M. 127
non-conformist monks 38–39, 44; expulsion 38
Nyāṇatiloka 84–5, 88, 118
Nyanatusita, B.: and Hecker, H. 85

Ober, D. 8, 16–36, 133–47
Obeyeseker, G.: and Gombrich, R. 178
O'Connell, D. 129
Olcott, Col H.S. 18–20, 23, 31, 66–7, 136, 178
Oldenberg, H. 44
Open Court, The 18, 21, 26
Oregon Historical Society 19
Orient 57
Oriental Esoteric Head Center 54
Orientalists' International Union of the Pacific Hemisphere 27–8
Oung, H. 86
Outlines of Mahayana Buddhism (Suzuki) 59

Pagan Chicago 180
Pagan Min (of Burma) 42
Pali Text Society (PTS) 43–4
Panchard McTaggart Lother 101
Paññāvaḍḍho 150–4, 158–64
Pantheism 57
parinibbana state 38–39
Pemberton, J. 79–1
Perera, C. 79–1, 84–5, 79n
Pfoundes, C. 4–6, 11, 51, 125, 128; advertisement pamphlets 19–2, **21**; biography 17–22; as difficult character 27; failed projects 24–8; international congresses/expositions 22–7; Irish Buddhist 17; marriage to Rosa Alice Hill 19–20, 32n; as Omoie Tetzunostzuke 6, 16, 31n; play on English name 31–2n; retirement from Admiralty 20, 33n; return to Japan 20; theosophy denunciation 20; two-centre event plans 24–5
pioneer European buddhists 3–16; early British (and Black) Bhikkhus 8; early conversions 8; failures and possibilities 4–6
polities 9
Pounds, James Baker 17; Pfoundes' father 17, 31n
Procter & Gamble 170
Prothero, S. 181
Purfurst, W. 148–65; and EST 149–50; first Englishman ordained in Thailand 150; as Kapilavaḍḍho 148–65; subsequent life 161–2

Quest 56

Radhakrishnan, S. 135
Rama I, King of Siam 103
Rama Tirtha, Swami 25

Rama VI, King of Siam 97
Rama VII, King of Siam 95
Ramanya Nikaya 41–3
Rangoon: Sixth World Council Synod 38, 44–6; Tavoy monastery 8
revivals 5, 10
Rhys-Davids, C. 83
Rhys-Davids, T.W. 83
Roerich, G. 141
Russo-Japanese war (1904–5) 9

Sadhāvaḍḍho 150–4, 158, 161, *see also* Albison, R.
St Louis 26, 29; *World's Fair Bulletin* 26
Sakya Buddhist Society (Madras) 128, 135
Sangha Act (1902) 95, 102, 109; rural/local Buddhist practices discrimination 97
sanghas 2, 38–43, 125, 129; purification 39; responsibility for Buddha's teachings 38–41; Sinhalese 40
Sāñkṛtyāyan, Rahul 8, 134–6, 139–5; as Baba Rāmodār Dās 139; as *bhik⊠u* 141; and Four Noble Truths 142; and lost Sanskrit manuscripts 139–1, 144–5n; passion for Marxist revolution and jail 142; travelling missionary 139–40; visits to Tibet 139–1, 144–5n
Sathienkoset 105, 111n
Satow, E. 27, 34n
Sāvarkar, V.D. 135
Sayajiroa Gaikwad, Maharaja of Baroda 137
Seager, R. 28
Shaku Sōen 54, 57
Shine, T. 151
Shingon sect 17, 60
Shin'ichi, Y. 7
Shotōkuji Documents Collection 52
Shugendo 51
Shwe Dagon Pagoda 86, 173
Siam Forest 100
Siddiqi, Y. 119
Sigāla Sūtta 137
Singapore: Buddhist Mission 17
Sinnett, A.P. 84
Sino-Japanese conflict (1894–5) 9
Skilton, A. 8, 148–67
Snodgrass, J. 56
Snyder, G. 118
Society for the Propagation of the Gospel 85
Sodh, Luang Por (Abbot of Wat Paknam) 148–65; disagreement with Kapilavaḍḍho 150–7; illness 157, 160
Soni, R.L. 171–7
Sri Lanka 39–7; tooth relic 42
Sri Lankan London Buddhist Vihara 150
Stars and Stripes 174–5
Sudhamma Nikaya monks 42
Suh, S. 182
Sumaṃgala Ven Hikkaḍuwē 83
Sumedho (disciple of Ajahn Chah) 162
Sutin, L. 116
Suzuki, B. 51–2, 55, 59–60
Suzuki, D.T. 7, 51–61
synods 6, 38–45; Fifth 42; forgotten 45; Kotte 41, 46; Mandalay 42, 47n; manuscript edit and print 43–4; Pataliputra 39; Pegu 45; significance 40; Sixth World Council (Rangoon) 38, 44–6; Vesali Second Council 39

Tai-Burmese-Lao Buddhisms 93–114
Taosim 53
Tavoy monastery (Rangoon) 8
Taylor, C. 140
teak business trading 100
temperance 11, 94; advocacy 69–3
temple documents discovery 7
Tendai sect 17, 51
Thai Forest Sangha (Ajahn Chah) 149
Thailand (Siam) 4, 94; Bangkok urban landscape transformation 99–100; and British centralization 95–7, 103–8; independence 9; inter-marriages with Lanna and Kengtung royalty 101–3; Jaroen Krung/Sathon Roads importance 99–1, 104; Lanna's integration 102; migration 100–1; railways 101; schools 106–8; Tai-Burmese-Lao Buddhisms 93–114; teak and rice trades 100–1; temples, political control and advantages 103–8; treaties 97–8
Thammayut sect 97, 102; hierarchy 98; privileged royalist monks 98–7
Thelle, N. 22
Theosophical Siftings 20
Theosophical Society 19, 59, 80; Brixton Lodge 80; Buddhist Lodge (London) 59; Esoteric School 81; India 52–3, 59; New York 19
Theosophist, The 56, 79
theosophy 19–20, 27, 61, 67
Theravada 6, 46, 54–5; communities 37–8; fountain crisis 40; Sinhalese-Mahavihara tradition 40; tradition emergence 39
Things Japanese (Chamberlain) 19

Thitavedo 149–5; dis-robing 161; disagreement with Sodh 151–7; disappearance from Wat Paknam 152–5; temple funds irregularities 165n
Time magazine 180
Times of India, The 16
Tittila 149
To Lhasa in Disguise (McGovern) 53
Transactions of the Royal Society of Literature 20
transnationalism 37–48 and Buddhist ecumene 38–41
treaties 97–8; Bowring 97–8; consequences 97–8; diplomatic, France and Siam 98
Trikāya 58
Turner, A. 7, 65–76, 177; Cox, L. and Bocking, B. 1–16
Tweed, T. 181

U Nu, of Burma 44
Udana Karana Order 181
United Press wire service (Hong Kong) 176
Unreformed Buddhist Church 181
upasaṃpadā (higher ordination) 78, 84, 150
Utsuki, N. 4, 7, 11, 52, 55, 58–61; biography 59–60

Vedanta philosophy 54
Vietnam: Cai Dai religion 52
Vijjāvaḍḍho 8, 148–61, *see also* Blake, George
Vinaya Pitaka (Oldenberg) 43
Vinaya rules 39
vipassana meditation 160
Virtual Orientalism (Iwamura) 178–80
Vishnu 135
Visuddha 128
Visuddhimagga 137
Viswanathan, G. 67
Vivekananda, Swami 24, 28, 135

Warrington, A.P. 52–3, 59
Wat Ban Thawai monastery (Bangkok) 8, 99, *see also* Wat Don Thawai
Wat Chonlaprathan 162
Wat Don Thawai temple 94, 100, 103–8; bilingual school 106–8, **107**; ethnic politics 125–6; Jan Janthasaro (Abbot) 103; Jangvang support and titles 104; sacred statue 105; Sangharat Pae Tissatheva 104
Wat Lao temple 94, 99–100, 103–8
Wat Paknam 148–67; Luang Por Sodh (Abbot) 148–60, *see also* English Sangha Trust
Wat Thathong 150
Wat Thung Kula temple 94, 99–100, 103–8; Min Ong (Abbot) 103
Wat Vivekārām (Chonburi) 158
Wat Yannawa temple 94, 103–8; bilingual school 106; royal Thai 99–100
Watts, A. 61, 181
West, Max R. 100
Wicked Proclamation to His Fellow Beings, A (Dhammaloka) 69
William Q 19
Williams, D. 101
Women's Christian Temperance Union 98
Woodhead, L.: and Heelas, P. 163
Woods, J. 137
World Buddhist Flag 175
World Fellowship of Buddhists 37, 44
World's Parliament of Religions, Chicago (1893) 6, 20, 23–4, 28

yoga 80–1
Yoshinaga, S. 9–11, 19, 27, 51–64
Young East 55
Young Folks Paper 20

Zen sect 17, 61; pioneers 61; Rinzai 51, 55; Samadhi Society 54–5, *see also* Mahayana Association